Wordsworth Dictionary of Idioms

The Wordsworth Dictionary of

IDIOMS

MARTIN H. MANSER

Wordsworth Reference

In loving memory of
MICHAEL TRAYLER
the founder of Wordsworth Editions

I

Readers who are interested in other titles from
Wordsworth Editions are invited to visit our website at
www.wordsworth-editions.com

For our latest list and a full mail-order service, contact
Bibliophile Books, 5 Thomas Road, London E14 7BN
TEL: +44 (0)20 7515 9222 FAX: +44 (0)20 7538 4115
E-MAIL: orders@bibliophilebooks.com

This revised edition first published in 2006 by
Wordsworth Editions Limited
8B East Street, Ware, Hertfordshire SG12 9HJ

ISBN I 84022-491 6

Typeset in Great Britain by Antony Gray
Printed and bound by Clays Ltd, St Ives plc

Introduction

This dictionary explains idioms and other phrases used in typical English conversations. Modern spoken English contains many phrases that the average English speaker scarcely thinks about and foreign learners find difficult. This dictionary is an attempt to explain such phrases.

Idioms are fairly fixed phrases that consist of more than one word, with a meaning that cannot be understood from putting together the meanings of the individual words. But this dictionary of idioms is different from other dictionaries of idioms. Such dictionaries often try to give a complete list of all idioms; in this book we have concentrated on phrases that are used in certain conversational situations. Clear examples are *How do you do?* when greeting, the exclamations *Good luck!* when wishing someone well and *Well I never!* when you are surprised, and sayings such as *Great minds think alike* and *Wonders will never cease*.

This book will be found useful by all speakers of English. Those with English as their native language will be surprised at the wide range of phrases used in everyday speech – think of *all right*, *I mean* and *you know*. Students learning English as a second or foreign language will find help here that is just not included in other reference books – so this dictionary will increase the understanding of what has been heard and will also develop a proficiency in using idioms. A further application is for writers who want to catch and use what people actually say, e.g. those who write cartoons or devise titles for books or articles, or programmes on television and radio.

The index brings an additional benefit: by consulting the list of subjects, the user is referred to appropriate phrases.

MARTIN H. MANSER

How to use this book

The book is in two parts: the dictionary and the index. The dictionary is an alphabetical list of idioms. The index classifies idioms according to their subject or function in the language. The notes here deal with the dictionary; a note on the use of the index is placed at the beginning of the index.

Arrangement of entries

Idioms in the dictionary are listed in alphabetical order of *keywords*. A keyword in an idiom is usually its first noun, or if it has no noun, its first verb; if it has no verb, then its first adjective. For example, *Be my guest!* is listed at *guest*; *That does it!* is listed at *do*; *Not bad* is listed at *bad*. A few items are not given under their first noun or verb, etc., or do not contain a noun, verb, or adjective, but in all these cases, cross-references are included at appropriate places to help locate the entry easily. Similarly, if you happen to look up a phrase in the wrong place, you will find a cross-reference to the right place, so you will be able to find the idiom you are looking for.

Where there is more than one idiom at a keyword, the idioms are listed at numbered entries in alphabetical order of the first word of the idiom. Note, too, that where an idiom has more than one meaning, the entry is subdivided into *a*, *b*, etc.

Each entry consists of the idiom, a definition of the idiom, and in nearly every case one or more examples. The definition is an explanation of the meaning of the idiom, and often contains notes on the situation in which the idiom is used. Examples, which are preceded by the symbol >, have been written to reflect usage of the idiom in natural English contexts. Dialogues between two speakers often draw out the sense. The examples are also intended to show the main grammatical patterns associated with the particular idiom.

Further information about the idiom is also given as necessary: *stress* or *pronunciation* is shown where this may prove difficult; common *variant spellings* are shown; *alternative phrases* with similar meaning are given; *etymologies* explain the origin of some idioms—where the idiom contains a proper name (e.g. *Gordon Bennett!*), in cases of Cockney rhyming slang, e.g. *head* being replaced by *loaf of bread* in the idiom *Use your loaf!*, and in other cases where the idiom has a clear origin, e.g. *Tell that to the marines!*

Certain types of phrases and idiomatic usage have been excluded from this dictionary. Proverbs have been omitted: these are dealt with in *The Dictionary of Proverbs* by G. L. Apperson, revised by Martin H. Manser and Stephen Curtis (Wordsworth) or *The Facts on File Dictionary of Proverbs* by

Martin H. Manser (Facts on File). Also excluded are: single words that are common in speech, e.g. *actually*; foreign expressions used in speech, e.g. *bon appétit!*; *bon voyage!*; speech expressions with obvious meanings, e.g. the dentist's *open wide!*; and taboo and other vulgar items.

Alternative forms of the idiom

Although many of the idioms listed in the dictionary have a fixed form, some variations are often possible. These are mainly of two types:

Alternative forms, shown by the use of *or* or *etc.*: *How* (or *what*) *about …?* Means that *How about …?* And *What about …?* are both used. *It's your* (*his*, *her*, etc.) *baby* means that *It's your baby*, *It's his baby*, and *It's her baby* all may be used, depending on the object intended. (Such items are normally listed under the *you* or *I* (or *me*) form.)

Optional forms, shown by the use of brackets ( ): *The* (*very*) *idea!* Means that *The idea!* and *The very idea!* are both used, and examples are often shown in instances of both.

Note … is used in an idiom to show that a word is missing; details of what kind of word this is can be deduced from the definition, and are clear from the examples given.

Style markers

Most of the idioms listed are not given any particular style marker; this means that they are used in informal everyday conversation, e.g. that used between friends. But some idioms are limited to a particular level or register of usage. Markers such as *Formal*, and *Slang* (to indicate a very informal style heard among people of the same age group, especially the young), *Humorous*, *Nonstandard* (for phrases not regarded as correct or acceptable by native speakers), and *Literary* (used in poetry, formal creative writing, etc.) are used. A number of idioms have been marked *Old-fashioned* or *Becoming old-fashioned*. This means that they are becoming rare in modern spoken English, but are still used, mainly by older speakers or in older written works. If learners use such expressions, their language will sound rather dated. Idioms belonging to a particular country are marked accordingly, e.g. *British* and *American* are used to show distinctive national varieties, although a detailed treatment of American English has not been attempted. Note that the style marker given under a main idiom entry also applies to the alternative forms listed, unless otherwise stated.

It is important to note that many of the idioms without a style marker may not be used in formal writing. Note too that expressions containing the word *God*, *Christ*, or *Lord*, are avoided by some speakers as they are thought to show a lack of respect towards God.

Acknowledgements

Obviously it has not been possible to compile such a dictionary without some recourse to the various standard dictionaries and reference books, and I gratefully acknowledge my debt to these as they provided a useful starting-point for my own work.

In particular I would also like to record my thanks to my wife Yusandra and other members of my family (especially Ben and Hannah), friends (notably the late Hermann Fink), and some organisations, for their help in working out some of the definitions and examples; to Roger Flavell for his many valuable comments on the typescript, to Gloria Wren for her meticulous typing of the manuscripts for the first and second editions, to Barry Evans and Margaret David of Aylesbury Keyboarding for their work in the production of the index, to Su Ong, David Kewley and Karen Jamieson of the publishers for their encouragement while writing this book, and to Emma Redfern for her checking the text for this edition.

A

ABOARD

All aboard! An announcement to passengers to get on a train, ship, etc., that is about to leave: > *'All aboard! The ship is about to sail.'*

ABOUT

1 How (or what) about ... ?
a An expression used to introduce a suggestion > *'How about a game of cards?'* > *'What about going out for a meal?'* > *'How about another piece of cake?'*
b What do you think of (something)?: > *'How about the other side beating us last night by three goals?'* > *'What about abortion? Is it a good or a bad thing?'*
c Have you heard about (an item of news)?; are there plans about (something)?: > *'What about the weather? Is it going to get worse?'* > *'How about Aunt Alice? We can't just leave her by herself, now that her husband has died.'*
d Used to ask for a decision or explanation, often as a reminder to someone: > *'I've never had an accident in my car.' 'How about that time you reversed in to your neighbour's van?'* > *'What about your library books?' Have you returned them yet?'* Sometimes *'How (or what) about'* is used as a rather rude reply > *'What about that offer of taking me out to dinner.' 'What about it?'*

2 How (or what) about that (then)!
An expression of surprise or praise: > *'I'm off to Africa next week.' 'Well, how about that!'* > *'How about that, then! Our school's finally beaten yours!'*

3 That's about it
a An expression used to summarise all one's knowledge: > *He seemed an ordinary fellow: he had a nine-to-five job, a few friends used to come to his bedsit; that's about it.*
b An expression used to close a conversation: > *'Well, that's about it ... I'd better be going. I'll see you next week then.'*

ABOVE

1 Above all An expression used to introduce the most important thing: > *'You should be kind to everyone, but, above all, to those who cannot look after themselves.'*

2 Above and beyond In addition: > *Above and beyond working hard all day, he spent his evenings helping in a youth club.*

ABSOLUTELY

Absolutely not Used as a strong way of saying no to something or disagreeing emphatically with someone: > *'Dad, can I borrow the car tonight?' 'Absolutely not!'*

ACCIDENT

Little Jimmy's (Johnny's, etc.) **had an accident!** *Euphemistic Jimmy (or another baby's name) has passed water onto the floor.*

ACCIDENTAL

Accidentally on purpose With the real intention of doing something, but making it seem to happen by chance: > *He used to buy bottles of drink and then drop them accidentally on purpose to get another one.*

ACCOUNT

1 **On account of** Because of: used to introduce an explanation: > *'He can't walk very far on account of his poor health.'*
2 **On no account** Used to say that something must not be done under any circumstances: > *'On no account must you play with matches.'*
3 **There's no accounting for tastes** *see* **Taste.**

ACHE

My heart aches for you *see* **Heart 7.**

ACID

The acid test A way of discovering whether something is really as good or effective as people think it is: > *The acid test is not whether people are interested in our new product but whether they will actually buy it.* The expression derives from the use of nitric acid to test whether a metal is gold or not.

ACT

1 **A hard act to follow** A very successful person or achievement that will be difficult for the next person to be as impressive: > *'James has been chairman for ten years. His breadth of experience means he'll be a hard act to follow.'*

2 **Act your age!** *see* **Age 1.**
3 **Get one's act together** To become more organised; to take greater, more effective control of yourself: > *After a report that the school was almost a failure, the governors need to get their act together quickly.*

ACTION

1 **A piece** (or **slice**) **of the action** A share in the exciting aspects of an activity; a share in the profits of a successful business: > *With all the fast-moving developments in the telecommunications industry, every firm wants a slice of the action.*
2 **Action stations!** A call to get ready and be at the point of duty: > *'Action stations, everyone! The royal couple will be here an hour from now!'* > *'Action stations! The programme goes on the air in one minute!'* Also, an order to soldiers, sailors, etc., to prepare themselves for fighting by getting into position.
3 **Actions speak louder than words** People take more notice of what you do, rather than what you say; sometimes used to express criticism of someone when he or she says one thing but does something different.

ACTUAL

Your actual ... *British* The real (person or thing): used to emphasise an expression: > *'So this is your actual automatic washing-machine!'* > *'I'm your actual expert, you know!'* Also spelt and pronounced (*slang*): *Yer actual.*

ADMIT

I must admit I freely acknowledge: > *'I must admit that I'm glad it's all over!'* > *'I must admit, I'm not as fit as I used to be.'* > *'That exam was very difficult, I must admit, even though I'd done a lot of revision.'*

AFRAID

I'm afraid I'm sorry: a polite way of expressing regret about having to refuse something, or about something bad that has happened or probably will happen: > *'I'm afraid I can't help you.'* > *'I've some bad news, I'm afraid – Gill's had an accident.'* > *'Can you drive me into town?' 'I'm afraid not; I'm too busy.'* > *'Were you beaten in the final?' 'Yes, I'm afraid so.'* In speech, *afraid* is often shortened to *'fraid*: > *'Sorry, 'fraid I don't know the answer.'*

AFTER

1 **After you** Please enter, go, etc., before me: > *'After you,' the gentleman said, opening the door to the lady standing by.* > *'After you sir.'* The stress falls on *after*.
2 **After you with ...** Please may I have (something) when you have finished with it: > *'After you with the salt, Jo.'*

AFTERNOON

Good afternoon *see* **Good 3.**

AGAIN

1 **Once again** *see* **Once 2.**
2 **There again** *see* **There 2.**

AGE

1 **Act (or be) your age!** Don't be so childish!: > *'Act you age, Jim, you're eighteen now!'*
2 **Age before beauty!** A humorous expression that an older person should go, enter, etc., before a younger, more good-looking person: > *'Age before beauty,' the young man said to his mother as he opened the door for her.*
3 **... in your old age** A humorous phrase added to something to mean that a person is at last doing something: > *'Have one of these apples!' 'Thanks – You're getting generous in your old age!'*

AGENDA

A hidden agenda A secret plan; a result of a plan which you want but which you do not tell other people about it: > *They're afraid that the chairman's statements on greater democracy are all really just part of his hidden agenda to reduce the power of the general committee.*

AGREE

1 **I couldn't agree less** I totally disagree: > *'This government's policies are really helping the country along.' 'I couldn't agree less; everything seems to have gone wrong for them.'*
2 **I couldn't agree more** I agree completely: > *'Harold will just have to do better at school, if he's to pass his exams.' 'I couldn't agree more – he's about halfway down the class in most subjects at the moment.'*

AID

What's ... in aid of? *British* What is the purpose of (something)?: >*'What are all these books in aid of? Don't tell me you've finally started your revision!'* > *'What are all these wires in aid of?' 'They connect the tape-recorder to the amplifier and the loudspeakers.'*

AIM

We aim to please A motto stating that the main purpose of a restaurant, shop, hotel, etc., is to provide a good service that satisfies its customers: often used as a response to a compliment made to those running the restaurant, etc.

AIR

1 **A breath of fresh air** *see* **Breath 1.**
2 **Clear the air** To talk openly about any misunderstandings or difficulty: > *'The organization suffers from the usual petty jealousies and problems. Some frank exchanging of feelings would clear the air and then everyone would work a lot better together.'*
3 **Hot air** Empty talk; mere words with no substance behind them. > *'All these politicians' promises at election time: everyone knows they're just a load of hot air.'*
4 **In the air** Used to describe an emotion or mood that is generally felt: > *A sense of excitement is in the air as the new session of parliament begins.*
5 **Up in the air** Not decided or settled yet: > *Plans for the new factory are still very much up in the air.*

ALIVE

You don't know you're alive *see* **Know 29.**

ALL

1 **After all**
   a In spite of everything: > *'It's only a game, after all.'*
   b Used to introduce a reason or argument that someone has forgotten or not considered: > *'Why can't I go to the party? After all, it is my birthday!'* > *'I do think we should let her go to town by herself. After all, she is ten now.'* In this sense, the stress falls on *all*.
   c Anyway: > *Ron didn't think he could see the football match, because he had so much work to do, but he managed to get it done and went after all.*
2 **All along** All the time: > *'I knew that all along.'* > *'I thought all along that you two would end up getting married, and you have!'*
3 **All in all** Taking everything into consideration: > *'All in all, this is the best party I've been to in years!'* > *'All in all, we see things pretty much in the same way, although we do disagree on minor details.'*
4 **All of** *Informal* Used to emphasise a distance, age, etc.: > *'It's all of millions of miles to the stars!'* > *'She's all of eighty years old, you know!'*
5 **All over** *Informal* Completely: > *'The man you've just described sounds like my neighbour all over!'* > *'Did he say you were mean with money? That's him all over!'*
6 **All right** Often spelt *alright*. Also **OK**
   a A conventional reply to a

greeting such as 'How are you?':
> *'How are you keeping, Jane?' 'All right, thanks. How about you?'*
Also used as a question to mean 'Are you well?': > *'All right?' 'Yes, thanks, and you ?'*
b Yes: used as reply to show agreement with a suggestion or plan: > *'Shall we go to Brighton this afternoon?' 'All right, let's!' > 'All right, we'll meet at six o'clock, then!'*
c Certainly: sometimes used with *but*: > *'Not much is happening on tonight's weather map. All right, there's some wind in the eastern part of the country, but that will soon die down.' > 'She's intelligent, all right, but not very good at making friends.' > 'We're agreed the country's in a mess, all right, but how are we going to get out of it?'*
d Used to express impatience or annoyance, or when you think someone is being unreasonable: > *'All right, don't take my advice if you don't want to, but don't blame me when you fail.'* The phrase can also be used a number of times to express extreme annoyance: > *'All right, all right, all right, I'm just coming!' > 'OK, OK, OK, there's no need to get so angry!'*
The phrase with the words repeated a number of times is also used humorously by comedians, music-hall artists, often to introduce something.
e Used to link parts of an explanation, meaning 'Do you understand me so far?': > *'You're going down the Bristol Road, then. All right, now you turn left at the bottom to get to the university.'*

7 **All the best!** *see* **Best 1.**
8 **All the same** *see* **Same 1.**
9 **All together now!** Let's say, sing, or act the words, song, etc. together: > *'All together now, children, "All things bright and beautiful ..."'*
10 **All well and good** *see* **Well 1.**
11 **And all** Pronounced *'n all.*
  a Including the people or things just mentioned; and a large number of the rest: > *'There were books, papers, magazines and all covering the whole of the floor.'* The phrase *Uncle Tom Cobbleigh and all* (from the ballad *Widdicombe Fair*) is becoming old-fashioned but is used humorously to mean 'and the rest': > *'Bill, Tom, Joe, and Uncle Tom Cobbleigh and all were at the party!'* Often the phrase *warts and all* is used to mean 'with all its faults as well as its good points': > *'Tell me what your new house is like, warts and all.'* This phrase can also function as an adjective in front of a noun: > *A warts-and-all account of life in our inner cities.* This comes from the instruction by Oliver Cromwell to the painter, Sir Peter Lely, to paint a true likeness of him with all his prominent warts.
  b And all that that means: > *'We never go out for meals these days, now that Bill's been made redundant and all.'*
  c Slang, British As well; too: > *'You can take that look off your face, and all, young Smith.'*
  d British Certainly: used at the end of a statement, to give

emphasis: > *'It's cold today, isn't it?' 'It is, and all!'*

12 **And all that** Used to make what has been said before sound less definite and sometimes even dubious: often introducing a further limiting phrase; followed by *but*: > *'The plot is very interesting and all that, but I still don't like it as a play.'* > *'Sorry and all that! I didn't realise that was your toe I'd trodden on!'*

13 **As all that** As might be expected or hoped: > *'He's not as clever as that, considering what his brothers are like.'*

14 **Evening all!** Good evening, everyone!: used supposedly by policemen, and made familiar as the opening words from the policeman George Dixon in the television programme, *Dixon of Dock Green*; now usually used in a rather staged, humorous way. *Morning all!* ('Good morning, everyone!') is also common.

15 **For all ...** So far as (something) is concerned; in spite of: > *'You might as well never have gone to college, for all the good it's done you.'* > *'He's been ill for two weeks, but for all that, he must be fit for next week's big match.'*

16 **For all I (you,** etc.**) know (**or **care)** As far as I (you, etc.) know (or care): sometimes used when the speaker is not really interested in the person or thing described: > *'He may be very rich, for all I know.'* > *'For all I care, Jim could be at the North Pole for the rest of his life – I'm never speaking to him again!'*

17 **I'm all right, Jack** *see* **Jack 2.**

18 **It's all right** *see* **Well 3.**

19 **It's all very well** *see* **Well 3.**

20 **Of all ...** Used to show surprise when mentioning a particular person, thing, or place: > *'Of all people, Harry, I would have expected better behaviour from you! I'm very disappointed in you.'*

21 **Of all (the) ...** Used to express annoyance: > *'Of all the stupid things to do!'* > *'Why choose me of all people to lead the team?'* > *'Of all the cheek – he's walked off with my sweets!'* The phrase can also be used without a following noun, to show annoyance: > *'Of all the ... someone's taken my bicycle!'*

22 **That's all** *see* **That 12.**

23 **That's (**or **it's) all right** There is no need to thank me or apologise: > *'Thank you for the present!' 'That's all right!'* > *'I'm sorry I trod on your toe!' 'It's all right, don't worry!'* > *'Thanks very much for coming to see us!' 'That's all right! Any time!'*

ALLOW

Allow me *Formal* Used as a polite way of offering to help someone: > *'Allow me to carry your suitcases, Madam,'* the porter said at the hotel entrance. Also **Permit me.**

ALSO

Not only ... but also *see* **Only 2.**

ALWAYS

... can (or **could) always ...** Used in making a suggestion or giving advice: > *'If she's not at Sue's, you could always try phoning her at Lynn's.'* > *'There's always the local college, if you don't get into university.'*

AND

1 **And all** *see* **All 11.**
2 **And all that** *see* **All 12.**
3 **And how!** see **How 1.**

ANOTHER

1 **Ask me another!** *see* **Ask 3.**
2 **Not just another ...** An expression used to describe an original, fresh approach to something: > *This is not just another dictionary; it has lots of additional exciting features.*
3 **Tell me another!** *see* **Tell 15.**
4 **You're another** *see* **You 4.**

ANYBODY

It's anybody's guess *see* **Guess 3.**

ANYONE

1 **It's anyone's guess** *see* **Guess 3.**
2 **It's anyone's game** (or **race**) The game (or race) can be won by any of the competitors: > *'With only 100 metres to go, it's still anyone's race.'*

ANYTHING

1 **Anything but** Far from (it); just the opposite (of): > *'He's anything but handsome.'* > *'I don't mean she's clever – anything but!'*
2 **Anything doing?**
   a What's happening?: > *'Anything doing tonight?' 'Yes, would you like to come and play football with us?'*
   b Will you be able to help?: > *'I'd like a lift into town this morning. Anything doing?'*
3 **Anything like** At all near; to any extent: > *'She isn't anything like as nice as her sister.'* > *'Winning first prize of £1,000 still doesn't mean we are anything like near being able to buy a house.'* Also **Anywhere near**: > *'Writing that essay shouldn't take you anywhere near two weeks.'* Also often in negative forms *Nothing like; Nowhere near*: > *'It's nowhere near as cold as it was last week.'*
4 **Anything you say** Used as a response to a request made to you, showing agreement with the request but often also an unwillingness to fulfil it: > *'Will you do the washing-up?' 'Anything you say.'*
5 **As ... as anything** Very: > *'She's as busy as anything, with a new baby, a job, and a house to run!'*
6 **Don't do anything I wouldn't do!** A friendly humorous way of saying goodbye: sometimes with sexual overtones: > *'Don't do anything I wouldn't do, Claire!' Sue said, winking at Claire. 'OK, cheerio, then!'* The catch phrase (*Be good and*) *if you can't be good, be careful!* has a similar meaning, and is a translation of the Latin *Si non caste tamen caute.*
7 **If anything** If there is any difference: > *'If anything, this glass has more in it than that one, but I can't really tell.'* > *'If anything, I prefer my new car to the older one, as it's more economical.'*
8 **Like anything** Very fast; very much: > *'He ran like anything down the street.'* > *'I adore chocolate like anything!'*
9 **Or anything** Used to introduce other indefinite possibilities as suggestions, not for a specific purpose: > *'If you want to ring me or anything, I'll be at the office all day.'*

10 Would not ... for anything
Would definitely not do something: > *'After all the fuss and bother of working with that company last time, I wouldn't do it again for anything.'*

ANYWHERE

1 Anywhere near *see* **Anything 3.**
2 We can't take you (him, her, etc.) **anywhere!** An expression used when someone has done or said something embarrassing, especially when visiting friends or in a restaurant: used humorously: > *'That's the sixth cake you've had so far! Honestly, Peter, we can't take you anywhere, can we!'*

APART

Apart from
a Used to introduce an exception to a general statement: > *'I feel fine, apart from my usual back trouble.'*
b Used to show an awareness of one aspect of something but to introduce an emphasis on another aspect that you consider more important: > *Quite apart from the purely technical con-siderations, the project would fail on the grounds of cost.*

APPEARANCE

To all appearances When you consider the way something generally seems to be: > *His second marriage was, to all appearances, happier than his first.* Also **By all appearances, from all appearances.**

APPLE

An apple a day keeps the doctor away A saying that if you eat an apple every day you will stay healthy and not be ill.

APRIL

April Fool! *see* **Fool 1.**

ARISE

Arise, Sir ... The expression supposedly used by the Queen or King of the United Kingdom when knighting a man: > *'Arise, Sir Matthew!' the Queen said to Sir Matthew Smith, knighted for service to his country and fellow men.* In fact, the monarch touches the new knight on both shoulders with the flat of the sword and then invests him with the insignia. However, no form of words is used at the actual ceremony. The expression is now chiefly used in films, sketches, etc., showing this scene.

ARM

1 Cost an arm and leg To be extremely expensive: > *'It cost us an arm and a leg to get these seats at the theatre. We're not going to walk out now, even though it's rubbish.'* > *Our new furniture suite won't cost you an arm and a leg.*
2 Give one's right arm To be prepared to do almost anything in order to obtain something that you want very much: > *'I'd give my right arm to be able to turn the clock back ten years and start out again fresh from university.'*
3 Twist someone's arm To persuade

someone strongly to do something: > *'I really didn't want to help out at the bazaar but Susie twisted my arm and I didn't feel I could say no.'*

4 **Up in arms** Very angry: > *Motoring organisations are up in arms against the increase in tax on petrol.*

5 **Welcome with open arms** To show that you are very pleased to see someone or that you are very enthusiastic about a plan, development etc.: > *The organisation has accepted the new safety report with open arms.*

ARMY

You and whose army! *Becoming old-fashioned* An expression used ironically in reply to a threat, to suggest that the person is too weak by himself or herself to carry it out: > *'If you don't shut up, I'll come and hit you!' 'Yeah – you and whose army?'*

AROUND

1 **Have been around** To have had a wide experience of different situations in life: > *'John's been around for a long while so he certainly knows what to do.'*

2 **The most exciting (interesting, etc.) ... around** The most exciting type of its kind that there is: > *That company is the most exciting fringe-theatre group around at the moment.*

ART

Have something down to a fine art To be extremely skilled and experienced at doing something: > *'Having spent months trying*

different routes to get to work, she's now got it down to a fine art and reckons she can be in the office within 45 minutes of leaving home.'

AS

1 **As against** In contrast to, in comparison with: > *Income was £1 million this year, as against only £800,000 last year.*

2 **As ... as they make 'em** *see* **Make 1.**

3 **As for** Concerning; used to elaborate further on an earlier statement: > *'We'll be able to have new science laboratories, but as for the project to rebuild the swimming pool, that'll have to wait – there simply isn't the money, I'm afraid.'*

4 **As if ...** An expression of annoyance, to show disapproval of a suggestion, statement, explanation, etc.: > *'As if you expect me to believe that story!'* > *'As if I cared whether you were here or not!'* Also used by itself, to show disbelief: > *'I'm going to take you out for a meal on Saturday!' 'As if! You've said that so many times before, and never done it.'*

5 **As it is** In reality; in the existing state of affairs: > *'As it is, I shall probably only just finish all my work today, without taking on any more.'* > *'The weather's awful today, as it is, so I've no hope of getting the washing dry.'* Also **As it turns out; As things stand.**

6 **As it were** If it might be expressed in this way; as if it were really like this: used with a strange way of saying something or to make a statement seem less definite: > *'Language is, as it were,*

a mirror of what a society is like.' > *'Our house in the country is our second home, as it were.'*

7 **As you were** An expression used to withdraw what has just been said: > *'The number is 720 ... No, it's not! As you were! It's 7202!'* Originally, a military order to return to the previous position.

8 **It's not as if** Used to state that something is most certainly not true: > *'You're not going to miss her much when she's gone, are you – it's not as if you were close friends.'*

ASK

1 **Ask a silly question** *see* **Question 1.**

2 **Ask for it** (or **trouble**) To behave in such a way as to invite or provoke trouble, punishment, etc.: > *'You were asking for it,'* Pat said as she hit her child. > *'If you turn up late when you promised to be early, you're really asking for trouble!'*

3 **Ask me another!** I do not know: > *'If the government knows how to run the country, why aren't things getting any better?' "Ask me another! – I've no idea either!'* Originally, said as a reply to someone asking an ordinary riddle. Also **Don't ask me!** The stress falls on *me.*

4 **... for the asking** Freely; you only have to ask for something and you can have it: > *'The job's yours for the asking.'*

5 **I ask you!** An expression showing surprise, disgust, or other emotion: > *'Peter says he's applying for a job as a policeman! I ask you! I know he's had a lot to do with them in the past, but that's*

been when he's been caught speeding!' > *'I ask you! He came in here and demanded the keys to my car! He could have been more polite about it!'* The stress falls on *ask.*

6 **If you ask me** In my opinion: but usually used with a statement that has not in fact been asked for: > *'If you ask me, Sally's a fool for going out with Alan – she's not his type at all!'* > *'I don't think you're as ill as you look, if you ask me.' 'I wasn't asking you, so shut up!'*

ASSURE

1 **I (can) assure you** Used to emphasise that something is true: > *'I assure you, your dog will be well taken care of by our specialist veterinary surgeons.'*

2 **(You can) rest assured** *see* **Rest 5.**

AT

1 **At that** Also: > *'He was very rich and a confirmed bachelor, at that.'*

2 **Where it's at** The place where exciting things happen: > *'I hear the new club in town is where it's at.'*

ATTENTION

(Your) attention, please Please listen carefully to what is about to be said: used in official announcements but also in informal situations: > *'Your attention, please. The train now standing at platform two is the fast service to London Euston.' > 'Attention please, everyone. Now's the time in the party when we're going to give Mum her present!'*

AUGHT

For aught I know (or **care**) *Old-fashioned or literary, becoming rare* If I know anything (or care) at all: often used when the speaker is not really interested in the person or thing described: > *'I've not missed seeing her all these years. She might even have emigrated, for aught I care.'* > *'For aught I know, he might be dead by now.'*

AUNT

My giddy (or **sainted**) **aunt!** *Old-fashioned* An expression showing surprise or amazement: > *'My giddy aunt! It's Joe Greenway! I've not seen him for years!'* > *'My sainted aunt! I've not heard that song for ages! Didn't we used to dance to it before the war?'* Also **Saints alive!**

AUTHORITY

Have something on good authority An expression used to say that you believe something is true because you trust the person who told you: > *'I have it on good authority that the secretary's job will become available in the next few weeks, if you're interested.'*

AVERSE

Not be averse to (doing) something *Formal* To like or want something slightly: > *'I would not be averse to spending more money, if that proved necessary.'*

AWAKENING

A rude awakening A sudden awareness of something unpleasant: > *'If you think everything will be easy once you've bought your own house, you're in for a rude awakening.'*

AWAY

1 **Away with ... !** A slogan used to show the speaker's disapproval of (someone or something): > *'Away with the old ideas and in with the new!'* > *'Away with her!'* > *'Away with the universities!'*
2 **Away with you!** *see* **Get 5.**
3 **They're away!** The horses, runners, etc., have set off!: > *'They're away! And it's* Magic Bullet *in the lead at the first fence!'*

AXE

Have an axe to grind To have a particular reason for doing something: > *'I'm merely making this suggestion; I have no axe to grind.'*

AYE

Aye, aye
   a *Nautical* Yes: an expression indicating agreement: > *'Aye, aye, sir, I'll see it's done immediately.'*
   b *British* An expression of surprise at seeing or finding someone or something, especially when this was expected: often used humorously and sometimes to indicate sexual overtones: > *'Aye, aye! So Neil and Lynette are together again!'* > *'Aye, aye! I suppose you gentlemen are just out for a walk at this time of night, are you? And you just happen to have jewels coming out of your pockets?'*

B

BABY

It's your (his, her, etc.) baby *Slang*
The task belongs to you (him, her, etc.) alone to deal with: >
'Jack, I need your help in working out the cost of the new centre.' 'Oh no, Freda, it's your baby, and you can work it out for yourself.' The stress falls on *your* (*his, her*, etc.).

BACK

1 **Back to square one** *see* **Square.**
2 **Back to the drawing board** *see* **Board 1.**
3 **Behind someone's back** In secret and in an unkind way: > *'They said all sorts of nasty things about me behind my back.'*
4 **Get off my back!** Leave me in peace!: > *'Get off my back, John, I've had enough of your chatter all morning; I must get on with some work.'*
5 **Get (or put) someone's back up** To make someone angry or annoyed: > *'Making me look a fool in front of all my friends really put my back up.'*
6 **Mind your back(s)!** Please let someone pass: > *'Mind your backs, please – Mr Jones wants to come through with the tea trolley.'*
7 **You scratch my back and I'll scratch yours** If you help me, then I will help you in return: > *'I'm snowed under with work at the moment. Could you possibly give me a hand, Victoria?' asked Sarah. 'Yes, I'm fairly quiet at the moment, but perhaps you could help me out with that rush job later in the month?' 'Certainly. You scratch my back and I'll scratch yours.'*

BACKWARDS

To know something backwards To know something very well: > *'He's been lecturing on heraldry for years. He knows it all backwards.'*

BAD

1 **(It's) too bad** It's a pity, but nothing can be done about it: > *'It's too bad that you've got to go now to catch your bus – still, we've had a good time together.'* > *'Too bad you couldn't come to the party – you'd have enjoyed yourself there.'* > *'It's too bad of you to have eaten all the biscuits.'* The stress falls on *too.*
2 **Not bad** Quite good, really: often used as an answer to a question about someone's health or welfare: > *'How are you today, John?' 'Not bad, thanks and you?'* Also **Not so bad; Not too bad.**
3 **Not half bad** *Becoming old-fashioned* Quite good really: > *'The weather's not half bad for this time of year, is it?'*
4 **That can't be bad!** An expression of approval or congratulation: > *'I've just heard I've won first prize in the competition – a trip to California!' 'Well, that can't be bad, can it!'*

BAG

1 **Bags I** (or **I bags**) ... *British school slang*
   a Don't touch it; it's mine, I claim it: > *'I bags that seat!'*
   b I want (to do something): > *'Bags I be goalie!'* > *'Bags I go first.'*

BALANCE

On balance Used to state a general opinion after you have thought about different opinions, facts, etc.: > *'Having thought through all the advantages and disadvantages of both the old and the new systems, on balance I think I prefer the older one.'*

BALL

1 **A whole new ball game**
   A situation that is completely different from a previous one or one experienced before: > *'I've no idea what to do. I used to live in a village. Living in the city is a whole new ball game.'*

2 **The ball is in your** (**his, her,** etc.) **court** It is your (his, her, etc.) turn to act now: > *'You've heard what he told you about the robbery and now you've got to decide whether to go to the police or not – the ball is in your court.'*

BANDWAGON

Jump (or **climb**) **on the bandwagon**
   To become involved in something that is fashionable and successful; often used to express disapproval of such involvement: > *'I don't think they're seriously interested in saving the planet – they're just jumping on the environmentalists' bandwagon.'*

BANG

1 **Bang goes ...** The chances of something happening suddenly disappear: > *'Mortgage rates going up again – bang goes our dreams of a new house.'*

2 **Bang on** *Slang* Exactly correct: > *'Your answer's bang on and you've won yourself £100!'* The stress falls on *bang*. Originally, an exclamation by fliers in bombers in World War II.

BARGAIN

1 **Into the bargain** As well; an expression used to emphasise something added: > *He had a full-time job but also regularly wrote long articles for his local newspaper into the bargain.*

2 **It's** (or **that's**) **a bargain!** I agree; I accept your offer: > *'You do the washing-up and I'll put the baby to bed!' 'Right, it's a bargain!'*

3 **More than you bargained for** More than you expected: > *'The time to write up my essay was much more than I'd bargained for.'*

BARGEPOLE

Not touch something with a bargepole Not to have anything to do with something: > *'I hear they're going to build a new factory right next to that house you've thought about buying. I wouldn't touch it with a bargepole.'*

BARK

His (or **her**) **bark is worse than his** (or **her**) **bite** He or she appears rougher, more bad-tempered, or more difficult than he or she really is: > *'Mr Pierson, our* *manager, isn't too bad really – his bark is worse than his bite.'*

BARN

He (she, etc.) must have been born in a barn A complaint when someone does not shut a door or window, when it is cold and windy outside: > *'He must have been born in a barn – he never shuts the door.'*

BARREL

Scrape the bottom of the barrel *see* **Bottom 3.**

BE

1 **Be a devil**! *see* **Devil 1.**
2 **Be my guest!** *see* **Guest.**
3 **Be that as it may** The facts concerning that state of affairs are of little importance: > *'I know I won't be here on Monday. Be that as it may, I intend that you should do some homework, so I'm setting it today.'*
4 **Be your age!** *see* **Age 1.**
5 **Have been and gone and …** To have (done something amazing or something not approved of): > *'After all the bother about his injury, he's been and gone and won first prize in the race!'* Also shortened to *Been and …* ; *Gone and …* ; > *'Who's been and gone and bought another block of ice-cream when we've still not finished this one?'*
6 **Have been and gone and done it** *Slang* To have done something extremely bad: > *'Mike's been and gone and done it now; old Jake must have seen him climbing on the school roof.'* Also shortened to *Gone and done it.*
7 **Well I'll be!** *see* **Blow 3.**

BE-ALL

The be-all and end-all The most important thing: > *'Winning is not the be-all and end-all of taking part in a competition, you know.'* The expression comes from Shakespeare's *Macbeth*, Act 1, Scene 7.

BEAN

Old Bean *see* **Boy 2.**

BEAT

1 **Beat it!** *Slang* Go away: > *The older boy hit the younger ones, shouting, 'Beat it, you lot we don't want you playing with us.'*
2 **Can you beat that!** *Slang* I am surprised!; have you ever heard anything so strange?: > *'Have you heard Carol's won that trip for two to California?' 'Well, can you beat that!'* The stress falls on *beat* and *that.*
3 **If you can't beat 'em, join 'em!** A saying used when a person fails in fighting for a particular idea or plan and therefore decides to move to the other, more successful side, *'em* is fixed in this phrase and is short for *them.*

BECOME

What has become of … ? What has happened to someone, especially someone you have not seen for a long time: > *'What became of that girl you knew at school? Julie, wasn't it?'* Also **What will become of … ?** What will happen to someone? > *'You know, I'm really concerned about Helen. What will become of her when Bob dies?'*

BEDPOST

Between you, me, and the bedpost
see **Between.**

BEE

1 **Have a bee in one's bonnet** To think something is so important that you keep talking about it: > *'He's got a bee in his bonnet about fresh air – that's why he's always opening up the windows and we have to sit here in the cold!'*

2 **He (or she) thinks he (or she's) the bee's knees** Someone thinks that they are the best person there is: > *'Now that he's at university, he thinks he's the bee's knees!'*

BEEN

1 **Have been and gone and ...***see* **Be 5.**

2 **Have been and gone and done it** see **Be 6.**

3 **Have been around** see **Around 1.**

BEG

1 **Beg the question** To base an argument on an assumption, the truth of which is the precise matter that is being argued about: > *'The idea of whether the motorway should be widened begs the question of whether we need more facilities for private transport in the first place.'*

2 **I beg to differ** *Formal* A polite way of saying that you disagree with someone: > *'I beg to differ from you on this point.'*

3 **I beg your pardon** *see* **Pardon.**

BEGGAR

Beggars can't be choosers An expression used to say that if only one course of action is offered to you, then you should accept that: > *Being unemployed means you may have to accept whatever job is available – beggars can't be choosers, you know.*

BELIEF

1 **Beyond belief** Incredible: > *'His crudeness is beyond belief.'*

2 **Contrary to popular belief** Used to introduce a statement that is the opposite of what most people generally believe: > *Contrary to popular belief, there are no more accidents on a Friday the 13th than there are on other days.*

BELIEVE

1 **Believe it or not** I am telling you the truth even if you don't believe me: > *'They were great fans of the Beatles, so believe it or not, when they had children, they called them John, Paul, George and Ringo!'*

2 **Believe (you) me** Please believe what I am saying: > *'I feel like the United States president with his finger on the nuclear button – believe me, I take the responsibility of this job seriously.'*

3 **Can't believe one's eyes** (or **ears**) Be so surprised at one you have seen or heard: > *He couldn't believe his eyes! Was he really face to face with his old schoolfriend, Tony?* > *She could scarcely believe her ears when he told her of his love for her.*

4 **... , I believe?** Am I right in thinking that you are (a particular person)?: > *'Mr Ronson, I believe?' 'Yes.' 'Then do come in.'*

5 I believe you, thousands wouldn't!
A rather humorous expression used to show mild acceptance of what someone has just said: > *'Excuse me, Kathy – Don't think I'm not sitting next to you because I don't like you or anything – it's just that I've seen Ruth over there, and I've not spoken to her for ages!' 'I believe you, thousands wouldn't.'*

6 If you believe that, you'd believe anything! An expression showing disbelief: > *'Here's a racing tip: Guide in the three o'clock at York.' 'If you believe that, you'd believe anything!'*

7 Not believe for a moment *see* **Moment 3.**

8 Would you believe A cry to catch and hold someone's attention: often used when there is some doubt about the truth of something: > *'Ladies and gentlemen, this is, would you believe, the last rabbit of its kind in the world,' the man at the fair shouted as he held up what looked like an old rag!*

BELL

1 Hell's bells *see* **Hell 2.**

2 Saved by the bell An expression said when something happens to someone in a difficult, embarrassing, or unpleasant situation that allows him or her to escape that situation: > *The awkward silence between them was broken by the sound of the phone ringing. 'Saved by the bell,' said Craig, as Rachel got up to leave.*

3 That rings a bell That sounds familiar; I seem to have heard the name, phrase, etc., somewhere before: *'Patrick Mann, you say? That name rings a bell. Ah yes, did you go to Bristol University?'*

BELT

Belt up! *Slang, becoming old-fashioned* Stop talking!: > *'Belt up, I'm trying to work!' Pat shouted impatiently.*

BEND

Bend over backwards To do all that you can to help people: > *'When we first moved into the town, all our neighbours bent over backwards to be kind to us.'*

BENEFIT

Give someone the benefit of the doubt To accept what someone is saying as true even though you are uncertain whether he or she is telling the truth or not: > *I'll give you the benefit of the doubt but next time, bring your membership card with you.'*

BENNETT

Gordon Bennett! *Old-fashioned* An expression showing great surprise: > *'Gordon Bennett! It's old Jake – how are you keeping these days? We've not seen each other for ages, have we!'* Gordon Bennett (1841–1918) was a proprietor of the *New York Herald*; his name is used as a euphemism to avoid calling upon the name of God directly.

BEST

1 All the best! May everything go well for you: used when saying goodbye to someone or at the end of a letter to a friend: > *'All the best then, Jean, and we'll see you* *in three weeks!'* Also used as a toast.

2 **Make the best of something** To accept an unsatisfactory situation and try to deal with it as best you can: > *'With only half the money that we asked for, we had to make the best of it.'* Also **Make the best of a bad job.**

3 **The best of British!** Good luck!: used to wish someone well, especially when the speaker doubts whether someone will succeed: > *'I'm off to take my driving test, and I've only had three lessons.' 'And the best of British to you – you'll need it!'* Originally, a phrase used in World War II, particularly when things were not going well for the British. The longer phrase *The best of British luck!* is also used.

BET

1 **Don't bet on it ...** Do not think that something is certain: > *'Don't bet on your friendship lasting for ever – that doesn't usually seem to happen these days.'*

2 **I bet**
a I'm sure; I should think: > *'After swimming the Channel, you were glad to see the White Cliffs of Dover, I bet.'* > *'I bet we run out of petrol before we reach Edinburgh! You last filled the tank up in Birmingham!'*
b I don't believe you: > *'He promised faithfully to be here at seven!' I bet! I've heard too many of his promises before!'*

3 **My bet is ...** Used to express one's own opinion about something, especially a future event: > *'My*

bet is that in ten years' time she'll be presenting her own TV show.'

4 **What's the betting?** Is it likely?: > *'What's the betting the bus will turn up late – it has done every day this week so far.'*

5 **You bet** *Slang* You can be certain: > *'Were you frightened by that bull?' 'Frightened? You bet I was; I was scared out of my skin!'*

6 **You (can) bet your bottom dollar** *Slang, becoming old-fashioned* You can be absolutely sure: > *'You can bet your bottom dollar that Roy will be away today, as we've got a history test.'* This idiom is American in origin. Alternatives to *You (can)* are *I will* and *I would* and alternatives to *bottom dollar* are *boots, life,* and *shirt.*

BETIDE

Woe betide *see* **Woe 1.**

BETTER

1 **Better safe than sorry** *see* **Safe.**

2 **For better or (for) worse** Whether the results of something are good or bad; used to express (sometimes resigned) acceptance of a state of affairs that cannot be changed: > *'This new school curriculum is, for better or worse, here to stay, so we might as well learn to live with it.'* The expression derives from the 'Solemnisation of Marriage' in the Book of Common Prayer: 'To have and to hold from this day forward, for better for worse, for richer for poorer, in sickness and in health, to love and to cherish, till death us do part, according to God's holy

ordinance; and thereto I plight thee my troth.'

3 Had better see **Have 1.**

4 That's better Used to express encouragement, praise or comfort: > *'Now, Daniel, let me have another look at your sketch. That's better, you've obviously tried very hard to get the perspective right this time.'*

5 What could be better than ... ? Something is perfect and cannot be improved upon: > *'What could be better than a month's holiday at our luxury hotel by the sea?'*

6 You (he, she, etc.**) would be better off** Used to express advice to someone to follow one course of action in preference to another > *'You'd be better off travelling by train – it's quicker than by car during the rush hour.'*

BETWEEN

Between you and me An expression used with the telling of a secret that the speaker wants only the person being spoken to to know and no one else: > *'Between you and me, I think Pete and Sarah's marriage is breaking up.'* This idiom is very commonly used wrongly in the form *Between you and I.* Also **Between ourselves; Between you, me, and the bedpost; Between you, me, and the gatepost.**

BEYOND

Be beyond you (him, her, etc.**)** Be too difficult for you (him, her, etc.): > *'Differential calculus is utterly beyond me, I'm afraid.'* > *'Why he should go and buy a new car is beyond me, considering he's completely penniless.'*

BIG

That's big of you (him, her, etc.**)** That's very generous, kind, of you (him, her, etc.): often said in a surprised tone, and used ironically: > *'That's big of you to help me wash the car – I thought you were far too busy to care about other people.'*

BIND

I'll be bound see **Bound 1.**

BIRD

1 A little bird told me I heard indirectly or unofficially from someone: used to avoid saying the source of some information: > *'A little bird told me you were moving soon!'* > *'How did you know Marcia was expecting a baby?' 'Ah, a little bird told me!'*

2 Kill two birds with one stone To do two things on one occasion: > *'We'll go to Manchester to do the shopping and we'll pop in to see Aunt Madge – we'll kill two birds with one stone.'*

BIRDIE

Watch the birdie! see **Cheese 2.**

BIRTHDAY

Happy birthday! An expression of greeting on someone's birthday, wishing a happy time: > *As Sarah came down to breakfast, the rest of the family cried, 'Happy birthday!'* > *'Let me be the first to wish you a happy birthday!'*

BISCUIT

That takes the biscuit Used to express surprise at the extreme example of something: > *'I've heard of lots of different excuses for being late but that one really takes the biscuit.'*

BIT

1 **Every bit as good (clever,** etc.**) as** Just as good (clever, etc.) as someone or something else. > *'She's every bit as clever as her sister.'*

2 **Not a bit** Not at all: often used as a reply: > *'Do you mind if I read your newspaper?' 'Not a bit.'*

BITE

1 **Bite off more than you (he, she,** etc.**) can chew** To accept responsibilities or tasks that are greater than you (he, she, etc.) can cope with: > *'You've taken on the school governorship and chair of the local sports league – don't you think you've bitten off more than you can chew?'*

2 **He (or she) won't bite** He or she will not harm you; used to say that there is no reason to be afraid of someone: > *'Why don't you ask her? She won't bite, you know.'*

3 **Once bitten, twice shy** You will be very careful about doing something a second time because on the first occasion you had a bad experience.

4 **What's biting you (him, her,** etc.**)?** *Slang* What is worrying or annoying you (him, her, etc.)?: > *'What's biting Geoffrey? He seems so nervous today.'*

BLAME

1 **Don't blame me** Do not hold me responsible for something; used when giving advice to someone not to do something: > *'If I were you, I wouldn't accept that job. Don't blame me if it all goes wrong.'*

2 **Have only yourself (himself, herself,** etc.**) to blame** You are responsible for what happens; used when the speaker is unsympathetically saying that someone's difficulties are his or her own fault: > *'You've only yourself to blame if you brush aside her advice.'*

3 **I don't blame you (him, her,** etc.**)** You were (he or she was, etc.) quite right: > *'I told her I thought she was the biggest fool I'd ever met.' 'I don't blame you – I think so too!'* > *'I don't blame him for walking out on her – I'd have done the same.'* Also **I can't say I blame you.**

BLAST

1 **Blast it (or you)!** *Slang, British* An expression of annoyance: > *'I can't get this screw into the wall, blast it!'* > *'Blast you, can't you shut up while I'm trying to read?'* > *'Blast this sticky tape! Why doesn't it ever work when I want it to?'*

2 **Full blast** At full power > *'Do you have to have your radio on full blast all the time?'*

BLAZE

1 **Go to blazes!** *Slang, old-fashioned* Go away!: > *'Can I have a word with you for a moment?' 'No, go to blazes!'*

2 Like blazes *Old-fashioned* Very fast; very much: > *She ran like blazes away from the scene of the explosion.*

3 What (how, when, where, who, why) the blazes? *Old-fashioned* Whatever (however, whenever, wherever, whoever, why ever): used in questions to emphasise a strong feeling such as annoyance or surprise: > *'What the blazes is going on here?'* > *'How the blazes did you get here? I thought you were on holiday in Canada!'*

BLEED

My heart bleeds for you *see* **Heart 7.**

BLESS

1 Bless you! An expression said to someone who has just sneezed.

2 (God) bless my soul! *Old-fashioned* An expression of surprise or pleasure: > *'God bless my soul! You've won first prize again – well done!'* Also **Bless me!; I'll be blessed!; Upon my soul!; (Well) I'm blest!**

3 God bless (you) An expression said at saying goodbye to close friends, wishing them well: > *As we stood at the gate, we shouted, 'God bless' to Johnny; he turned round and waved goodbye as he walked slowly down the lane.*

4 (God) bless you (him, her, etc.**)** An expression of thankfulness, fondness, or well-wishing: > *'Bless you, Martha, you shouldn't have bothered to buy me these flowers, but it really is very kind of you.'* > *'There were many of us who had good reason to be thankful, for the school, God bless it, had*

encouraged us greatly.' Also **Bless your (his, her,** etc.**) heart,** and to small children **Bless his (her,** etc.**) (little) cotton socks.**

BLESSING

1 A blessing in disguise Something that at first seems to be a cause of difficulties but in the end proves to bring benefits: > *'Jo's illness proved to be a blessing in disguise: it brought her and George much closer together.'*

2 Count your blessings To remember the good things in one's life instead of moaning: > *My gran always used to say, 'when you feel down, count your blessings.'*

BLIND

It makes you go blind *see* **Make 3.**

BLOOD

1 Like getting blood out of a stone Used to describe something extremely difficult: > *Trying to get some companies to pay money they owe you is like getting blood out of a stone.*

2 Make your (his, her, etc.**) blood boil** To make someone extremely angry: > *'To think what some people do to young children really makes my blood boil.'*

BLOW

1 Blow it! Used to express annoyance: > *'Blow it! I just can't get this wallpaper straight! Will someone come and help me, please?'*

2 Blow me (down)! Used to express surprise: > *'Blow me, if it isn't old Charlie – I've not seen you for years: how are you, old friend?'* > *'I asked him twice to remember to post the* *letters, and blow me down if he didn't forget all about it!'*

3 (Well) I'll be blowed! *Slang* Used to express surprise or annoyance: > *'I'll be blowed if I'll help him: he never helps me when I need him.'* Also shortened to **(Well) I'll be ...!** (where ... shows a pause) to express surprise: > *'Well, I'll be ..., the horse has won another race!'*

BOARD

1 Back to the drawing board We must go back to the beginning: used when an invention or design has gone wrong: > *'Have you heard, the new car we're working on blew up this afternoon?' 'Well, it's back to the drawing board, then, I suppose!'*

2 Take something on board To accept an idea, a proposal, etc.: > *'We'll certainly think about your comments and may well take them on board.'*

BOAT

1 Miss the boat To miss a chance to do or have something and so not have another opportunity: > *'You'll have to apply for the post soon or else you'll miss the boat.'*

2 Push the boat out To spend a lot of money on something, especially a celebration: > *'Michelle's our only daughter so we thought we'd really push the boat out for her wedding.'*

3 Rock the boat To upset a calm situation by disagreeing with others: > *'I don't want to rock the boat but I think someone should stand up for what's right.'*

BOB

(And) Bob's your uncle *Becoming old-fashioned* (And) everything will work out well; everything will be all right: > *'You turn left at the roundabout, go straight on for a little way, and, Bob's your uncle, you're at the motorway.'* The origin is unknown.

BODY

Over my (his, her, etc.) dead body Not if I (he, she, etc.) can stop it happening: used to show opposition to what has just been said: > *'Can I borrow the car tonight, Dad?' 'Over my dead body, son, you've crashed it once this week already.'* > *'A wage freeze – over our dead body,' the trade union leaders cried.*

BOLD

If I may be so bold Used as a polite way of asking or suggesting something without offending anyone: > *'If I may be so bold as to say so, I think we should ask the opinion of someone who has had experience in this matter.'*

BONE

1 Feel in your bones To know something in a strong and definite way without being able to explain why. Also **have a feeling in your bones**: > *'I've got a feeling in my bones that you're going to lose disastrously today.'*

2 I've a bone to pick with you I've something I want to complain to you about: > *'Ah, there you are, Audrey, I've a bone to pick with you – why didn't you tell me you'd be* *out all night? I was worried stiff about you!'*

3 Make no bones about it! *see* **Make 5.**

BOOK

1 In my book In my opinion: > *'In my book, not being dressed smartly for work was a major misdemeanour.'*

2 In your (his, her, etc.) bad (or good) books To have done something that has annoyed (or pleased) you (him, her, etc.): > *'From the way the teacher's looking at you, I think you're in her bad books.'*

3 That's a turn-up for the book! *see* **Turn 1.**

4 Throw the book at someone To punish someone very severely, because he or she has broken the rules: > *'If you misbehave again, they'll really throw the book at you.'*

BOOT

1 To boot As well; an expression used to emphasise something added: > *'They're offering two weeks' holiday at a special cut-price rate and they're throwing in free car hire to boot.'*

2 You (can) bet your boots *see* **Bet 6.**

BORN

1 He (or she) must have been born in a barn *see* **Barn.**

2 I wasn't born yesterday I am not easily fooled: > *'I won't let you take the car away till I know the money's actually paid into my bank account. I wasn't born yesterday, you know!'*

3 In all my born days *see* **Day 6.**

4 There's one born every minute There really are a lot of fools

about: > *'We were trying to sell our house for a long time and then suddenly someone came up and offered us thousands more than it's really worth: there's one born every minute!'*

5 You don't know you're born *see* **Know 29.**

BOTHER

1 Bother (it)! *Old-fashioned* An expression of annoyance: > *'Bother it! I've forgotten my keys.'*

2 It's no bother I'm happy to help you and it will take little effort: > *'It's no bother just to drop you off at the station.'*

BOTTOM

1 Bottoms up An expression used when drinking with other people.

2 From the bottom of your (his, her, etc.) heart Very sincerely: > *'I'd like to thank you all from the bottom of my heart. You've been so helpful to me over these last few weeks.'*

3 Scrape the bottom of the barrel To do or use something of very low quality, often because higher-quality material has already been used or taken: > *The artists were really scraping the bottom of the barrel when they designed this new type style.*

BOUND

1 I'll be bound *Becoming old-fashioned* I'm quite sure: > *'The bus will be late again, I'll be bound.'*

2 I'm bound to say Used to introduce something that the speaker finds unwelcome or unsuitable: >

'I'm bound to say I think you're in danger of making a serious mistake.'

BOY

1 **(Oh) boy!** An expression of excitement, surprise, pleasure, etc.: > *'Oh boy, our team's going to win! How fantastic!'* Also **Boy, oh boy!**

2 **Old boy** A familiar, friendly way of talking to a man or male animal: > *'Well, Jim, how are you today, old boy?'* > *'Come on, old boy, eat up your biscuits and then I'll take you out for a walk.'* Also **Old bean** (*British, old-fashioned*); **Old chap; Old fellow** (*British, old-fashioned*); **Old fruit** (*British old-fashioned*); **Old man** Old man is used especially to refer to a person's husband or father: > *'The old man's just gone out.'*

3 **There's** (or **that's**) **my boy!** An expression of encouragement, approval, excitement, or delight: > *'There's my boy! First again! Well done!'*

BRAIN

1 **Have something on the brain** To think constantly about something: > *'He's always had football on the brain ever since he was little.'*

2 **Pick someone's brains** To ask someone for help or information on something because that person has a lot of knowledge on the subject: > *'Do you mind if I pick your brains for a moment? I need to buy a new computer printer and I wondered if you knew which was the best one to buy.'*

BREAK

1 **Break it up!** Stop fighting!; move!: > *'Break it up! Move along there,'* the police called out to the rival gangs of teenagers milling around in the town square.

2 **Give me a break** *Slang* Stop annoying me by what you are talking about or what you are doing: > *'Give me a break, will you. All you ever talk about is your wretched music. I've had enough of it!'*

3 **You're breaking my heart** *see* **Heart 7.**

BREATH

1 **A breath of fresh air** Something that is exciting and new: > *'Jason's ideas are a real breath of fresh air. They're original and creative – just what we need.'*

2 **Don't hold your breath** There is no need to wait eagerly for something; used when you think something is unlikely to happen: > *'The politicians tell us that one day we'll get back to full employment but don't hold your breath.'*

3 **In the same breath** Used when you are talking about two things that contradict each other: > *'You can't talk about a higher quality of education and in the same breath think of reducing government funding to schools.'*

4 **Take your breath away** To be extremely beautiful or pleasing: > *The view of the mountains from her window really takes your breath away.*

5 **Waste your breath** To continue talking without having any effect

on your listeners because they are not taking any notice of you: > *'Don't waste your breath. They'll carry on doing their own thing, whatever you say to them.'*

BREATHE

As I live and breathe *see* **Live 1.**

BRITISH

The best of British! *see* **Best 3.**

BROAD

As broad as it is long It makes no difference whichever way you consider it or whatever you do, it comes to the same thing: >*'Whether we travel south first down the main road and then east along the motorway or east along the main road and south down the motorway is just the same: it's as broad as it is long.'*

BROTHER

Oh brother! *Becoming old-fashioned* An expression of mild annoyance, impatience, or surprise: > *'Oh brother, the phone's ringing again! That's the tenth time this morning – who can it be now?'*

BUCK

The buck stops here (or **with me**) The final responsibility for something rests with me, not anyone else: > *'The buck stops with me. I'm in charge and I'll have to accept the blame if anything goes wrong.' The US President Truman had a sign on his desk with the words 'The buck stops here.'*

BULL

1 **A bull in a china shop** Used to describe someone who is insensitive and who rashly says things that upset other people.

2 **Like a red rag to a bull** Very likely to make someone extremely angry: > *'Telling them that you want to leave college is like a red rag to a bull.'*

3 **Take the bull by the horns** To act with determination: > *'I know it's a difficult decision but it's time to take the bull by the horns and tell him that resigning is the only course of action open to you.'*

BULLY

Bully for you (**him, her,** etc.) *Slang, old-fashioned* An expression used in reply to someone's boasting, especially when the speaker is jealous; and in an ironical tone: > *'We're flying to America for a month next week.' 'Oh, bully for you. I suppose I've got to stay here and work all the time you're away.'*

BURN

Feel one's ears burning *see* **Ear 2.**

BUSH

Not beat about the bush To speak directly and clearly about something: > *'Let's not beat about the bush. Tell me honestly – did you take the money or didn't you?'*

BUSINESS

1 **Business is business** A saying used to state that in commercial dealings, matters such as friendship should not be allowed to interfere with the aims of

efficiency and making a profit:
> *'We shouldn't let the fact that we've just got engaged affect our relationship at work – business is business, you know.'*

2 **Mind your own business!** An expression used as a warning not to interfere in other people's concerns: > *'Can you tell me what you're doing?' 'No; mind your own business!'* This phrase is offensive in direct speech.

3 **None of your business** Not something that you have a right to be concerned about: > *'It's none of your business what I do in my private life.'*

BUT

1 **But for ...** Except for; without: > *'But for Mark's quick response in the emergency, Sharon would not be alive today.'*

2 **But me no buts** Rare Don't give me any of your excuses: > *'But me no buts this time, just do what I tell you and do it at once!'*

3 **But then** Used to introduce qualifying conditions that make what has just been said appear less true: > *'The score at half-time was 4-0 to us. Most teams would have increased their lead to 6-0 or 7-0 but then, most teams don't have such a poor defence as ours, so we ended up drawing 4 all.'*

4 **Not only ... but also** *see* **Only 2**.

5 **There are no buts about it** There is no doubt about it: > *'I saw you steal the money from the drawer. There are no buts about it. You can't defend yourself because I caught you in the act.'*

BUTTER

Butter wouldn't melt in his (or her) mouth He or she appears to be kind and well-behaved, but isn't really: > *'She looks as if butter wouldn't melt in her mouth, but she's not so harmless really!'*

BUY

I'll buy it *Slang* I don't know the answer – you tell me: > *'What did the gum say to the glue?' 'Go on, I'll buy it.'; 'Find a good thing and stick to it.'*

BUZZ

Buzz off! *Slang, chiefly British, becoming old-fashioned* Go away!: > *'Buzz off, I'm trying to work.'*

BY

By and large *see* **Whole**.

C

CAKE

1 **A piece of cake** *see* **Piece 2.**

2 **You can't have your cake and eat it** You cannot have the benefit of the two things you want; only one is possible: > *'We won't let you work shorter hours and get more money – you can't have your cake and eat it.'*

CALL

1 **Don't call us, we'll call you** An expression humorously used to say that someone is not really interested in another person, especially having someone work for the other person: > *'I've been trying to get work from that firm for a long time, but they don't seem to like me.' 'Don't call us, we'll call you, you mean?' 'I suppose so.'* Also **Don't ring us, we'll ring you.**

2 **Nature calls** *see* **Nature.**

3 **(Now) that's what I call ...** An expression of great praise or admiration for (something or someone): often said in a surprised tone: > *'Now that's what I call a meal! It was delicious, dear.'* > *'Just look at that sunset! That's what I call beautiful.'*

4 **There is no call for ...** There is no need to behave in such a rude way: > *'There's no call for such bad language – we know you're already doing all you can.'*

CAN

1 **Can I (you, etc.) ...?** Used in making a request or asking for permission: > *'Can I have a cup of tea, please?' 'Yes, here you are.'* > *'Can you hold the ladder a minute, please?'*

2 **How can you ...?** *see* **How 12.**

CARE

1 **A (fat) lot you (I, etc.) care!** You (I, etc.) don't care at all: > *'A fat lot you care about whether I've got a job or not – you don't help me to find one.'*

2 **For all I (you, etc.) care** *see* **All 16.**

3 **For aught I care** *see* **Aught.**

4 **Have a care!** *Old-fashioned* Please be more careful: > *'Have a care, James, you nearly knocked over that pile of books!'*

5 **(I) couldn't care less** I am not in the least bit interested: often used when the speaker is angry, frustrated, or bored: > *'I couldn't care less what you do with those old boxes. They've been there for months. Just get them out of here.'* > *'Didn't you realise that was the headmaster you were so rude to?' 'Couldn't care less, I'm leaving next term, anyway.'*

6 **I didn't know you cared!** *see* **Know 10.**

7 **Not care a damn** *see* **Damn 6.**

8 **Take care!** Be careful!: often used (especially in American English) when saying goodbye to someone: > *'Take care then, Nancy!' 'Yes, I will – cheerio, Amy!'* > *'Do take care when you're crossing the road!'*

9 **What do I (you, etc.) care?** I (you, etc.) do not care at all about

something: > *'What do you care? You're only interested in yourself.'*

10 **Who cares?** It doesn't matter; I don't care: > *'This is the problem, Sue – if you don't apply for college by January, you won't have a chance of a place!' 'Who cares? I'm not really interested in studying, anyway!'*

11 **Would you care for ... ?** Would you like something? Used in making a polite request: > *'Would you care for another cup of tea?' > 'Would you care to join us for a drink?'*

CAREFUL

You can't be too careful Used for giving advice to someone to take every possible precaution to avoid danger or trouble: > *You can't be too careful as far as fire is concerned.*

CARPET

Sweep something under the carpet To try to forget something bad: > *'He wanted to sweep his years in prison under the carpet.'*

CASE

1 **A case in point** A good example (of something that has just been mentioned): > *Museums need not be boring. A case in point is the new County Museum's display of local history with lots of hands-on activities for children.*

2 **In any case**
a Whatever may happen; even if other things change, one part of a situation is not changed: > *'I don't know whether the doctors could have saved her. In any case it's all too late now – she's died, hasn't she?'*
b Anyway: said before the main point is mentioned, to bring out a contrast with something just said: > *'What an awful time you must have had. In any case you're safe, which is the main thing.'*

3 **In that case** Used to describe possible results or circumstances if something actually happens: > *'I've decided I'm not going to the party.' 'Well, in that case, I'm not going either.'* Also **That being so.**

4 **(Just) in case** So as to be safe if something happens; used to advise caution: > *At your fireworks display always have a bucket of sand available near your bonfire, just in case.*

CAT

1 **(Has the) cat got your tongue?** *Old-fashioned* Can't you speak?: sometimes used to a child who refuses to say anything: > *'What's the matter, Ronny? Has the cat got your tongue?'*

2 **Let the cat out of the bag** To give away a secret: > *'Trust Malcolm to let the cat out of the bag and tell Jane we're having a party!'*

3 **Who's she? The cat's mother?** *Old-fashioned* Used when someone, especially a child, refers to a lady not by name, but with she: > *'She comes and sees us every Saturday.' 'Who's she? The cat's mother?' 'Mrs Robinson, I mean.'*

CATCH

1 **I wouldn't be caught dead** *see* **Dead 2.**

2 **You wouldn't catch me doing something** I would never do something: > *'You wouldn't catch me handing in my homework late.'*

CEASE

Wonders will never cease *see* **Wonder 6.**

CHALK

Not by a long chalk (or **shot**) Not by any means: > *I've not given up my hopes of becoming a famous footballer, not by a long shot.*

CHANCE

1 **(A) fat chance!** *see* **Hope 3.**

2 **Any chance of ...** Used when asking to have something: > *Is there any chance of someone opening a window? It's so stuffy in here.* > *'Any chance of a cup of tea?'*

3 **By any chance** Used when politely asking a question to find out whether something is true: > *'You wouldn't be Mr Sargeant by any chance?'*

4 **Chance would be a fine thing** Used to say that what you want to happen is extremely unlikely: > *'If he asked me out, then I'd jump at it.' 'Chance would be a fine thing!'*

5 **Give me (him,** her, etc.**) a chance!** Give me (him, her, etc.) the opportunity to do something: used when what is being expected is thought unreasonable: > *'Have you done the washing-up yet?' 'Give me a chance – I've only just finished my meal!'*

CHANGE

1 **A change is as good as a rest** A saying that just a change in one's activities or environment is very valuable or has the same value as doing nothing: often said when one has a busy holiday, for example spent in decorating one's home, after one has worked hard in one's job.

2 **All change!** The train, bus, etc., ends its journey here, sometimes also meaning that passengers must board another one to continue travelling: > *'All change!' the guard shouted as the train drew into Amersham station.*

3 **Change the subject** *see* **Subject.**

4 **For a change** Used when describing an action or experience that is pleasantly different from what usually happens: > *'For a change, why don't you let me drive so that you can see the sights?'*

5 **It makes a change** Something different from the everyday routine is very pleasant: > *'Having pizzas is nice! It makes a change from the usual pie and chips!'* > *'We went to Bournemouth for our holidays. The sea air made a welcome change for Ruth and myself.'*

CHAP

Old chap *see* **Boy 2.**

CHEEK

What a cheek Used to express anger or shock when someone has spoken to you rudely or behaved toward you very disrespectfully: > *'What a cheek! He borrowed my car without even asking me.'*

CHEER

1 **Cheer up!** An expression of encouragement; you can be happy: > *'Cheer up, Pete, we're winning by three goals, and there's only ten minutes left!'* Sometimes a

phrase is added, such as *Cheer up – the worst is yet to come!*

2 **Three cheers!** Three cries of *hurrah* said by a group of people to praise a person, event, etc.: > *'Three cheers for the cricket team! Hip, hip, hurrah! Hip, hip, hurrah! Hip, hip hurrah!'* The person leading the cheers cries *hip, hip* and everyone shouts *hurrah*; this all happens three times.

3 **Two cheers!** There is little enthusiasm for what is suggested: > *'Two cheers for your plan to go to the National Park on a coach outing – we'd much rather watch the football on television!'*

CHEESE

1 **Hard cheese!** *Becoming old-fashioned* An expression of sympathy at someone's misfortune; but usually now only used when the speaker does not really care about the other person's trouble: > *'I failed my driving test again.' 'Oh, hard cheese – what went wrong this time?'* > *'I've got to go out tonight.' 'Hard cheese!. You've been in all day, so the fresh air will do you good!'*

2 **Say 'cheese'!** An expression used by a photographer when trying to get the people he or she is about to photograph to smile. This phrase is used because when one is saying the word cheese, one's lips spread to form part of a smile. Also **Watch the birdie!** This phrase is perhaps used so that the people will look at the camera in a lively, expectant way, as if gazing at a bird.

CHILD

My child A way of addressing someone: used by an older person when speaking to someone much younger or by a priest to a person confessing his or her sin: > *'My child, I remember years ago when all this was just fields, and how we used to go for long walks in the summer.'* > *'My child, you may go in peace, knowing that God has forgiven your sins.'*

CHIN

(Keep your) chin up! Keep cheerful; don't give up: > *'Chin up, Freddie, it's not far to go now – we're almost home.'* Also (*slang, British*) **Keep your pecker up!**

CHIP

He's (she's, etc.**) got a chip on his (her,** etc.**) shoulder** He (she, etc.) bears a grudge or feels bitter or resentful about something: > *'He's got a chip on his shoulder because he can't read or write.'*

CHOP

Chop, chop Used to ask someone to act more quickly: > *'Come on children, chop, chop. The bus leaves in two minutes.'*

CHRISTMAS

Merry (or **Happy**) **Christmas!** An expression of greeting at Christmas, wishing a happy time: > *'Merry Christmas, everyone!'* > *'I wish you all a very happy Christmas!'*

CHUCK

Chuck it (in)! *Slang* Stop what you're doing!: *'Chuck it in, Ted, or I'll go and tell your Dad.'*

CIRCUMSTANCES

1 **In** (or **under**) **the circumstances** Used with a statement to show that a particular situation is different from what is normally expected: > *'Under the circumstances I think we can waive the usual rule about having to live in the area for two years.'*

2 **Under any circumstances** Used to emphasise that something definitely must not happen: > *They're against abortion under any circumstances – even if the mother's life is threatened.* > *Under no circumstances are you allowed to leave the building.*

CLEAR

1 **All clear** There are no obstacles in our way; we can now do what we want: > *'The teachers have all gone now. All clear! We can climb over the fence!'*

2 **Clear off!** Go away! > *'You children are not supposed to come into this room – now clear off!'*

3 **Do I make myself clear?** Used for emphasis when one is angry with someone: > *'I won't stand for such behaviour in my class. Do I make myself clear?'*

CLOUD

On cloud nine Extremely happy: > *'She's been on cloud nine ever since she heard she passed the exam.'*

CLUB

Join the club! Well done!: said when something (usually bad) that has already happened to the speaker and to other people happens to the person being talked to: > *'I've failed the exam!' 'Join the club! Lots of us have as well, don't worry!'*

CLUE

Not have a clue Not to know anything about something or what to do: > *'So we're in Warrington, and now where do they live?' 'I haven't a clue.'* > *'I haven't a clue what I want to do with my life.'*

COBBLEIGH

Uncle Tom Cobbleigh and all *see* **All 11a.**

COBBLER

What a load of (old) cobblers! *see* **Load 2.**

COIN

1 **On the other side of the coin** *see* **Side.**

2 **To coin a phrase** *see* **Phrase.**

COLUMBUS

Christopher Columbus! *Old-fashioned* An expression showing great surprise: > *'Christopher Columbus! What are you doing here? I thought you were still in Edinburgh!'* The name of the Spanish navigator and explorer (1451–1506).

COME

1 **As ... as they come** *see* **Make 1.**

2 **Come again?** I didn't hear what you said, or I didn't understand what you said; could you say it again, please?: > *'I hope this diagram is clear.' 'Come again?' 'I said, I hope this diagram is clear.'* > *'Mum's won £100 in the lottery!' 'Come again?' 'You know that lottery Mum tries every week –*

well, she's just won £100!' Also (*rare*) **Say again?**

3 Come and get it! The food is now ready for you to come to eat: > *'Come and get it!' Jo called to the children, and they all came running downstairs to the dining-room.* Originally used in the army.

4 Come back ..., all is forgiven! *Humorous* An expression used when (someone) has left a place or job and is missed: > *'If only she were here now ... Come back, Freda, all is forgiven!'*

5 Come, come! I don't believe what you've been saying; think again; let's settle the matter: sometimes used to express the speaker's annoyance or impatience: > *'Come, come, what were you really doing behind the bicycle sheds? I think you've been telling me lies so far.'* Also **Come now:** > *'Come now, let's not get angry about your results in the exams, but see if we can talk about them calmly.'*

6 Come off it! Stop trying to deceive people!; stop your boasting!: > *'Come off it, Henry, we know you're only joking!'* > *'As I was saying to the President only last week,' Penny began. 'Oh, come off it, Penny, you've never even met him,' Susie interrupted.*

7 Come on Also **Come along**
a An expression used to encourage or persuade a person to do something: > *'Come on, Rosalind, you can tell me – I promise I won't tell anyone else.'* *'Come along, boys, one of you must know who wrote* Macbeth.*'*
b Move more quickly; hurry up: > *'Come on, Jackie, we've not got*

all day. The train's leaving in five minutes!'

8 Come to that An expression used to add to and modify a previous statement: > *'I remember we didn't have much money at the time. Come to that, none of us did.'* Also **If it comes to that:** > *'I don't think I've seen Jim for ages now. If it comes to that, I've not seen his brother, either.'*

9 Come what may Whatever happens: > *They are determined come what may, to make sure that the cease-fire holds.*

10 ... coming up Food or drink (at home or in a café or restaurant) is ready to be served: > *'Sausage and chips coming up!' the lady behind the counter called out.*

11 Do you come here often? Traditionally held to be a comment that someone makes in order to start a conversation with a person who he (or she) does not know but who they find sexually attractive.

12 Don't come the ... with me Do not pretend to behave in a certain way: > *'Don't come the innocent victim with me! I know that you're lying through your teeth.'*

13 How come ... ? Why is it that ... ? How did it come about that ... ?: often used when the speaker is surprised: > *'How come you're back from holiday a week early?'* > *'You're late, Doris, how come? You're usually so punctual.'*

14 If the worst comes to the worst *see* **Worst.**

15 (Now I) come to think of it Now that (or when) I stop to think

41

about it: > 'Now I come to think of it, Robby does look like his mother, as you said.' > 'I've not had a letter from Hugh for a few weeks, but come to think of it, I've not written to him.'

16 **What is ... coming to?** What is happening to (something)?: > 'What is this city coming to; people get mugged, women get raped – what's happening to us all?'

17 **When it comes down to it** Used to introduce an important aspect of something: > We can discuss this all day but we know that when it comes down to it nothing is going to change.

COMFORT

Too close for comfort Too near so that it makes someone afraid or anxious: > The bombs fell in the surrounding street, too close for comfort.

COMMENT

No comment I don't want to answer your question; I've nothing to say on this subject: > After the important meeting, the minister firmly said, 'No comment' to the waiting reporters and quickly got into his car. > 'For the moment I'm still an honest businessman.' 'For the moment?' 'No comment!' > 'I'm a bit impatient at times, aren't I?' 'No comment!'

COMPANY

1 **Present company excepted** Not including the people who are here now: used as a polite comment by a speaker to tell his or her listeners that his or her unfavourable or critical comments do not apply to them: > 'Present company excepted, I don't think many people realise the full significance of this project.'

2 **Two's company, three's a crowd** It is all right to have two people together by themselves, but a third person is not wanted; said for example by a boyfriend and girlfriend to a third person who wants to join them.

COMPLAIN

Can't complain A reply to a greeting such as 'How are you?', saying that one's health and well-being are really not too bad: > 'How are you, Carol?' 'Can't complain, I suppose, but I've got a lot of shopping to do today.' Also **Mustn't grumble**: > 'How's things?' 'Mustn't grumble – I've finished most of my work and I'm just about to go home.'

COMPLIMENT

1 **My** (or **our**) **compliments to the chef** Formal An expression of praise to be passed on to the person who has cooked a good meal in a restaurant: > 'My compliments to the chef; that fish was very tasty!' Also **Please present** (or **give**) **my** (or **our**) **compliments to the chef.**

2 **The compliments of the season** Best wishes for a particular time of year: mostly used at Christmas: > 'The compliments of the season to you, Jack!' 'Thank you, sir, and I wish you the same.'

CONCERN

As far as I'm concerned What I think is this: used to give a personal view; sometimes used in a situation which the speaker finds unpleasant: > *'As far as I'm concerned you're welcome to come to the lecture, but the Head of Department may not agree.'* > *'As far as I'm concerned, you can leave now – we've got nothing more to say to each other.'*

CONCLUSION

In conclusion Used to show that one is finishing what one wants to say: > *'In conclusion, ladies and gentlemen, I'm sure we would all like to express our appreciation to tonight's speaker for her most interesting lecture.'*

CONFESS

I must confess I freely acknowledge or admit: > *'I must confess I'm glad the holidays are over and the children are back at school.'* > *'I must confess I cried a bit in that film – it was all too sentimental for me.'*

CONFOUND

Confound it (you, etc.)! *Old-fashioned* An expression used to show anger or annoyance: > *'Confound this nail! Why won't it go into the wall?'*

CONFUCIUS

Confucius, he say ... *Humorous, becoming old-fashioned* An expression used before relating a traditional wise thought: > *Confucius, he say, 'You take no umbrella – it rains, you get wet!'* Unorthodox grammatical verb forms are used to imitate Chinese grammar.

CONTRARY

On the contrary Used to express complete disagreement with what had just been said: > *'I'm sorry I didn't quite say all that I could have done about Matthew.' 'On the contrary, I found you refreshingly honest.'*

COOKIE

That's the way the cookie crumbles That is the state of affairs and nothing can be done about it: used (often humorously) when something unfortunate has happened: > *'Sorry to hear you've failed your exam again, Sarah, but that's the way the cookie crumbles.'* This phrase is American in origin. Also **That's the way it goes.**

COOL

Cool it! *Slang* Stop getting so excited or angry: > *'Cool it, you two, let's see if we can discuss this more calmly.'* This phrase is American in origin.

CORRECT

1 **Correct me if I'm wrong** Used to emphasise that the speaker is not completely sure whether what he or she is about to say is true or not: > *'Correct me if I'm wrong, but I think it was in 1979 that Margaret Thatcher became Prime Minister.'*

2 **I stand corrected** *Formal* Used by the speaker to admit that something he or she has just said is wrong, after someone else has pointed out that it is wrong.

COST

1 **At all costs** Whatever happened; under no circumstances: > *'Over the next few weeks, you must avoid outside distractions at all costs, to maintain your fitness for the big match.'*

2 **It will cost you** Something will be expensive: > *A few copies of the first edition are still available but they will cost you.*

COTTON

Bless his (her, etc.) (little) cotton socks see **Bless 4**.

COULD

1 **Could I (you, etc.) ...?** Used in making a polite request or asking permission: > *'Could you open the window slightly, please – it's very hot in here.'* > *'Could I ask you to help me if you've got time?'* This is rather more hesitant than using *can*.

2 **How could I have ...?** see **How 8**.

3 **How could you ...?** see **How 12**.

4 **I couldn't** Used to refuse, in a polite manner, something offered: > *'Would you like another piece of cake?' 'No thanks, I couldn't.'*

5 **If you could** see **If 4**.

6 **You could ...** Used in making a polite suggestion, invitation, etc.: > *'You could always try the library to see if they might be able to help you.'*

COUNT

Count to ten (before you lose your temper)! Don't lose your temper!: > *Colin looked furious, but Josh tried to calm him down and told him, 'Count to ten!'*

COUNTRY

It's a free country! Surely I can do what I am suggesting!; I am certainly within my rights: > *'But it's a free country, Mum, why shouldn't I stay out all night if I want to?'*

COURSE

1 **Of course**

a Certainly: > *'Are you taking me into town?' 'Of course!'* > *'Of course Pete's coming – he always comes to our parties!'*

b As expected; what I am saying is true: used when the speaker knows that the other person knows what he or she is saying already, and sometimes said before adding some modification to the opinion: > *'The orchestra was good, of course, but it was hardly worth the price we paid for the tickets!'* > *'The weather's bad again, so the buses are late, of course.'*

2 **Of course not** Used to give emphasis to saying no: > *'Do you think Gary will mind if I borrow his football?' 'Of course not.'*

COURT

The ball is in your court see **Ball 2**.

COURTESY

1 **By courtesy of** Provided by, or given out of kindness; not paid for: > *As this is a special celebration, all drinks tonight are by courtesy of the management.*

2 **Courtesy costs nothing** Used as a response to a rude or offensive statement offered by someone else or to suggest that that

person could at least have been polite.

COW

1 **Holy cow!** *see* **Holy.**
2 **... till the cows come home** For ever: > *'You could argue with him till the cows come home, but he'll never change his mind.'*

CRACK

Get cracking! Start doing the job quickly; do the job more quickly: > *'Get cracking, Mary, you've got all your packing to do by six o'clock and it's five o'clock now.'* > *'I'd better get cracking on the painting, as it'll take me a long time.'* Also **Get weaving!**

CRIME

Crime doesn't pay A saying that crime is not worthwhile because criminals may well get caught.

CROSS

1 **Cross one's fingers** *see* **Finger 1.**
2 **Keep one's fingers crossed** *see* **Finger 2.**

CROW

Stone the crows! *see* **Stone.**

CRUMBLE

That's the way the cookie crumbles *see* **Cookie.**

CRY

1 **A far cry** Something very different: > *Preparing a speech in your study is a far cry from delivering it in front of hundreds of people.*
2 **For crying out loud!** An expression of impatience, anger, etc.: > *'For crying out loud, please shut the door!'* > *'For crying out loud, why do you worry about the children all the time?'*

CURIOUS

Curiously enough *see* **Enough 5.**

CURIOSITY

Curiosity killed the cat Don't interfere in affairs that do not concern you or you will suffer harm yourself: > *'Where were you two last night?' 'I'm not saying. Remember curiosity killed the cat!'* The expression is sometimes alluded to in the phrase *You know what happened to curiosity.*

CURSE

1 **Curse it (you, etc.)!** An expression used to show anger or annoyance: > *'Curse it, why does the phone always ring just when we're eating our meal?'*
2 **Not care** (or **give**) **a tinker's curse** *see* **Damn 6.**

CURTAINS

It'll be curtains for ... Someone or something will experience a lot of trouble or difficulty, come to an end, or die: > *It'll be curtains for this shop if business doesn't improve.*

CUSTOMER

The customer is always right A motto that the customers in a hotel, bank, shop, etc., are important, and are to be considered right in any dispute, even when they may be wrong.

CUT

1 Cut it (or **that**) **out!** Stop what you're doing: > *'Cut it out, you two, or one of you will get hurt,'* *Adam said, as he tried to stop the fight.*

2 To cut a long story short *see* **Story** 5.

D

DAMAGE

What's the damage? *Slang* What is the price of a service given or an article that is being bought?: > *'Thanks for mending the car; what's the damage?'*

DAMN

1 As near as damn it *see* **Near 1.**

2 Damn all *Slang, chiefly British, old-fashioned* Absolutely nothing: > *'You men sit around all day, doing damn all, and expect to get paid for it!'*

3 Damn it (**you**, etc.)! *Slang, chiefly British* An expression used to show annoyance, impatience, etc.: > *'I can't remember his name, damn it! What did you say it was?'* > *'Damn that fool who left his bike in front of the door!'*

4 Damn me! *Slang, chiefly British* An expression used to show surprise, anger, etc.: > *'Well damn me, if it isn't my old schoolmate, Peter; I wonder what he's doing here in California!'* Also **I'll be damned!; I'm damned!:** > *'I'll be damned if I'll help him: he never helps me when I need him.'* > *'Well, I'm damned, it's started snowing!'*

5 Do one's damnedest To do your utmost: > *'I'll do my damnedest to be with you by nine o'clock.'*

6 Not care (or **give**) **a damn** Not to care in the slightest: > *'Shall I come by car or walk here tomorrow?' 'I don't care a damn how you come here, on foot, in a car, or by jet plane: just make sure you're here by nine o'clock!'* > *'Ken couldn't give a damn about what other people think of him, he's only interested in himself.'* Alternatives (*old-fashioned*) to *a damn* are *a fig, a tinker's curse, two hoots,* and *two pins.*

DARE

1 How dare you! How can you be so rude!: > *'How dare you speak to me like that! You must apologise at once!'*

2 I dare say *see* **Say 10.**

3 (Just) you dare! Used to discourage someone from doing something: > *'Can I jump off that tree?' 'You dare!'* Also **Don't you dare!:** > *'Mummy, look – I'm going to fly through the air!' 'Don't you dare!'*

DARKEN

Never darken my (**our, this**, etc.) **door again!** *see* **Door.**

DARN

1 Darn it! *Slang, chiefly British, becoming old-fashioned* Used to express annoyance, impatience, etc.: > *'Darn it! I've missed the last bus home!'*

2 I'll be darned *Old-fashioned* Used to express anger, surprise, dissatisfaction, etc.: > *'It's not me I'm worried about, but I'll be darned if my children have to grow up in such a world of inequality and injustice!'* In both **1** and **2**, *darn* was originally a euphemism for *damn*.

DASH

Dash it! *Slang, chiefly British, old-fashioned* Used to express annoyance, impatience, etc.: > *'Dash it all, old chap, when I say I'll pay you back, I mean it!'* *Dash* was originally a euphemism for *damn*.

DAY

1 Any day of the week Always and under any conditions: used to show what one would prefer to do or when one is sure of one's opinions: > *'I'd rather be on holiday in Florida any day of the week than stuck in this office all of the time.'* > *'I'm a far better footballer than he is, any day of the week.'*

2 Don't give up the day job *Humorous* Used to tell someone that he or she is not very good at the activity he or she is undertaking and if he or she were to do it as a full-time job, he or she would fail at it.

3 Give me ... any day! Used to express a strong preference for someone or something: > *'I'm fed up with listening to all your pop music – give me a Beethoven symphony any day!'*

4 Good day *see* **Good 4.**

5 Have a good (or **nice**) **day** *Chiefly American* I hope that (the rest of) your day is pleasant; an expression used when leaving people.

6 In all my (**his,** her, etc.) **born days** In the whole of my (his, her, etc.) life: used to add emphasis to what the speaker says and often to show surprise: > *'I've never heard such nonsense in all my born days.'*

7 (It's) all in a day's work These things are unpleasant but have to be accepted as part of life: > *'Don't you mind running round town with all these messages that Mr Brown gives you?' 'Oh no, it's all in a day's work.'*

8 It's not every day Used to say that a particular occasion is special and therefore worth marking in a memorable way: > *'Come on, let's splash out and celebrate! It's not every day that you pass your exams!'*

9 It's not my (**his,** her, etc.) **day** So many unfortunate things have happened to me (him, her, etc.) today: > *'The washing-machine flooded this morning; I burnt the dinner; it's just not my day.'*

10 Live to see the day To experience something that was previously thought unlikely: > *'I never thought I'd live to see the day when the Channel Tunnel was actually built.'*

11 Not have all day Not to have a lot of time; used to ask someone to hurry up: > *'Come on Emma, we've not got all day! We said we'd be at Peter's in half an hour.'*

12 One of these (fine) days Some time in the future: > *'One of these fine days, I'll get round to decorating the living-room.'*

13 One of those days A day on which many things go wrong: > *'I lost my purse in town, missed the bus, and got soaked walking home: it's been one of those days.'*

14 That'll be the day! I will be very surprised when what you say actually happens: used when the speaker does not really believe what the other person says will happen: > *'I'll get round to putting that shelf up soon.' 'That'll be the day!'* > *'Me get married? That'll be the day!'*

15 Those were the days! There were good or happy times in the past: > *'I used to go to school by steam train.' 'Ah – Those were the days!'* > *'Those were the days when you could buy a big bar of chocolate for half the price it costs now!'*

DAYLIGHT

Daylight robbery An unreasonably high charge: > *'£100 for a haircut? That's daylight robbery!'*

DEAD

1 Drop dead! *see* **Drop 1.**

2 I wouldn't be seen (or **caught**) **dead** Used to express a strong disapproval of particular clothes, places, or activities: > *'I wouldn't be seen dead in those trousers – they're so old-fashioned!'*

3 Strike me dead! *see* **Strike.**

DEAL

1 Big deal! *Slang* I do not think what you're saying is important; I am not impressed by it: used to take away a person's boasting, excitement, or keenness: > *'I'm going to America for three months next summer.' 'Big deal! I was a student there for two years!'*

2 It's a deal Used to express agreement to an arrangement: > *'£1,000 for the two batches?' 'OK, it's a deal.'*

DEAR

1 My dear A way of addressing someone in a friendly way: > *'How lovely to see you, my dear!'* Also used in more formal, humorous, or condescending situations: > *'My dear sir, may I take your coat?'* The phrase is *My dears* when used to more than one person: > *'My dears, come in and tell me all your news.'*

2 Oh dear! An expression of sadness, sympathy, or anxious surprise: > *'Oh dear, where can Harry be? He should have been here an hour ago.'* Also **Dear, dear!; Dear me!; Dear, oh dear!; Deary me!**: > *'Dear me, where have I put my keys?'*

DEATH

... will be the death of you (him, her, etc.) (Some bad experience, a naughty child, etc.) is or will be very terrible for you (him, her, etc.); often used in an annoyed tone or humorously: > *'Going out without a coat will be the death of you!'* > *'That child will be the death of me!'*

DEBT

Owe a debt (of gratitude) to someone
To be extremely grateful to
someone: > *'I really don't know
what to say. We owe a debt of
gratitude to you all for your care
and love over the years.'* Also **Be in
someone's debt.**

DECENCY

Have the decency to do something
To behave in such a way that
conforms to the basic principles
of ordinary human relationships:
> *'He should at least have had the
decency to have asked my permission
before he borrowed my DVD
player.'*

DECENT

Do the decent thing To behave in
such a way that conforms to the
moral principles which are
generally accepted: > *Politicians
who get caught up in scandals
should do the decent thing and
resign.*

DECLARE

Well I (do) declare! An expression of
surprise, annoyance, or disbelief:
> *'Well I do declare, this is an awful
mess you've got us in!'*

DEFINITION

By definition Simply because of
what it is: > *Teaching has not been
effective, by definition, if learning
has not taken place.*

DEFY

1 **Defy description, understanding,**
etc. To be so extreme, strange,
etc., that it is almost impossible
to describe or understand: > *How
someone could shoot another human
being in cold blood defies description.*
2 **I defy you (to do something)** I
challenge you to do something;
used when the speaker is asking
someone to do something
impossible: > *'I defy you to prove
that you were at home by yourself
last night, as you said you were.'*

DELIVER

Stand and deliver! *see* **Stand 2.**

DEPEND

1 **It (or that) all depends** I am not
sure about it (or that): > *'Can you
come to the party tonight?' 'It all
depends when I finish my work.'*
2 **(You can) depend on it** You can be
quite certain about this: > *'We'll
be there at six, you can depend on
it.' > 'Depend on it, I'll finish
making the bookshelves by Monday.'*

DESERT

His (her, etc.) just deserts The
punishment that he (she, etc.)
deservedly received for doing
something bad.

DEUCE

**What (how, when, where, who, why)
the deuce?** *Rare, old-fashioned*
Whatever (however, whenever,
wherever, whoever, why ever):
used in questions to emphasise a
strong feeling such as annoyance
or surprise: > *'Where the deuce did
I put my keys? I can't seem to find
them anywhere.'*

DEVIL

1 **Be a devil!** An encouragement for someone to be bold on this one occasion: > *'Come on, Joe, be a devil and have another drink!'*

2 **Be the very devil** To be very difficult, awkward, or annoying: > *'My new car is super to drive, but it's so big it's the very devil to find a parking place for it.'*

3 **Better the devil you know (than the devil you don't)** Used to say that it is better to choose someone or something whose faults you know, rather than to choose someone or something who you do not know at all and whose faults might be even worse.

4 **Go to the devil!** *Slang, old-fashioned* Go away!: used to express annoyance with someone: > *'Go to the devil, Jo. I'm sick of your questions all the time.'*

5 **Lucky devil** Used to refer to someone that the speaker is slightly jealous of, because he or she has been successful, fortunate, etc.: > *'I hear Wayne's been promoted again.' 'Lucky devil.'*

6 **Talk (or speak) of the devil!** A phrase used when a person who has just been discussed unexpectedly appears: > *'Peter really is a bit of a fool, isn't he? – Oops, talk of the devil, here he is!'*

7 **The (or a) devil of a ...** *Slang* (Something) that causes great difficulty: > *'We had the devil of a job to get the wardrobe upstairs!'*

8 **The devil take the hindmost** Used to describe a situation in which people think only about what is best for themselves and do not care about other people.

9 **The devil you (he, she, etc.) do (will, have, etc.)!** Used as an answer to a statement to express anger, disbelief, or other strong feeling: > *'I came first in the exam.' 'The devil you did!'* > *'Peter said I'd drive him into town – the devil I will!'*

10 **There'll be the devil to pay** There will be trouble to be faced because of an action: > *'There'll be the devil to pay if we're caught breaking into this room, you know!'*

11 **To the devil with you (it, etc.)!** *Old-fashioned* I do not care at all about you (it, etc.): > *'To the devil with you all! You amateurs don't know how to run a gardening club at all!'*

12 **What (how, when, where, who, why) the devil?** *Slang* Whatever (however, whenever, wherever, whoever, why ever): used in questions to emphasise a strong feeling such as annoyance or surprise: > *'How the devil do I know where your book is! When were you last reading it?'*

DICE

No dice *Slang* No: used when refusing to do something or when there has been no success or luck: > *'Did you get him to drive you into town?' 'No dice.'* > *'I tried to get him to back us with £1,000. But no dice. He just wasn't interested.'*

DICKENS

What (How, where, who) the dickens? Whatever (however, wherever, whoever): used in questions to express surprise or anger in a strong but fairly polite way: > *'What the dickens are you doing here?'* Originally, a euphemism for *devil*, *dickens* is an altered form of *devilkins*, a small devil.

DIE

1 **Be dying for** (or **to do**) **something** To want (to do) something very much: > *'I'm dying for a cup of tea.'* > *'I'm dying to talk to you again after all these years.'*

2 **I almost died** Used to express great emotion, e.g., surprise, embarrassment, shock: > *'I almost died when I heard the news.'* Also **I nearly died; I could have died:** > *'It was so upsetting that I could have died.'*

3 **Never say die!** *see* **Say 26.**

DISGRACE

Be a disgrace to someone To behave in such a bad way that causes someone to feel ashamed: > *'You're a disgrace to the school. You should be expelled immediately.'*

DISRESPECT

No disrespect Used when criticising someone or something to show that one does not wish to seem rude: > *'No disrespect to Kevin but he's not the world's most eloquent lecturer.'*

DO

1 **... and have** (or **be**) **done with it** And finish the job completely: often used in a humorous suggestion: > *'You've broken four out of the six windows – why don't you smash the other two and be done with it?'*

2 **Anything doing?** *see* **Anything 2.**

3 **Did you ever?** A way of expressing surprise, amazement, etc.: > *'Well, did you ever! Mary's finally marrying Dave after all!'*

4 **Do as you're told** Used to tell children to behave in the way that one has asked them to.

5 **Do me** (or **us**) **a favour!** *see* **Favour.**

6 **Don't do anything I wouldn't do!** *see* **Anything 6.**

7 **Don't ... me!** Used to show annoyance at (the use of a particular word in addressing the speaker, originally said by the other person and repeated by the speaker): > *'Come on, dear!' 'Don't "dear" me, you nasty man!'*

8 **Easy does it** Do it slowly and carefully: > *'Easy does it!'* Steve said as he and Leslie lifted the wardrobe through the narrow door.

9 **Fair do's**
   a Let's have fair shares: > *'I want a bigger slice of cake, Mummy.' 'So do I, Mum' 'Fair do's, children; you can each have a piece the same size.'*
   b Please be fair with me: > *'Fair do's, Jane, I only said I might phone you, not that I definitely would.'*

10 **Have been and gone and done it** *see* **Be 6.**

11 **How are you doing?** *see* **How 6.**

12 **How do you do** A polite conventional way of greeting someone when people meet each other, especially for the first time: > (John talking to Peter) *'Peter, I'd like you to meet Mr Duckworth.'* (Peter to Mr Duckworth) *'How do you do, Mr Duckworth.'* (Mr Duckworth to Peter) *'How do you do.'* The stress falls on *do*. Very

informally, the expression may be shortened to *How do*.

13 How do you do it? How is that done?: often said with a note of surprise: > *'How do you do it, Tony? You travel long distances every day – I just don't know where you get the energy from!'*

14 I (he, she, etc.**) could do with ...** I need (he or she needs, etc.) or can make use of (something): sometimes used as an indirect way of asking someone to do something? > *'I could just do with a nice cup of tea.'* > *'I think the car could do with a good clean.'*

15 Nothing doing
a Nothing is happening: > *'Nothing doing tonight – there's only an old film on at the cinema, the bowling alley's closed down, so we're staying at home.'*
b No; I refuse: > *'Will you help me with the washing-up?' 'Nothing doing. I must go and get my work done.'* > *'I've got no money. Have you got a bed for tonight?' 'Sorry, nothing doing unless you've got some money.'*
c A way of reporting failure, refusal, or a lack of success: > *'I tried to get a job at the factory but every time I rang, it was always nothing doing.'*

16 Sure do! Yes please: > *'Do you want an ice-cream?' 'Sure do!'* This phrase is American in origin.

17 That does it! I cannot bear any more!; I am now going to take some action: said after a series of unfortunate events have happened: > *'That does it! You've been rude so many times tonight*

that I'm sending you straight up to bed!' The stress falls on *does*.

18 That will do No more is needed or wanted; enough has already been done: used to express a wide range of feelings from politeness to anger: > *'I think that will do, Mr Smith. Thank you very much for coming to speak to us.'* > *'Children, that will do! How many more times do I have to tell you to be quiet?'* When expressing anger, the stress falls on *do*.

19 That's done it! Something bad has been done now!: > *'Why did you have to break the window? That's done it now! Mum'll be furious with us.'* The stress falls on *done*. Also **Now you've (he's, she's,** etc.**) done it!**

20 Well done! An expression of praise and congratulation: > *'I came first in the history exam!' 'Well done!'*

21 Well I never did!
a An expression of surprise or astonishment; what I've heard or seen is amazing: > *'Ros went to America for the weekend, you say? Well I never did!'* Sometimes shortened to *Well I never!*
b An expression of surprise mixed with disapproval: > *'After all the nasty things he's said about me, he now wants me to help him!' 'Well I never did!'*

22 What can I do for you? see **Help 1.**

23 What do you do (for a living)? What is your job?: > *'What do you do, Martin?' 'I write dictionaries.'*

24 Whatever you do don't do something Whatever happens, do not do something mentioned; > *'Whatever you do, don't tell Roseanne that we're having a party.'*

25 What's ... doing ...? Why is (something) (in a particular place)?: often expressing disapproval: > *'What's that coat doing on the floor?'*

26 Why don't ...? Used in making a request, invitation, etc.: > *'Why don't you shut up?'* > *'Why don't you come round for dinner one evening?' 'I'd love to, but I'm rather busy at the moment.'*

27 Will do! I will do that: > *'Can you go upstairs and get my jacket?' 'Will do!'*

28 You (he, she, etc.**) could do worse than do something** Used to show that the speaker thinks that it would be quite good if you (he, she, etc.) did the thing mentioned: > *'You could do worse than try the local college.'*

29 You do that Yes, do it: > *'Shall I try some of your chicken pie?' 'You do that.'* This phrase can also be used to discourage someone from doing something: > *'Mummy, I'm going to turn on the television!' 'You just do that!'* The stress falls on *do*.

30 You know what you can do with ... *see* **Know 33.**

31 You would do well to Used when giving advice to someone: > *'You would do well to avoid East Cheam this afternoon because of a major accident in the town.'*

DOG

1 A dog's breakfast A mess, something very untidy or badly done: > *'You've, made a real dog's breakfast of the new arrangements for the committee.'*

2 Dog eat dog Used to describe a situation of intense competition in which everyone wants to succeed even at the expense of harming other people: > *In today's business world it's really dog eat dog.*

3 It's a dog's life *see* **Life 4.**

4 Not have a dog's chance Not to have any chance at all.

DOLLAR

You (can) bet your bottom dollar *see* **Bet 6.**

DOOR

Never darken my (our, this, etc.**) door again!** *Old-fashioned* Stay away from here!; you must never come back again!: > *'Go away and never darken my door again.'* > *'You must promise never to darken these doors again, as long as you live.'*

DOUBT

1 Be beyond (reasonable) doubt To be certain: > *'It's beyond reasonable doubt that Jones was not there at the time the robbery took place.'*

2 No doubt I am sure; I suppose; probably: > *'You must be hungry after your journey. No doubt you'd like something to eat.'* > *'You've no doubt heard the news that the president's been shot.'* No doubt can also be used as a polite way of persuading people to do something: > *'No doubt you'll be paying us your rent soon, Mr Bannister?'*

3 Without doubt Used to emphasise that an opinion is true: > *'Without doubt this will be the most important year of your life at college.'*

DOWN

Down with ...! A slogan used to show disapproval of something or someone: > *'Down with school!'* > *'Down with the king!'* > *'Down with the government!'*

DOZEN

Six of one and half a dozen of the other There is no difference between two things or two ways of dealing with a difficulty; both sides seem equal: > *'It's six of one and half a dozen of the other – the fares on the bus or the coach are the same.'* > *'Aunt Edith's been complaining about her neighbours talking about her behind her back, but if you ask me, it's six of one and half a dozen of the other!'*

DRAT

Drat it (you, etc.)! An expression used to show anger or annoyance: > *'Drat this pen, it never writes when I want it to!'* *Drat it* was originally a euphemism for *God rot it*.

DREAM

1 Dream on Used to tell someone that what they want will not happen: > *'You're hoping for an easy life once you leave college? Dream on!'*

2 I wouldn't (or shouldn't) dream of

it Certainly not: > *'Would you ever think of smoking inside a church?' 'I wouldn't dream of it!'*

3 In your dreams Used to say that something that someone wants is unlikely to happen: > *'I know I'm going to win the lottery.' 'In your dreams!'*

4 Sweet dreams! Sleep well: said especially to children when wishing a good night's rest: > *'Sweet dreams!' Mummy whispered, as she kissed Hannah goodnight.*

DRINK

I'll drink to that Used to express agreement with what someone has just said. To *drink to* someone or something is also a toast.

DROP

1 Drop dead! *Slang* Go away!; stop bothering me!: > *'Drop dead!' shouted John to his older brothers who were interfering with his electronics kit.*

2 The penny dropped *see* **Penny 2.**

DRY

Dry up! Be quiet!: > *'Dry up, Rick! I'm fed up with hearing your voice.'*

DUCK

1 Lovely weather for ducks! *see* **Weather 1.**

2 Take to (something or someone) like a duck to water To find something such as learning a language easy to learn or do; get to know a person very quickly: > *'He took to German like a duck to water.'*

DUE

To give someone his (her, etc.) due
Used when one is criticising
someone to say that as well as
the bad thing he (she, etc.) has
done, he (she, etc.) also has good
points: > *'He failed his exams but,
to give him his due, he did do some
work for them this time.'*

E

EACH

Each and every Used for emphasis
to refer to every member of a
group: > *'And I want each and
every one of you to arrive punctually
in future.'* > *Death comes to each
and every one of us.*

EAR

1 **(Could I have) a word in your ear?**
see **Word 1.**

2 **Feel one's ears burning** To think
that other people are talking
about one: > *'We talked last night
for a long time about you and Jim.'
'That's funny – I thought I felt my
ears burning!'* Also **My ears are** (or
must be) burning.

3 **Play it by ear** To decide something at the moment you need to
and not before: > *'We'll play it by
ear what time we should leave.'*

EARTH

1 **Cost the earth** To cost a lot of
money: > *'Our new car cost the
earth, I can tell you!'*

2 **What (how, where, who, why) on
earth?** Whatever (however,
wherever, whoever, why ever):
used to add strength in
questions: > *'How on earth can you
wear that hat? It looks awful!'* >
'Why on earth did we have to go out
*this evening – I'd much rather have
stayed at home!'*

EARTHLY

Not have an earthly Not to have the
slightest chance at all; not have
any real idea about something: >
*'Do you think John will get through
the exam?' 'No, he hasn't an
earthly; he's not worked all term.'* >
*'Have you any thoughts on what
you'd like to do after you finish
college?' 'Not an earthly.'*

EASE

At ease! A command, especially to
soldiers, to stand in a relaxed
manner with feet apart: > *When
the ceremony had finished, the
officer shouted, 'At ease!' and the
men could move again after
standing still for so long.*

EASY

1 **Easy does it** *see* **Do 8.**

2 **Go easy (on ...)** *see* **Go 5.**

3 **I'm easy** *Chiefly British* I have no
special desire for any of the
choices offered; I will accept
whichever you want to do: >
*'Francis, would you like to go to the
cinema or go out for a meal
tonight?' 'I'm easy – which would
you like to do?'*

4 It's easy for you to say (or **talk**)
Used to express a rather angry
response to someone's advice
when that person does not truly
understand one's situation: > *'It's
easy for you to talk. You've never
lost your husband like Gillian has.'*

5 Take it easy! *see* **Take 7.**

EAT

1 I'll eat my hat *see* **Hat 3.**

2 What's eating you (**him, her,** etc.)?
What is worrying you (him, her,
etc.)?; why are you (is he, she,
etc.) so unhappy and worried?: >
*'What's eating you, Anne? You look
so miserable.'*

EFFECT

In effect Used to describe what
something really is, as a
summary of a situation or in
contrast to the way it appears to
be: > If the rate of inflation is
three per cent and our wages rise
by only two per cent, we will in
effect be one per cent worse off.

EGG

Good egg! *Old-fashioned* I am
pleased!: used to express delight:
> *'We thought of going out for a
drive in the car this afternoon, Jamie.'*
'Oh, good egg, Mother, I'd love that!'

ELBOW

More power to your elbow! *see*
Power.

ELEMENTARY

Elementary, my dear Watson! *Old-
fashioned* An expression used in
connection with an explanation
that makes something clear and
that is obvious to the speaker: >

*'I can't get this tape-recorder to
work. Can you help me?' 'Ah!
You've not plugged it in! There you
are – elementary, my dear Watson!'*
From the Sherlock Holmes
stories by Sir Arthur Conan
Doyle, though this exact phrase
is not found in the original texts.

ELSE

1 If nothing else Used to express
the fact that there is only one
good point to a situation: > *'The
whole day wasn't a complete
disaster. You did get to see the shops,
if nothing else.'*

2 Or else! Or something terrible
will happen!: used after a
command as a threat or warning:
> *'Hand over the money or else!'* >
'Do what I say or else!' The phrase
may also be followed by a verb: >
'Do as I say or else leave the room!'

END

1 At the end of the day After all the
facts, possibilities, etc., have been
considered: > *This strike can go
on, but at the end of the day, the
unions and managers are going to
have to sit round the table and work
out a solution.*

2 In the end After thinking about
all the relevant facts: > *'I thought
about going away to college but in
the end decided to live at home and
commute.'*

3 It's not the end of the world It's
not really as bad as it seems: used
to bring comfort when someone
has suffered a misfortune: > *'It's
not the end of the world, Suzie.
You'll soon forget Peter and there
are lots of other nice boys around!'* >
'We'd like to have won, but losing

in the first round isn't the end of the world.'

4 **The (absolute) end** The limit of what I can endure: > *'This car of mine is the end. I've had nothing but trouble with it since I bought it.'* Also **The (absolute) limit:** > *'That child is the absolute limit! He howls every night and keeps us awake all the time!'*

ENOUGH

1 **Enough is enough!** I cannot bear what is happening, being done, etc., any more: > *'Enough is enough. Can't you talk about anything else but politics?'* Often shortened to *Enough's enough!*

2 **Enough of ...** Stop (something); I cannot bear it any more: > *'Enough of your rudeness! Come here at once and apologise!'*

3 **Enough said** *see* **Say 29.**

4 **Fair enough!** That is reasonable; all right; I agree: > *'I'll give Pat and Judy a lift home if you take Charlotte and Margaret.' 'Fair enough.'*

5 **Funnily enough** It is strange, but ... : > *'Funnily enough, Alan, we were just talking about you and here you are!'* Also **Curiously enough; Oddly enough; Strangely enough:** > *'Oddly enough, Peter hasn't said anything about it.'* > *'No one, strangely enough, has ever noticed this mistake before.'*

6 **Right enough** *see* **Sure 8.**

7 **Sure enough** *see* **Sure 8.**

8 **That's enough!** No more is needed or wanted; stop!: > *'That's enough now, children! Stop playing and put your toys away, please.'*

ESSENCE

In essence Used to state the most basic or most important aspect of an idea, situation, etc.: > *'In essence what you're saying is that you don't trust me.'* > *Time is of the essence when working for yourself.*

EVEN

1 **Even so** Used to introduce something surprising, especially as a contrast to what one has just said; nevertheless: > *'She assured me that all the arrangements would work out well Even so, I still felt a little anxious.'*

2 **Even then** In spite of what has just been mentioned or what has just happened: > *The operation is performed using the latest hi-tech equipment but even then there is no guarantee of success.*

EVENING

1 **Evening all!** *see* **All 14.**

2 **Good evening** *see* **Good 5.**

EVENT

1 **In any event** Whatever may happen; anyway: > *The city's tight policy on expenditure has in any event ensured that it won't make a deficit this year.* Also **At all events.**

2 **In the event** What actually happened, in contrast to what might have happened: > We took our umbrellas but in the event we didn't need them.

EVER

1 **Did you ever?** *see* **Do 3.**

2 **Ever so** *Slang, chiefly British, old-fashioned* Very much: > *'That was*

a smashing tea! Thanks ever so!'
Also **Ever so much.**

3 ... for ever! A slogan used to show support and approval: > *'Scotland for ever!'* > *'QPR for ever!'*

EVERYTHING

1 Everything in the garden is lovely *Becoming old-fashioned* A saying that everything is just as one could want and needs no improvement: > *'We've just moved to a lovely house; Roger's settled in his job, and Ruth is doing well at school. Everything in the garden is lovely.'*

2 Hold everything *see* **Hold la.**

EXACT

To be exact Used when you are making a more precise statement about something or making a small correction to what one has just said: > *'He's eighty this year, on 7 May to be exact.'*

EXACTLY

Not exactly

a Used as a polite reply to someone saying that he or she is not wholly accurate or correct in what he or she has just said: > *'So you don't love him any more?' 'Not exactly, it's just that our relationship has changed over the past few months.'*

b Used to emphasise an ironic or sarcastic attitude in what is being said: > *'She called me stupid.' 'He's not exactly the world's greatest brain, is he?'*

EXAMPLE

For example Used to introduce a specific instance that illustrates

or explains an argument, opinion, etc.: > *The tour takes in many of the city's sights, for example Buckingham Palace and the Tower of London.*

EXCEPT

Present company excepted *see* **Company 1.**

EXCUSE

1 Can (or may) I be excused? May I leave the room?: used, especially by children at school, when they want to go to the lavatory: > *'Can I be excused please, Miss?' 'Yes, Jason.'*

2 Excuse me Often pronounced *'scuse me.*

a An expression used before the speaker does or says something that could annoy someone else; used to attract someone's attention: > *'Excuse me, could I come past?'* > *'Excuse me, is this the way to the post office?'*

b An expression used to apologise for expressing a disagreement with someone else; forgive me: > *'Excuse me, but I think you're wrong.'*

c An expression showing annoyance: > *'Excuse me, but isn't that my parking place you've put your car in?'*

3 Excuses, excuses! You always make excuses!: used to show disbelief at what has just been said: > *'The bus was late, Mr Faversham. Honest, sir!' 'Excuses, excuses, my boy!'*

EXPECT

1 Expect me when you see me I'm not sure when I'm coming back: > *'Expect me when you see me,*

Mum,' Pete said as he walked out of the door. The person who is staying behind may say: *'We'll expect you when we see you,'* meaning that the person leaving may return whenever he or she wants.

2 **I expect** Used to state that you think a statement is probably correct or true: > *'I expect you'll be back late tonight, as usual.'*

3 **What do (or can) you expect?** Used for emphasis to show that you are not surprised by something, especially something disappointing: > *'No wonder you're ill. You've been working too hard recently and haven't had any time off. What (else) can you expect?'*

EYE

1 **Eyes down!** A call to start playing the game of bingo or said by schoolchildren as the teacher approaches.

2 **Here's mud in your eye!** *see* **Mud 1**.

3 **My eye!** *Old-fashioned* What you are saying is nonsense!: used to express disagreement, surprise, or astonishment: > *'I'll have finished my work by seven o'clock.'* *'My eye! You'll still be working at midnight!'* Also (*old-fashioned*) **That's all my eye!; That's all my eye and Betty Martin!:** > *'I'm going to climb the Empire State Building!' 'That's all my eye! You won't even climb a ladder by the side of the house!'* It is not certain who Betty Martin was.

4 **One in the eye for someone** Something will be an annoying disappointment for someone; used when the speaker is pleased about such a disappointment: > *'Losing 3-0 at home. That's one in the eye for Gavin!'*

5 **There's more to ... than meets the eye** A situation is more complicated than it appears to be.

6 **You must have eyes in the back of your head!** You've got a good instinct or intuition: said when the speaker discovers that someone is aware of something that could not normally be known: > *'You must have eyes in the back of your head – how did you know I'd come in!' 'I just knew you had!'*

F

FACE

1 **Let's face it** Let us look at the matter, problem, etc., as it really is; let us accept a fact honestly: > *'Let's face it, Jim, you never were very good at playing the guitar.'* > *'This country has, let's face it, been going downhill for years.'*

2 **Not just a pretty face** Used humorously to describe a person who is more intelligent and able than others might think: > *'Gone to university, got a BA and a doctorate – not just a pretty face, are you!'*

3 **On the face of it** When one first considers something; apparently; on the surface: > *On the face of it, it seemed like a simple case of suicide. But the detectives are now having second thoughts.*

4 **Shut your face!** *see* Shut.

5 **Was my face red!** Used to express embarrassment or shame that the speaker felt: > *'I got into the compartment on the train and a few minutes later saw that it was for "ladies only"! Was my fed red!'*

FACT

1 **As a matter of fact**
a Used to introduce an answer that the previous speaker is not expecting and will find surprising: > *'I hear Mr Duckworth is leaving. I wonder who will get his job.' 'I am, as a matter of fact.'*
b Used to add strength to what is said, by making it more

definite or giving more details; indeed: > *'I didn't go to the club on Saturday. As a matter of fact, I've not been for months.'* Also **For that matter; In actual fact; In fact; In point of fact; The fact is; The fact of the matter is:** > *'This book will fascinate all students of the English language, and for that matter, all speakers of the language, too.'* > *'I could come and see you tonight, or I could come now, in fact.' 'I've not read the books, and the fact is neither has anyone else.'*

c In reality; actually: > *'Was the play good?' 'Yes, as a matter of fact, it was fantastic.'* Also **In actual fact; In fact; In point of fact:** > *'It was a very cold day. In fact, it was -10° Centigrade.'*

2 **The fact remains** Something is true; used for emphasis when the speaker wants others to realise this: > *'You may wish that he hadn't resigned but the fact remains that he has, so we might as well all accept that and discuss what our plans for the future should be.'*

FAIL

Words fail me *see* Word 14.

FAINT

Not have the faintest idea *see* Foggiest.

FAIR

1 **Fair do's** *see* Do 9.
2 **Fair enough!** *see* Enough 4.
3 **Fair's fair** What is being suggested really is just and right: > *'Fair's fair, children; Paul can*

stay up late tonight because I let Roger stay up late last night.'

4 To be fair Used to add a positive or favourable comment about someone or something that has just been criticised: > *'I know Jason failed his exams again but, to be fair, this time he did make a genuine attempt to revise.'* Also **In all fairness.**

FALL

1 **Fall between two stools** *see* **Stool.**
2 **It** (or **they**) **fell off the back of a lorry** *see* **Lorry.**

FANCY

Fancy that! An expression used to indicate surprise or disbelief, often as a reply: > *'I met Elsie Griffiths the other day. I'd not seen her for years!' 'Fancy that!'* Also, **Just fancy!**

FAR

1 **As** (or **so**) **far as I know** (or **remember**) Used when giving an opinion and one is unsure of all the facts: > *'As far as I remember, the hall was built about 1970.'* > *'As far as I can tell, his condition hasn't changed overnight.'*

2 **Far be it from me** Although I really should not; I am unwilling- > *'Far be it from me to interrupt your conversation, but I couldn't help overhearing what you were saying.'* > *'Far be it from me to correct you, but I think you've made a serious mistake.'*

3 **Far from it** Not at all: > *'Are you cold in here?' 'Far from it – we're boiling!'*

4 **Far out!** *Slang, old-fashioned* That's wonderful!; that's fantastic!: an expression of amazement or delight: > *'Far out, man! This music's great!'* This phrase is American in origin.

5 **So far, so good** Up to now all has gone well: usually said when difficulties or trouble may be coming: > *'The new president has been in office for a year now – so far, so good; but I don't know whether he'll last another year.'*

FAST

Not so fast Wait a moment: often used when the speaker thinks something may be wrong: > *'Not so fast, young man, let me check your ticket.'*

FATHER

Like father, like son A saying that a son behaves just like his father.

FAVOUR

Do me (or **us**) **a favour!** *Slang*
a Please (do something)!: > *'Do us a favour, Ken, go and annoy someone else!'* > *'Do me a favour, John, sit still and stop messing about!'*
b I (or we) can't possibly believe what you're saying!; do you think I am (or we are) foolish enough to believe you?: > *'Do you expect me to pay £100 for this heap of old metal that you call a car? Do me a favour!'*

FEAR

1 **Never fear!** That is not likely; don't worry: > *'I won't tell him you came, never fear!'* Also **Have no fear!**: > *'Have no fear, I'm not going yet!'*

2 No fear! Not likely; certainly not!: > *'You didn't agree to go to the States with him did you!' 'No fear! I'm staying right here in London!'*

FEATHER

A feather in his (her, etc.) cap Something to be proud of that brings honour or respect: > *Being promoted to Senior Salesman was a real feather in his cap.*

FEEL

1 Feel free Please do as you want: > *'May I sit down?' 'Feel free.'* > *'Feel free to come and go as you want.'*

2 I feel I think: used to make an opinion sound less strong: > *'I really feel you're making a big mistake.'*

FEELING

1 Have a feeling in your bones *see* Bone 1.

2 I know the feeling I've had the same thought or experience: > *'I realised that the other people being interviewed were more qualified than me.' 'I know the feeling. It was like that when I went for a job once.'*

3 No hard feelings I have no feelings of anger or bitterness towards you: used to be friendly to an opponent after a competition, race, etc.: > *'Sorry we treated you so badly last night!' 'Oh, no hard feelings!'* > *'At last I've finished in front of you after all these months of running – no hard feelings, are there?'*

FELLOW

Old fellow *see* Boy 2.

FIG

Not care (or give) a fig *see* Damn 6.

FIGHT

Be looking for a fight *see* Look 1.

FIGURE

That figures!
a That seems reasonable and logical; it is as I expected: > *'He said he wouldn't come if the weather was bad. It's pouring with rain and he's not here.' 'That figures!'*
b An expression said disparagingly of someone: > *'He missed the first train, then he missed the next one because he went for a cup of coffee.' 'That figures, knowing him!'*

FINAL

And that's final And that decision cannot be changed: > *'I don't want to discuss this matter any more, and that's final.'*

FINDER

Finders keepers Whoever finds something has the right to keep it: said when someone, especially a child, finds something by chance: > *'Finders keepers, I don't have to give the pen back, do I, Mum?'* Also **Finding's keeping.**

FINE

That's fine by me (him, her, etc.) I (he, she, etc.) agree(s) with the suggestion: > *'How about having a pizza tonight?' 'That's fine by me.'*

FINGER

1 Cross one's fingers To put one finger over the next one on the same hand (especially behind one's back), as a sign of excusing one from the lie being told: used mainly by children: > *Perry had his fingers crossed when he told his dad the lie.*

2 **Keep one's fingers crossed for (someone or something)** To wish someone well for a particular event; hope that something will be successful: said sometimes at the same time as actually putting one finger over the next one on the same hand: > *'We're keeping our fingers crossed for you on Thursday with the exam.'* > *'Now let's see if the light works. Keep your fingers crossed and I'll switch it on.'*

FINISH

When you've quite finished! *see* **Quite 3.**

FIRE

Fire away! Start speaking; start asking questions: > *'Can I ask you something?' 'Yes, fire away!'*

FIRST

1 **First off** Before anything else: > *'First off, let's find out how much money we've got to spend.'*
2 **First things first** *see* **Thing 3.**
3 **I'd ... first** Used to emphasise that the speaker does not want to do something: > *'Stand up in public and give a lecture? I'd kill myself/ die first!'*
4 **Not have the first idea** *see* **Foggiest.**

FISH

1 **Like a fish out of water** Awkward and uncomfortable, because you are in strange surroundings: > *When he first joined the company he felt like a fish out of water because he didn't know anybody.*

2 **There are plenty more (or other) fish in the sea** Used to comfort someone whose close relationship has just ended, and to reassure him or her that there are many other people with whom a new relationship is possible.

FIVE

Give me five To hit the palm of someone's hand with one's own palm, to show pleasure or as a greeting.

FLAT

(And) that's flat That's my final decision: used to add strength to a (usually negative) statement: > *'I will not go to your mother-in-law's, and that's flat!'*

FLATTER

You flatter yourself You think too highly of yourself: > *'Look, don't I look great in this new outfit! Won't they all be looking at me tonight!' 'You flatter yourself, Henrietta! You look just like you always do!'* > *'I wonder if they'll invite me to the cocktail party.' 'You flatter yourself – why should they invite you?'*

FLY

1 **Go fly a kite!** *see* **Kite.**
2 **Pigs might fly** *see* **Pig.**
3 **There are no flies on him (her, etc.)** He (she, etc.) is not a fool and is not easily deceived: > *'You can't get through without showing your ticket to old Parkey, you know – there are no flies on him!'*
4 **... wouldn't hurt (or harm) a fly** Used to emphasise that someone is very gentle: > *'Why are you*

afraid of Mike? He wouldn't hurt a fly.'

FOGGIEST

Not have the foggiest (idea) Not to have any idea at all: > *'Where's old Sam these days?' 'I haven't the foggiest idea.'* Also **Not have the faintest (idea); Not have the first idea; Not have the remotest idea:** > *'How long will it take you to do this work?' 'I haven't the faintest.'*

FOLLOW

Follow that! Say something that will be as significant as what the last speaker has just said, when the previous speaker has just done something very well that will be difficult for the next person to follow: > *'That's the answer to the problem. I'm sure you're all surprised at how easy it all was.' 'Follow that, Jim!' called out a number of people.* Sometimes the phrase is *I can't follow that:* > *'The plan I am proposing is undoubtedly the best scheme ever put forward for this redevelopment. Peter, let's hear your plan in similar detail.' 'I'm afraid I can't follow that, but here are a few of my rough ideas.'*

FOOL

1 **April fool!** Said to someone just after that person has been deceived by a trick on April Fool's Day, 1 April, telling him or her, in a mocking way, it was a trick.

2 **More fool you (him, her,** etc.**)!** I think you were (he or she was, etc.) stupid to do that: > *'More fool you for believing him: you should have known he only wanted*

your money.' > *'Darren's just eaten some strange berries.' 'More fool him. They could be poisonous!'*

3 **You could have fooled me** Used to show that one does not believe what someone has just told one: > *'That's Bruce dressed up as Father Christmas!' 'You could have fooled me!'*

FOOT

My foot! An expression used to show disagreement, surprise, or disbelief: added at the end of a comment, usually repeating the particular word that the speaker disagrees with: > *'This is glass, isn't it?' 'Glass, my foot! It's made of plastic – can't you see?'* > *'He didn't know, my foot! Of course he knew!'*

FOR

Oh for … ! I would very much like (something)!: rather old-fashioned, but also used humorously: > *'Oh for a good drink!'* > *'Oh for spring to come!'*

FORBID

God (or **heaven**) **forbid** *Becoming old-fashioned* I hope it will not happen; I hope that is not true: > *'God forbid that something should happen to Jackie, she's our only child.'* > *'I'm sorry to have to tell you that your son is one of the missing people!' 'Oh no, heaven forbid!'*

FORGET

Forget it! Let everything stay as it is; there is no need for an apology, paying money back, thanks, etc.: > *'I'm sorry, I've broken a cup. Let me pay for it.' 'Oh, forget it, they* were only very cheap ones.' > 'What about the money I owe you?' 'Forget it.' > 'How can I thank you enough for a lovely time this weekend, Jennifer?' 'Oh, that's all right, forget it!' Also used when it is clear that the person being spoken to has not understood something: > 'If you're after the manager's job when you've only been here two months, forget it!'

FORGIVE

1 **Forgive me, but ...** A polite way of asking a question or disagreeing with what someone has done or said: > 'Forgive me, but I think you're wrong.' Also in the form Forgive my ...: > 'Forgive my ignorance, but just who is it you're talking about?'

2 **May you be forgiven!** An expression used to excuse someone after they have done or said something bad: > 'Sheila really is a very nasty piece of work!' 'May you be forgiven – she's one of the nicest people I know!'

FRANK

To be frank Used with a statement of honesty, that the listener might not like: > 'To be frank with you, I think the idea is ridiculous.'

FREE

1 **Feel free** see Feel 1.
2 **Free, gratis, and for nothing** Absolutely free: often used humorously: > 'Yours for free, gratis, and for nothing, this set of wooden spoons when you buy this bowl!'

FRENCH

Pardon my French Please excuse my bad language: often used humorously: > 'Pardon my French, but can you turn that ... radio down a bit, please?' (... indicates a swear word.)

FRIEND

1 **Some of my (your, etc.) best friends are ...** Humorous An expression said in reply to and often to excuse unreasonable criticism of (a group of people), but often not when one's friends really are as stated: > 'I can't stand Spaniards!' 'Some of my best friends are Spaniards!'

2 **(To) absent friends!** An expression used when taking a drink with other people, wishing the prosperity of the missing friends of those gathered: > At the college reunion, the president called a toast, 'To absent friends!'

3 **We're just good friends!** Our relationship has no physical or sexual element: sometimes said as a public statement to stop rumours to the contrary: > At the airport, as the two filmstars flew off to Brazil together, they told the waiting reporters, 'We're just good friends!'

4 **What's ... between friends?** (A difficulty or the spending of time or money) does not really matter when compared to our friendship: > 'Let me pay for the petrol.' 'What's a few pounds between friends?'

5 **Your friend and mine** Our good friend: used in announcing or presenting an actor, singer, etc.:

> *'Here he is, your friend and mine, the greatest comedian in the world, Dickie Duckworth!'*

FROG

Have a frog in my (his, her, etc.) throat To speak in a husky voice because a small amount of mucus is lodged in your throat: > *'I'm sorry, I've a frog in my throat. It's this cold I've had all week.'*

FRUIT

Old fruit *see* **Boy 2.**

FUNERAL

It's your (his, her, etc.) funeral That is your (his, her, etc.) concern; if you do that, you will have to accept the consequences: > *'If you break into the factory, it's your funeral – don't expect us to help you if you're caught.'*

FUNNY

1 **Funnily enough** *see* **Enough 5.**
2 **Funny peculiar or funny ha-ha?** When you say 'funny', do you mean strange or amusing?: > *'A funny thing happened to me today!' 'Funny peculiar or funny ha-ha?'*

G

GAD

By Gad! *Old-fashioned* An expression of surprise, disbelief, anger, etc.: > *'By Gad, it's time for dinner already!'* Also **By gum!** *Gad* and *gum* are euphemisms for *God.*

GAME

1 **It's anyone's game** *see* **Anyone 2.**
2 **(So) that's your (his, her, etc.) little game** I have now discovered the trick, etc., that you are (he or she is, etc.) trying to do without being noticed: > *'So that's your little game, Smith: stealing other boys' textbooks and selling them back to them. Well, we've caught you now!'*
3 **The game is up** What you were trying to do without anyone noticing has been discovered; there is no chance of success: > *'We've discovered your plan to escape! The game is up!'*
4 **Two can play at that game** I can also do the unpleasant thing you are doing to me, and I can do it better than you and will beat you in the end: used as a threat or warning: > *'Two can play at that game,' said Rick as he was tripped up playing football, so later in the game he tackled the boy in the other team viciously.*
5 **What's the game?** What is happening; what are you doing: > *'I thought we were all supposed to meet at six, and there's only you and me here. What's the game?'*
6 **What's your (his, her, etc.) little game?** What trick are you (is he, she, etc.) planning?: > *'What's his little game now? How is he going to stop them beating us this time?'*

GARDEN

Everything in the garden is lovely *see* **Everything 1.**

GATEPOST

Between you, me, and the gatepost *see* **Between.**

GATHER

From what I can gather According to what I have found out to be true; often used about information obtained indirectly: > *'From what I can gather, she doesn't seem very happy working for that company.'* Also **As far as I can gather.**

GEE

1 **Gee up!** Go on; go faster: used as an encouragement to a horse.
2 **Gee whiz!** An expression of surprise, excitement, etc.: > *'Gee whiz, I never thought I'd pass that exam!'* A distortion of the word Jesus.

GENTLEMAN

Ladies and gentlemen *see* **Lady 1.**

GEORGE

By George! *Old-fashioned* An exclamation of surprise, disbelief, excitement, etc. > *'By George, you're right. How amazing!'*

GET

1 **Don't get me wrong** Don't misunderstand me: > *'Don't get me wrong, Charles, I wasn't trying to do your job for you. I just worked out some of the figures for last year's trading for the report I'm writing.'*
2 **Get a load of this!** *see* **Load 1.**
3 **Get a move on!** *see* **Move.**
4 **Get a word in edgeways** To have an opportunity to speak: > *'Once Joe starts talking, it's almost impossible to get a word in edgeways.'*
5 **Get along with you!** An exclamation expressing slight annoyance, impatience, disbelief, etc.: > *'Get along with you! I've heard that excuse before and I just don't believe you!'* > *'Get along with you! You don't really mean all those nice things you've said about me, do you?'* Also **(Get) away!; (Get) away with you!; Go along with you!:** > *'We walked twelve miles today.' 'Get away! It seemed like nearer twenty!'* > *'Away with you! What nonsense you do come out with!'*
6 **Get cracking!** *see* **Crack.**
7 **Get it?** Do you understand?: also used as a request to obey what has been said: > *'You're to sit here and keep quiet, get it?'*
8 **Get knotted!** *see* **Knot.**
9 **Get lost!** *see* **Lost.**
10 **Get off and milk it!** An expression shouted at someone who is riding a bicycle slowly.
11 **Get off my back!** *see* **Back 4.**
12 **Get stuffed!** *see* **Stuff 1.**
13 **Get weaving!** *see* **Crack.**
14 **Get you!** *Slang* I don't believe what you're saying: used as a reply to someone who is boasting: > *'I went to America for three months this summer and stayed on a cowboy ranch!' 'Get you!'* The stress falls on *you.*
15 **Got it in one** You have understood something immediately or guessed something correctly first time.
16 **How lucky,** etc., **can you get** Used to express surprise that someone could be so lucky, etc.: > *'How silly can you get? I don't believe that anyone could be so*

stupid as to try to climb a lamppost in their pyjamas.'

17 I get it I understand what you're trying to say; I understand the joke: *'I get it. You mean if we go earlier, we'll have time to do some shopping.' 'Yes, that's right!'* Also **I have it.**

18 It really gets me Something annoys me very much: > *'The way she keeps on saying 'you know' really gets me.'*

19 I've got it I know the answer: > *'I've got it! I've worked out how to open the safe!'* Also **I have it.**

20 There's no getting away from ... Something is true even if it is not liked: > *'There's no getting away from the fact that we're not earning enough money. If we don't cut back on expenditure, we'll soon be bankrupt.'*

21 You've got me there Also **You have me there.**

  a Your idea in the argument is a good one, and I will have to think about how I can answer it: > *'Why did you decide to put a fifth leg on the table?' 'You've got me there, I was hoping you wouldn't ask me that!'*

  b I don't know: > *'How many goals did your team score two years ago?' 'Ah, you've got me there – I'll have to look that up.'*

GIRL

1 Old girl A familiar, friendly way of talking to a woman or usually female animal: > *'Come on, old girl, you can look happier!'*

2 What's a nice girl like you doing in a place like this? Traditionally held to be a comment that a

man makes in order to start a conversation with a girl who he does not know but who he finds sexually attractive.

3 Who's the lucky girl, then? *see* **Lucky 1.**

GIVE

1 Don't give me that Don't expect me to believe that: > *'Would you like to go out for a meal on Saturday?' 'Don't give me that! You've been saying you'd take me out for months now, and you've not done so yet!'*

2 Give it a rest! *see* **Rest 3.**

3 Give me ... I like (something) most of all: > *'Give me a nice old-fashioned cup of tea any day!'*

4 Give me (him, her, etc.**) a chance!** *see* **Chance 5.**

5 Give or take Plus or minus: > *'I'll be there at one o'clock, give or take ten minutes.'* > *'Give or take a few minor mistakes, your essay is very good.'*

6 Give over! *Slang* Stop (doing something); be quiet: > *'Do give over! I can't work with all that noise!'* > *'Give over eating all my chocolates, will you?'*

7 I give up I'm stopping trying to guess what the joke, story, etc., means: > *'OK, I give up; you tell me what happened to the princess!'*

8 I wouldn't have it if you gave it to me! *see* **Have 5.**

9 I'd give anything (or **my right arm**) **...** I am extremely keen to do or have something: > *'I'd give anything to be on holiday right now.'*

10 I'll give you that I admit that you are right in saying that; used when the speaker does not like what is being said or disagrees with aspects of it: > *'He's clever enough, I'll give you that; it's just that his manner is so pompous all the time.'*

11 Not give a damn *see* **Damn 6.**

12 What gives? *Chiefly American* What's happening?: > *'What gives? What's everyone looking at?'*

GLAD

Glad to meet you! *see* **Meet 1.**

GLORY

Glory be! *Old-fashioned* An expression of surprise or pleasure: > *'Glory be! The coat that woman is wearing looks just like mine!'* > *'Glory be! All the flowers are for me – what a delight!'*

GO

1 As the saying goes *see* **Saying.**

2 Go along with you! *see* **Get 5.**

3 Go (and) jump in the lake! *see* **Lake.**

4 Go back to sleep I can see that you are not interested in what I am saying and you can return to your state of not being alert: > *'Go back to sleep, Catherine – it's useless trying to explain things to you when your mind is somewhere else.'*

5 Go easy
a Be moderate (with something): > *'Go easy on the milk – that's all we've got till Monday.*
b Do not exert yourself too much physically: > *'Go easy while you feel strong, so you'll have some strength left later when you're tired.'* Also **Go easy (with ...).**

6 Go fly a kite! *see* **Kite.**

7 Go for it Do all that you can to achieve something.

8 Go man, go! *see* **Man 2.**

9 Go on
a I don't believe you; don't exaggerate: > *'I'm sixty on Sunday.' 'Go on – you only look about forty-five!'* Also **Go on with you:** > *'I'm sure there were over 10,000 people at the demonstration.' 'Oh, go on with you – it looked like a few hundred, that's all.'*
b I dare you to (do something): used as an encouragement: > *'Should I ring him or not?' 'Oh, go on, you'll never make any friends if you don't.'*

10 Go to it Do something with much energy and effort; begin something: > *'Go to it, Robert – if you work hard, you'll have it finished by lunchtime!'*

11 Going, going, gone
a The announcement by an auctioneer that the bidding for a particular article is closing: > *'Any more offers for this fine vase, then? Going, to the man in the black suit, going, going, gone!'*
b An expression used to describe a thing or person that is disappearing, especially below the surface of the water: > *'My little boat's sinking! Going, going, gone; now it's sunk!'*

12 Here goes! I am about to do something: used before starting something that needs courage: > *'Here goes then! I'll see you in three hours, after the exam!'* > *'Now you've mended the television, let's try it.' 'OK, here goes!'*

13 Here we go again The same events are happening again: used especially of things that are unpleasant: > *'Here we go again,' muttered Sue as she left the* waiting-room to go into the dentist's surgery for the sixth time that year.

14 How's it going? An informal greeting; how are you?; what's happening?: > *'How's it going, Jane?' 'OK, thanks. And how are you?'* Also **How are things going?; How goes it?**

15 I (or **we**) **must be going** Used as a way of closing a conversation in saying that one has to leave: > *'It's getting late now. I think I must be going.'* Also **I've** (or **we've**) **got to go.**

16 It goes without saying Something seems so obvious that it hardly needs mentioning: > *It goes without saying that a teacher should always respect students' views, even if the teacher does not always agree with them.*

17 It just goes to show A statement just made or experience just referred to proves a particular point: > *More broken promises! It just goes to show that you can't trust politicians!* Also **It just shows.**

18 (It's) no go It's impossible; it can't happen: > *'It's no go, I'm afraid – that plan will never work.' 'Will the boss let you have next week off?' 'No go, I'm afraid.'*

19 My heart goes out to you *see* **Heart 7.**

20 Off we go! Let's go; now we're going: > *'Off we go, then,' said Dad as he drove off at the beginning of the family holiday.*

21 That's the way it goes *see* **Cookie.**

22 There you go again You are doing what you usually and repeatedly do: > *'There you go again, chewing your food loudly – I've told you not to do that lots of times, now stop it!'* Also used with *he, she,* etc.: > *'There she goes again, telling stories about other people!'* The stress falls on *there.*

23 Where do we go from here? What do we do next?: > *'We've cut all the pieces of card out. Where do we go from here? Do we stick them all together or paint them first?'*

24 Who goes there? The words of challenge by a soldier standing on guard: > *'Halt! Who goes there?' shouted the guard at the front of the palace.*

GOD

1 For God's sake! *see* **Goodness 1.**

2 For the love of God *see* **Love 1.**

3 God bless my soul! *see* **Bless 2.**

4 God bless (you) *see* **Bless 3.**

5 God bless you (**him, her,** etc.) *see* **Bless 4.**

6 God forbid *see* **Forbid.**

7 God grant *Formal* May it happen that: > *'God grant you much happiness in your marriage!'* > *'God grant that I never have to see this essay again once I've finished writing it!'*

8 God help him (**you, her,** etc.) *see* **Help 2.**

9 God knows *see* **Know 8.**

10 God preserve us! *see* **Preserve.**

11 God save ... May God keep and protect (a person): > *'God save the Queen!'* > *'God save the Prince!'*

12 God save me (**him, her,** etc.) **from ...** May I (he, she, etc.) be protected from (the interference of other people): > *'I* *know her approaches are well-meant but may God save me from her constant offers of help!'*

13 **God willing** If circumstances allow it; if all goes well: an expression of hope: > *'I'll see you again next Tuesday, God willing.'* Also the Latin phrase *Deo volente* or *DV*, used especially in church announcements.

14 **Good God!** *see* **Good 7.**

15 **Honest (to God)** Honestly: used to add strength to a statement of the speaker's truthfulness: > *'Honest to God, sir, I wasn't anywhere near the garden at the time of the accident.'* Also **Honest to goodness.**

16 **I wish (hope, swear,** etc.**) to God that** Used to emphasise something that is wished, hoped, promised, etc.; > *'I wish to God that Philip was here now.'*

17 **In God's name** *see* **Heaven 9.**

18 **Oh God!** An expression of surprise, disbelief, fear, etc.: > *'Oh God! I wish this pain would stop!'* Also **God almighty!**; **My God!**; **Oh Lord!**

19 **Please God** I hope; if all goes well: > *'We'll be married this time next year, please God.'* > *'If everything works as I've planned it, we should have enough money one day to retire to the country, please God.'*

20 **So help me God** *see* **Help 6.**

21 **Ye gods!** *Old-fashioned* An expression of surprise: > *'Ye gods'. I didn't expect to see you here – I thought you were on the other side of the world!'*

GOLLY

1 **By golly!** *Old-fashioned* An expression of surprise, disbelief, etc.: > *'By golly, that's Pete Bates over there!'* > *'Be quick about it or, by golly, you'll be punished!'* > *'By golly, if you buy a present, you certainly buy expensive ones, don't you!'*

2 **Golly gumdrops!** *see* **Gumdrop.**

GONE

1 **Have been and gone and ...** *see* **Be 5.**

2 **Have been and gone and done it** *see* **Be 6.**

GOOD

1 **A good one** Sometimes written (*slang*) a good *'un*.
   a That is unbelievable: > *'My dad earned £100,000 last year!' 'That's a good one – I suppose he'll earn twice that much this year!'* > *'The bus never turned up, sir!' 'That's a good one, Smith – I was on it myself, so where were you?'*
   b That is a good joke!: > *'A good 'un, Freddie!' they cried, as they bent double with laughter.*

2 **(And a) good job** (or **thing**) **too** Used as a reply, expressing approval of what has just been said: > *'I complained about the broken bag they'd sold me and the shop gave me my money back.' 'A good job too!'* > *'Pete's rung to tell me not to come this weekend.' 'And a good thing too – if you'd driven all that way and found no one there, you'd have been very annoyed.'* Also **It's a good job** (or **thing**).

3 **Good afternoon** An expression used when greeting or leaving people in the afternoon

4 **Good day** *Formal, becoming rare* An expression used when greeting or leaving people during the day.

5 **Good evening** An expression used when greeting, or, less commonly, leaving people in the evening.

6 **Good for you (him, her, etc.)!** An expression of congratulations; well done!; well said!; etc.: > *'I got three grade A's, you know!' 'Good for you!'* > *'Good for Pete – I'm glad he's beaten John at the long jump at last!'* An alternative in British English for *for* is *on*: *Good on you!*

7 **Good gracious!** An expression of surprise, disbelief, annoyance, etc.: > *'Good gracious, you should have done your homework by now! It's ten o'clock already!'* Also **By heaven!** (*old-fashioned*); **Good God!**; **Good heavens!**; **Good Lord!**; **Goodness gracious (me)!**; **Goodness me!**; **My goodness!**

8 **Good grief!** *see* **Grief.**

9 **Good morning** An expression used when greeting or leaving people in the morning: used especially on the speaker's first meeting of the day with the person spoken to.

10 **Good night** An expression used when leaving people in the late afternoon, evening, or at night, especially when going to bed or to sleep.

11 **If you can't be good, be careful!** *see* **Anything 6.**

12 **It's a good thing** *see* **Thing 7.**

13 **So far, so good** *see* **Far 5.**

14 **That's a good one** An expression of disbelief at what someone has said, often used when the speaker thinks what has been said is a joke: > *'You've won the lottery! That's a good one!'*

15 **Very good** Yes; of course: used as a polite way of showing agreement: > *'Get my suit out, please!' 'Very good, sir!'*

16 **Would you be so (or as) good as to ... ?** *Formal* Would you please (do something)?: > *'Would you be so good as to open the door for me?'* Also **Would you be good enough to ...?**

GOODNESS

1 **For goodness' sake!** An expression of impatience, anger, surprise, etc.: often used in questions or requests: > *'For goodness' sake, man, pull yourself together!'* > *'Be quiet, for goodness' sake!'* Also **For God's sake!; For heaven's sake!; For mercy's sake!; For Pete's sake!; For pity's sake!:** > *'Yes, you can see some of the most famous pictures in the world. They're all on show at your local gallery, right here, now, in Wolverhampton, for heaven's sake!'*

2 **Goodness gracious (me)!** *see* **Good 7.**

3 **Goodness knows** *see* **Know 8.**

4 **Honest to goodness** *see* **God 15.**

5 **My goodness!** *see* **Good 7.**

6 **Thank goodness!** *see* **Thank 3b.**

7 **... to goodness** An expression used to add strength to (a wish or hope): > *'I hope to goodness James will be back soon.'* > *'I wish to goodness you'd shut up!'* Also **Surely to goodness:** > *'Surely to goodness, you don't expect me to believe that!'*

GRACIOUS

Good gracious! *see* **Good 7.**

GRANT

1 **God grant** *see* **God 7.**
2 **Granted that** Used to say that something is accepted as true: > *'Granted that they broke the law, what do you consider would be a suitable punishment?'*
3 **I grant you** I accept that what you say is true: > *'Their team may not be the world's greatest, I grant you, but neither are they at the bottom of the league.'*

GRAPE

Sour grapes An expression used to describe the bitterness a person feels, prompted by envy, when pretending to dislike something that he or she likes really but cannot do or get himself or herself: > *'He said that the book I wrote is not worth reading, but that is sour grapes because he'd like to write one himself.'*

GRASS

The grass is (always) greener on the other side A saying that life is more comfortable, pleasant, etc., in a different place or situation from the one a person is in at the moment.

GRATIS

Free, gratis, and for nothing *see* **Free 2.**

GREAT

That's great! That's fantastic!; that's excellent!: > *'I've just passed my driving test!' 'That's great!'* Also used sarcastically: > *'It's just started to rain.' 'That's great – what are we going to do now?'*

GREEK

It's all Greek to me It's too difficult for me to understand: > *'That lecture on biochemistry – I'd no idea what he was saying; it's all Greek to me!'*

GRIEF

Good grief! An expression of surprise and sometimes horror: > *'Good grief! It's Jill Winter – how are you? We've not seen each other for years, have we?'* > *'Good grief! How am I going to manage now my wife's left me?'*

GRIN

1 **Grin and bear it** To accept and suffer difficulty, hardship, or pain without complaining: > *'I'm not sure how I'll fit in this extra work when I'm so busy already, but I suppose I'll just have to grin and bear it.'*
2 **Take** (or **wipe**) **that grin** (or **smile**) **off your face** Stop laughing at what I'm saying: > *'Take that grin off your face for a start, Jones – this is serious. I'm going to find out who broke that window!'*

GROAN

Groan, groan! An expression of humorous disapproval: used as a reply to a joke that is not very funny: > *'Call me a taxi!' 'Right oh – you're a taxi!' 'Groan, groan!'*

GROW

Grow up! Stop behaving like a child!: > *'Grow up, Michael – when are you going to stop hitting boys younger than yourself?'*

GRUMBLE

Mustn't grumble *see* **Complain.**

GUESS

1 **Guess what** Here is something that I think you will find surprising: > *'He's a great fan of the Beatles – and, guess what, he's called his boys John, Paul, George, and Ringo!'*

2 **I guess** *Chiefly American* Used to show reluctant agreement: > *'Mummy, can I play with Snoopy?' 'Sophie, you know dinner's nearly ready. But I guess it's all right.'*

3 **It's anybody's** (or **anyone's**) **guess** It is difficult to predict; there is no certain way of knowing: > *'It's anybody's guess who will win the next race!'* Also note that *anybody's* (or *anyone's*) *guess* can stand on its own: > *'What will happen next is anyone's guess!'*

4 **Your guess is as good as mine** I know as little as you do about it; I don't know either: > *'When is the bus coming?' 'Your guess is as good as mine! They seem to turn up whenever they want to!'*

GUEST

Be my guest! Please feel free to do as you like; I do not mind if you do: often used in reply to a question: > *'May I use your phone?' 'Be my guest!'* > *'Can I have another piece of cake?' 'Be my guest!'*

GUM

By gum! *see* **Gad.**

GUMDROP

Golly gumdrops! *Old-fashioned* An exclamation of surprise or wonder: > *'Golly gumdrops! You're back already – that was quick!'*

GUN

1 **Jump the gun** Do or say something before you should: > *'We jumped the gun by saying that you could buy televisions more cheaply. There is a plan to do this, but it is not yet in operation.'* The phrase comes from athletes beginning a race before the starter's gun goes off.

2 **Son of a gun** *see* **Son.**

HAIR

1 **Keep your hair on!** *see* **Shirt 1.**

2 **Let your hair down!** Relax and
enjoy yourself; behave as you
want: > *'Go on, let your hair down
this evening. You deserve it after the
busy week you've had at work!'*

HALF

1 **A ... and a half** A very big or good
example of (a thing or person): >
*'That's a car and a half you've got
there – it's far too large for the two
of you and it'll never fit in your
garage!'*

2 **Half a moment** *see* **Just 3a.**

3 **Half a tick** *see* **Just 3a.**

4 **My better half** My wife; my
husband: usually used
humorously: > *'I'll have to talk to
my better half about that.'*

5 **Not half** *British*
a Very: > *'It isn't half cold in this
room.'* > *'That chicken wasn't half
nice!'*
b Very much: > *'He doesn't half
swear!'* > *'It didn't half rain!'*
c Yes; certainly: used as a reply
to a question: > *'Would you like to
come with us?' 'Not half!'* > *'Did
you like the film?' 'Not half I did!'*

6 **Not half bad** *see* **Bad 3.**

7 **The half of it** Only part of the
whole story, trouble, etc.: > *'I
went out of the house this morning,
lost my keys at the shops, got soaked
walking to school, and that's not the
half of it – I've had an awful day!'*

8 **Too ... by half** *British* Far too
(something): > *'He's too cocky by*

*half!' > 'I'm no chef.' 'You're too
modest by half.'*

HAND

1 **A big hand for ...** Please welcome
(usually a famous person) by
clapping: > *'A big hand for Toby
Tootall, the greatest circus acrobat of
all time!'*

2 **All hands on deck!** Everyone must
play their part with the work to
be done: > *'All hands on deck! We
need everyone's help to get us out of
this mess!'* Also **All hands to the
pumps!**: > *'We've got so much work
to do, it'll be all hands to the pump
for weeks now!'* Both these
expressions were originally used
on ships.

3 **Cold hands, warm heart** An
expression that someone says
when he or she shakes one's
hand to find it cold; used to
show that although a person may
feel cold, he or she has a kind
and generous nature.

4 **Hands off!** Don't touch; don't
interfere: > *'Hands off that
machine – it's dangerous, you
know!'* > *'Hands off! She's my
girlfriend, if you don't mind!'* >
'Hands off our schools!' – the slogan
had been painted on the wall by
the protesters against cuts in
government spending on education.

5 Hands up!
a Please raise your hands if you
... : used to ask members of a
group (to agree to something): >
'Hands up all those who want to go

swimming,' the teacher said. >
'Hands up if you know the answer.'
b Put your arms above your
head: used by gunmen to the
people they want to rob, etc., to
get them to surrender: > *The
armed men burst into the shop.
'Hands up everyone! Hand over the
money!'* Also **Put** (or **stick**) **'em up!**

6 **I've only one pair of hands** *see* **Pair**.

7 **On the one hand ... and** (or **but**)
on the other ... Used to contrast
two ideas, statements, etc.: > *'On
the one hand, it's a very economical
car, but on the other, it's not much
to look at, is it?'*

8 **Shake hands** To take hold of
another person's hand and move
it up and down when greeting or
coming to an agreement or
reconciliation: > *When I was
introduced to Mr Page, we shook
hands.* > *They shook hands after
their quarrel.*

HANG

1 **Hang in there!** *Chiefly American*
Keep at it!: an expression of
encouragement to persevere
when things are difficult.

2 **Hang it (all)!** Used to express
annoyed dissatisfaction,
disappointment, etc.: > *'I've
forgotten my keys, hang it – how
am I going to get in?'* > *'Hang it
all! You've had three weeks to plant
the seeds and you say you've not
even started?'*

3 **Hang on**
a Please wait a moment: used
especially to someone on the
telephone but also in other
contexts: > *'Hang on – I'll just get
a pencil and jot down the details.'* >

*'Can I speak to Mr Jones, please?'
'I'll see if he's in – just hang on.'*
b Be reasonable; I want to make
a comment or objection: > *'Hang
on, old chap, who are you calling a
liar?'* Also **Hang about**.
c An expression of surprise or
amazement: > *'Hang on – don't I
know you? Weren't we at school
together?'*

4 **I'll be hanged** Used to express
anger, surprise, dissatisfaction,
etc.: > *'I'll be hanged if I'll apologise
this time – he should say he's sorry
first.'* Also **I'm hanged:** > *'I'm
hanged if I know the answer!'*

5 **Let it all hang out** *Slang* Be
completely free to express
yourself as you want: > *'We're
just off to the party.' 'Enjoy
yourselves – let it all hang out!'*

6 **Thereby hangs a tale** *see* **Tale**.

HAPPEN

1 **As it happens** An expression used
at the beginning of a statement
to link it with what has just been
said; often used to introduce
something surprising: > *'As it
happens, I know a colleague at work
who may be able to help you.'*

2 **It's all happening** There's a lot of
successful activity: > *'It's all
happening here today!'* > *'It's all
happening in Birmingham at the
moment: it's got a new shopping
centre, good concert halls, and an
excellent library – what more could
you want?'*

HARM

1 **It wouldn't do any harm** Used as a
way of suggesting a possible
course of action that could be

useful: > *'It wouldn't do any harm ringing them up first to see if they've got some in stock.'* > *'It wouldn't do you any harm to get some on-the-job training.'*

2 **No harm done** Used as a way of telling someone that he or she need not worry because no serious damage or hurt has been done.

HAT

1 **Hang onto your hats** An expression said when the weather is very windy, or when a journey or mode of transport is rather bumpy.

2 **Hats off to ...** An expression of admiration towards someone: > *'Hats off to you for your most interesting lecture.'*

3 **I'll eat my hat** *Becoming old-fashioned* I will be proved wrong; I will be surprised: used to show that the speaker does not really believe that something is true or that something will happen: > *'If that old horse of yours does come first in the race, I'll eat my hat!'* > *'If it wasn't Richard who broke the window, I'll eat my hat!'*

4 **My hat!** *Old-fashioned*
   a What nonsense!: > *'Seventy, my hat! Surely you're only around fifty!'* > *'My hat! You don't expect me to believe that story, do you? Where were you really last night?'*
   b An expression of surprise: > *'My hat, it's cold today, isn't it!'*

HATCH

Down the hatch! An expression used when taking a drink with other people.

HATE

1 **I hate to interrupt (bother, disturb, etc.) you** Used to apologise that one has to interrupt, bother, etc. someone: > *'I hate to interrupt you but I wonder if you could just help me for a few minutes.'*

2 **I hate to mention it, but ...** *see* **Mention 2.**

3 **I hate to say this** Used to express sorrow or reluctance that one has to say something embarrassing or unpleasant: > *'I hate to say this but I don't believe you trust us.'* Also **I hate to have to say this; I hate to tell you.**

4 **I hate to think** Used to emphasise that one finds something unpleasant: > *'I hate to think what might have happened if you hadn't telephoned just then.'*

HAVE

1 **... had better ...** (Someone) ought to (do something): > *'I'd better check that I've locked all the doors before I go out.'* > *'You'd better not go there this evening – / think he'll be busy.'* Sometimes used as a threat: > *'I'll pay you back on Friday.' 'You'd better!'* > *'I promise I'll return the car.' 'You better had!'*

2 **Have ... , will ...** An expression used to show a willingness or ability (to do something, especially go somewhere), because you have (something): > *'"Have car, will travel" as the saying goes – so we've been to Scotland for the week-end!'*

3 **I have and I haven't** An ambiguous, rather defensive, reply to a question, showing that the speaker has partly done or

undertaken something, and often used when the speaker purposely does not want to be clear: > *'Have you spoken to Mr Smith about a pay rise?' 'I have and I haven't – not directly, yet, but I promise to tomorrow.'* > *'Have you got any work for me to mark?' 'Well, I have and I haven't.'*

4 **I have it** *see* Get 17,19.

5 **I wouldn't have it if you gave it to (or paid) me!** I'm not accepting what you're offering: > *'That car of yours is so old, I wouldn't have it if you gave it to me!'*

6 **I'm (he's, she's,** etc.**) not having it** I'm (he, she, etc.) is not tolerating something: > *'I tell you, I don't want any of that kind of nonsense going on in my house. I'm just not having it.'*

7 **Let's be having you** A firm request to move somewhere quickly: used by attendants at a public place, foremen to workers, and supposedly by policemen: > *'Come along now, let's be having you, please!'* > *'Ladies and gentlemen, let's be having you: the museum closes in ten minutes.'*

8 **Thanks for having me** *see* **Thank 7.**

9 **What have you** Other similar people, things, etc.: > *On sale at the jumble sale were clothes, toys, bric-a-brac and what have you.*

10 **You have me there** *see* Get 21.

11 **You shouldn't have** It is very kind of you: used in accepting a gift: > *'Auntie, we've brought you some flowers, and all the family hope you'll get better soon.' 'Oh, you shouldn't have! Aren't they lovely!'*

HEAD

1 **Heads or tails?** An expression used when throwing a coin into the air to decide who will start a game, etc., the result depending on which side shows upwards: > *'Heads or tail?' Gerald called. 'Tails!' said Pat, but it was heads, so Gerald decided that his team should play downhill.* > *'Let's toss for it – heads or tails?' 'Heads!' 'Heads it is!'* Also used in the phrase *Heads I win, tails you lose,* a false bet, as whatever the result, the speaker will benefit.

2 **Heads will roll** Dismissals or resignations will take place: > *Heads might well roll this coming weekend as the new television company responds to its critics.* Originally the reference was to the execution of people.

3 **Mind your head(s)!** Be careful; something may hit your head or you may hit your head on something: > *'Mind you heads!' the workmen shouted to the people below as the tiles fell off the roof.* > *'Mind your head! it's a low ceiling!'*

4 **Off with his (or her) head!** Execute him!; execute her!: > *The women sat knitting in front of the guillotine. 'Off with his head!' they shouted.*

HEALTH

Your health! An expression used before drinking to wish that someone will remain well and be successful: > *'Your health, Pat – may you have a prosperous time in Scotland!'* Also **Good health!; Your good health! Your very good health!**: > *The whole gathering raised*

*their glasses and the chairman spoke,
'Your very good health, Colonel Digby!'*

HEAR

1 **Do you hear (me)?** Used to
emphasise that one wants
someone to pay attention to
what one is saying; often said in
an angry tone: > *'I won't tolerate
such disobedience. Do you hear me?'*

2 **Hear! hear!** An expression of
agreement and approval: called
out by someone at a public
meeting: > *'The government may
decide in certain circumstances to
reduce the amount of tax paid.'
'Hear! hear!'* Also used in more
informal contexts: > *'I think I'd
better go and do the washing-up!'
'Hear! hear!'*

3 **I hear what you are saying** I have
listened to what you are saying
and I understand the importance
of it.

4 **I wouldn't hear of someone doing
something** I refuse to let someone do something: > *'I wouldn't
hear of you paying this time.
Tonight's meal is on me.'*

5 **I've heard that one before!** I don't
believe you: often used in reply
to an excuse that has just been
given: > *'The bus didn't turn up.'
'I've heard that one before! Be
honest now, why were you late?'* >
*'Let's go to the disco on Friday!'
'I've heard that one before – you
always say that and then forget
about it later!'*

6 **You heard!** Used to add force to
a command, especially when the
speaker is impatient: > *'Get this
lorry out of the car park. You heard
– move it!'*

HEART

1 **Bless your (his, her, etc.) heart** *see*
Bless 4.

2 **Cross my (your, etc.) heart** I (you,
etc.) promise; I swear that I am
telling the truth: used to express
emphatically one's sincerity: >
*'Are you sure you don't know who
broke the window? Cross your
heart?'* Also **Cross my (your, etc.)
heart and hope to die** Often used
by children: > *'I won't tell your
secret to anyone else, cross my heart
and hope to die!'*

3 **Eat your heart out ...** Used to
compare the actions of two
people, one of whom is famous;
used to suggest that the named
person would be jealous of the
other person: > *Their new records
are selling millions. Eat your heart
out, Paul McCartney!*

4 **From the bottom of your heart** *see*
Bottom 2.

5 **Have a heart** Be kind or
sympathetic: > *'Have a heart,
Dick! I've been ill for six months –
can't you give me a bit more time to
catch up on the work?'* > *'I think
you could have been more reasonable
with Jane for being late; have a
heart – after all, she has travelled
all day to get here.'*

6 **His (her, etc.) heart is in the right
place** He (she, etc.) is kind and
generous although he (she, etc.)
has some weaknesses of
character: >*He may be a bit wild at
times but his heart is in the right
place.*

7 **My heart bleeds for you (him, her,
etc.)** *Often humorous* I feel very
sorry for you (him, her, etc.) but
often used when the feelings are

not really of sorrow: > *'I've got to be up by seven tomorrow morning to get to work early.' 'My heart bleeds for you – I get up at six every day at the moment.'* Alternatives to *bleeds* are *aches* and *goes out*. The phrases may also be used in the plural: > *'Our hearts went out to her when she had a miscarriage, just after we'd had a baby.'* Also **You're breaking my heart.**

8 **Put your (his, her, etc.) heart and soul into (something)** To give a full commitment to some work or activity; make the strongest possible effort: > *'I put my heart and soul into writing that speech, so don't tell me it wasn't worth it!'*

HEAVE

Heave ho! The cry of sailors when lifting the anchor up, and, more widely, to encourage someone when pushing or pulling something.

HEAVEN

1 **By heaven!** *see* **Good 7.**
2 **For heaven's sake!** *see* **Goodness 1.**
3 **Good heavens!** *see* **Good 7.**
4 **Heaven forbid** *see* **Forbid.**
5 **Heaven help him (her, you, etc.)** *see* **Help 2.**
6 **Heaven knows** *see* **Know 8.**
7 **Heaven preserve us!** *see* **Preserve.**
8 **Heavens above!** An expression of surprise, disbelief, annoyance, etc.: > *'Heavens above! That's Jane Mitcham over there – I've not seen her for years!'* > *'Heavens above, child! Can't you be quiet for two minutes?'* Also (slang, old-fashioned) **Heavens to Murgatroyd!**
9 **In heaven's name** An expression

used to add strength to a question, request, etc.: > *'Where in heaven's name did you put my keys?'* Also **In God's name.**
10 **Thank heavens!** *see* **Thank 3.**

HECK

1 **What (how, etc.) the heck?** *see* **Hell 6.**
2 **What the heck!** *see* **Hell 7.**

HELL

1 **Go to hell!** Go away; stop talking!: a strong expression: > *'Can I have a word with you for a moment?' 'No, I'm tired of you annoying me all day – go to hell!'*
2 **Hell's bells!** *Becoming old-fashioned* A strong expression of anger, annoyance, etc. > *'Hells bells! How many more times do I have to tell you to shut up?'* Also **Hell's teeth!**
3 **Like hell**
   a Very much, fast, etc.: > *'He always works like hell before exams.'* > *'We ran like hell to get away from the police.'*
   b An expression of strong disagreement: said as a reply to the previous statement, request, etc.: > *'Will you buy me that book I wanted?' 'Like hell I will: you never get me things when I ask you!'* > *'Like hell he paid for the holiday! We had saved for months and months to pay for it ourselves.'* Also (slang) **The hell you will** (or **won't**); **The hell he (or she) can** (or **can't**), etc.: > *'Mary says she'll help you learn to drive.' 'The hell she will – she's only just passed the test herself!'*
4 **There'll be hell to pay** People will get into serious trouble: > *'If they*

ever find out what you two have been doing, there'll be hell to pay.'

5 To hell with ... I (or we) do not care about; I'm fed up with (something or someone): > *'To hell with this essay – I've spent hours on it already, but I don't seem to be getting anywhere!'* > *'To hell with the lot of you – we're going home!'*

6 What (how, where, who, why, etc.) the hell? Whatever, (however, wherever, whoever, why ever): used in questions to emphasise a strong feeling such as annoyance or surprise: > *'What the hell are you doing in my workshop?'* > *'How the hell are we going to get out of this mess?'* An alternative to *hell* in these expressions is *heck*: > *'Who the heck do you think you are, coming in here without even knocking?'*

7 What the hell! An expression used to reject a difficulty or problem, showing that the speaker does not care: often used in a resigned tone: > *'What the hell, the company's paying for the meal, so let's have the most expensive dish!'* > *'So Jo's not in – what the hell – we can come back tomorrow instead!'* > *'OK – so I failed the exam. What the hell, I can always try again!'* Also **What the heck!**: > *'After he'd crashed the car, Pat just said, 'What the heck – my Dad'll buy me another one.'*

HELLO

1 Hello, hello, hello! *British* An expression supposedly used by policemen on finding something strange: but used humorously in real life: > *'Hello, hello, hello! What's all this then? A pot of gold hidden in the bushes!'* This phrase is pronounced and often written *'ello, 'ello, 'ello.*

2 Hello, stranger! *see* **Stranger.**

3 Hello there! A cry for attention when entering a house or when you cannot see: > *'Hello there! Is anyone in?'* Jean called out as she went through the door of the dark old house.

HELP

1 Can I help you? An expression used by a shop assistant in serving a customer: > *'Can I help you, sir?' 'Two boxes of matches, please.'* Also **What can I do for you?**

2 God (or heaven) help me (you, etc.) A cry requesting help from God: > *'God help us all at this time of national disaster.'* > *'Heaven help Mary in this crisis in her life.'* Also used humorously to express mild sympathy: > *'Heaven help the man who marries Kitty!'*

3 I (he, she, etc.) can't help I cannot control something: > *'I know I shouldn't but I couldn't help laughing at them.'* > *'I can't help thinking that she's making a big mistake.'*

4 Not if I can help it Only against my agreeing to it: > *'I won't pay the money on time, not if I can help it.'* > *'I'm coming round this evening to put an end to our arguments once and for all!' 'Not if I can help it, you won't!'* Also **Not if I know it**: > *'Not if I know it, you won't borrow my car!'*

5 So help me Used in emphasising

a promise: > *'I'll get revenge on you, so help me!'* > *'If you're not at the theatre tonight, so help me, I'll resign as your agent!'*

6 So help me God

a Although this may seem strange, I am speaking the truth: > *'I really did see a flying-saucer, so help me God.'* Sometimes

b Used to emphasise a hope or wish: > *'I never want to see you again, so help me God!'*

HERE

1 Here goes! *see* **Go 12.**

2 Here we go again *see* **Go 13.**

3 Here you are

a An expression used when giving something to someone; this is what you wanted: > *'Here you are, madam, what you ordered, roast chicken and peas.'*

b An expression used to call attention to something: > *'You say you want to go to the States in July but, here you are, it's January already and you've still not got any money – you'd better start saving, my lad!'* Also **Here we are.**

4 Here's how! An expression used when taking a drink with other people.

5 Here's to ... An expression used when drinking, to wish (someone or something) well: > *'Here's to the bride and groom.'* > *'Here's to your new job!'*

HESITATE

Don't hesitate to contact (call, etc.**) me** Do not worry about disturbing me: > *'Don't hesitate to ask if there's anything you don't understand.'*

HEY

Hey presto!

a An expression a conjuror says as he or she comes to the main part of a trick: > *'Do you see this smart top hat? Hey presto, here are two rabbits jumping out of it!'*

b Used to announce a surprising change or sudden appearance: > *The doorbell rang. I went to see who it was. Hey presto! It was my brother, Jason, who I'd not seen for years!'* > *'No one had arrived for the party – the room was empty. But hey presto, in five minutes all my friends were suddenly there!'*

HIDING

Be on a hiding to nothing To have no chance at being successful at something: > *'You're on a hiding to nothing, trying to get more money out of your boss.'*

HINT

Hint, hint! An expression used when making a small, indirect suggestion to do something: > *'It's ten o'clock, hint, hint!' muttered Sue quietly. Sam understood. 'Yes, I think it's time we went,' he said.* > *'A cup of tea would be nice – hint, hint!'*

HIP

Hip, hip, hurrah! An expression used to introduce cheers: > *'Congratulations to the team for coming first in the competition! Hip, hip, hurrah! Hip, hip, hurrah! Hip, hip, hurrah!'* The expression is usually called out with the person leading the cheers crying *Hip, hip* and everyone shouting *hurrah*. This all happens three times.

HISTORY

... and the rest is history *see* **Rest 2.**

HIT

Hit it off To have a good friendly relationship with someone: > *'From the first time they met, they hit it off.'*

HOLD

1 **Hold it**
   a Stop everything!; stop what you're doing, wait a moment: > *'Hold it, son, where do you think you're going with that picture under your coat?'* > *The armed men made their way into the bank. 'Hold it, everyone – don't anyone move: now tell us where the safe is!'* Also **Hold everything!**
   b Keep still: said by a photographer who wants people to stay in the same position: > *We stood around chatting to one another after the ceremony. 'Hold it!' Ian shouted, as he took a picture of us all.*

2 **Hold on!** Please wait a moment: used especially to someone on the telephone, but also in other circumstances: > *'Is Mr Jackson there, please?' 'Hold on, I'll see if he's available.'* > *'Hold on a minute! Aren't you the man the police are looking for in connection with the robbery?'*

3 **Hold your horses!** *see* **Horse 1.**

HOLE

1 **Need something like a hole in the head** Definitely not to need or want something: > *We need more ideas on how to change the world like we need a hole in the head.*

2 **Top hole!** *British, rare, old-fashioned* Excellent!; splendid!: > *'We're going to take you to the circus at Christmas!' 'Top hole!' cried Andrew with delight.*

HOLY

Holy smoke! *Old-fashioned* An expression of strong feeling such as surprise, delight, or anger: > *'Holy smoke! What are you doing here? I thought you were in America still!'* Also **Holy cow!; Holy mackerel!; Holy Moses!:** > *'Holy mackerel! Can't you children ever learn to be quiet?'*

HOME

1 **... go home!** A slogan used to show the speaker's disapproval of (someone): > *'Prime Minister go home!'* > *'Foreign troops go home!'*

2 **Home, James!** A humorous way of asking the driver to drive the car home: > *The children got into the back of the car and called out, 'Home, James!' to their father.* Originally, *Home, James, and don't spare the horses!*, an order to the driver of a carriage or coach, and later the chauffeur, to return home.

3 **Make yourself at home!** Please relax and do as you would in your own home: > *'Do come in and make yourself at home! Would you like something to eat?'* > *'Sit down and make yourself at home, while I put the kettle on for a cup of tea.'*

4 **Who's ... when he's (she's,** etc.) **at home?** I've never heard of (someone): used to ask who the

person just mentioned really is: > *'I'm off to see Tracy Rossiter.' 'Tracy Rossiter? Who's she when she's at home?'*

HONEST

1 **Honest to God** *see* **God 15.**

2 **To be honest** Used in a frank expression of one's opinion, sometimes when one thinks that the speaker will not like what one says: > *'To be honest, I've been worried about Rob for several months now.'* Also **In all honesty.**

HONOUR

1 **Be honoured to do something** To be very pleased to do something; used as a polite and formal expression of agreement: > *'I'd be honoured to be a godparent to Damien.'*

2 **Do the honours** To act as host or hostess by doing something such as pouring drinks or serving food: > *'Will you do the honours and carve the meat, while I go and bring in the vegetables?'* > *'Patrick, you do the honours and propose the toast.' 'All right, then. Ladies and gentlemen; here's to your new job, Elizabeth!'*

3 **God's honour!** Used to strengthen a promise, agreement, or state-ment: > *'God's honour! I'm telling the truth!'* Also *(old-fashioned)* **Scout's honour!; Honour bright!** *(British school slang)*: > *'I really am going to finish my work tonight, Scout's honour!'*

4 **On my honour** I assure you: used to emphasise a promise: > *'On my honour, we will do all we can to help you.'*

HOOT

Not care (or **give**) **two hoots** *see* **Damn 6.**

HOP

Hop it! *Slang, British* Go away!: *'Hop it, Pete, we don't want you around!'*

HOPE

1 **I hope you feel proud of yourself!** I hope you feel pleased with yourself: but used when the person has nothing to be proud of and has, in fact, in the speaker's opinion behaved badly: > *'I hope you feel proud of yourself, Sarah! Your silly behaviour in the restaurant really made your mother and me feel embarrassed!'*

2 **Not have a hope in hell** To have absolutely no chance of doing something: > *'At his age, he's not got a hope in hell of getting another job.'*

3 **Some hope(s)!** There is little or no chance that what you want will actually happen: > *'Some hopes of playing games today – it's been raining since early this morning!'* > *'I want to sail around the world one day!' 'Some hope!'* Also **(A) fat chance!; Not a hope!**

HORROR

Horror of horrors Used as an expression of shock, sometimes humorously: > *'Horror of horrors: a police officer turns into a crook.'* Also **Shock horror!**

HORSE

1 **Hold your horses!** Don't be too hasty to do something; be more patient!: > *'Hold your horses! We don't need to ring for the ambulance – it's only a slight cut.'* > *'Why do*

you have to get so angry about something as unimportant as that? Hold your horses!'

2 **I could eat a horse** I am extremely hungry: > *'I've not eaten anything since breakfast. I could eat a horse.'*

HOST

Mine host A humorous way of talking to one's host or, often, the landlord of a pub.

HOW

1 **And how!** Very much so: used to express strong agreement with what has just been said, but sometimes also used to express the opposite of this: > *'Goldie's beautiful, isn't she?' 'And how!'* > *'So you had a good time in London?' 'And how! It was all so dirty, the hotel was expensive, the trains were all late – we're never going back there!'*

2 **Here's how!** see **Here 4.**

3 **How ... !** Used to introduce an exclamation: > *'How kind you are!'* > *'Treacle tart! How lovely!'* > *'How she's grown!'* > *'How polite her behaviour is these days!'*

4 **How about. ... ?** see **About 1.**

5 **How about that!** see **About 2.**

6 **How are you?** A conventional greeting, often also a definite enquiry about someone's health and welfare: > *'How are you, Paula?' 'Very well, thanks, and you?' 'OK, thanks.'* > *'How are you, Mr Dickson?' 'Fine, thank you; how are you?' 'Fine, thank you.'* When used as a question, the stress falls on *are*; if used in a reply, the stress falls on *you*. Also **How are you doing?; How are (or how's) things?; How are you**

keeping? (*becoming old-fashioned*); **How's yourself?** (*slang*): > *'How are you doing, Vic? I've not had a chance to talk to you for ages!'*

7 **How come ... ?** see **Come 13.**

8 **How could I have ...?** Used in an apology when one has (done something foolish): > *'How could I have been so stupid? I'm sorry I stepped on your toe!'*

9 **How do you do** see **Do 12.**

10 **How is it?** Why?; what is the reason?: > *'How is it you always arrive late on Mondays?'*

11 **How is it for ...?** Is this satisfactory regarding (a particular feature): > *'Do you want to try on this coat?' 'Yes, let's.' 'How is it for size?'*

12 **How (or however) could (or can) you ... ?** You shouldn't have (done something): used to express sorrow and surprise that someone has acted in a certain way: > *'How could you have said such rude things to him?'* > *'How can you speak to her like that?'* > *'However could you have forgotten my birthday?'*

13 **How so?** Why?; why is it like that?: > *'I thought the concert was very disappointing.' 'How so?' 'The lead singer didn't turn up, and the understudy couldn't reach the high notes properly.'*

14 **How's it going?** see **Go 14.**

15 **How's that?**
a What do you think of that?: > *'There, the picture's on the wall – how's that?' 'I don't think you've got it quite straight.'*
b Why?; what is the reason?: > *'I'm not sure I'll be able to come and visit you again.' 'How's that?'*

c *Cricket* Is the batsman out?: said to an umpire: > *The shouts of 'How's that?' were loud enough to be heard outside the cricket ground.* Sometimes written and pronounced (*slang*) *Howzzat?*
d Please repeat what you said: > *'I'm going to be an astronaut when I grow up.' 'How's that?' 'I said I'm going to be an astronaut when I grow up.'*

16 How's that for ... An expression used to praise or draw attention to (a particular feature of something): > *'How's that for economy! It's the cheapest small car available!'* > *'How's that for the best float in the parade!'*

17 That's how it is *see* **That 16.**
18 This is how it is *see* **This 1.**

HOWEVER

However could you ...? *see* **How 12.**

HURRY

There's no hurry There is no need for you to do something immediately: > *'There's no hurry. We can wait till after Christmas.'*

HURT

It won't hurt Used as a way of suggesting a useful course of action: > *'It wouldn't hurt for you to do a good day's work for a change.'*

ICE

Break the ice To make the shyness and embarrassment less, for example when people meet for the first time: > *'Fortunately, we had the baby with us when we went round there for tea, so that helped to break the ice.'*

IDEA

1 Not have the foggiest (idea) *see* **Foggiest.**

2 Not my (his, her, etc.**) idea of ...** This is the opposite of what I (he, she, etc.) think of as (something): > *'Sitting on a beach all day is not my idea of a holiday – I prefer doing something active like looking round the area or climbing mountains.'* > *'Camping in the rain is not my idea of fun!'*

3 That's an idea What you are suggesting is worth considering: > *'Shall we go to Ilfracombe for the day?' 'That's an idea! I'd never thought of that!'*

4 That's the idea That's about right: > *'Listen, Mum, to me playing this piece by Mozart.' ... 'Yes, that's the idea! You're coming on very well now.'*

5 The (very) idea! What you are suggesting is most unreasonable: > *'The very idea of you staying out late makes me shudder!'*

6 What's the (big) idea? Why are you doing that?; how dare you do that!: used as an accusation: > *'What's the idea – coming into my workshop without even knocking?'* > *'What's the big idea of gossiping about me behind my back?'*

7 You have no idea Used when the speaker is emphasising that something is extremely good or extremely bad: > *'You have no idea what it was like being with Grant. I was absolutely awful.'*

IF

1 **As if** ... *see* **As 4.**
2 **If I were you** An expression used in giving advice: > *'If I were you, I'd accept that job.'* > *'If I were you, I'd be thinking about getting rid of that old car.'* A rather rude reply to this is sometimes *but you're not*: > *'I'd think about resigning, if I were you.'* *'But you're not, so shut up!'*
3 **If only** ... I wish: often used about (something that is very unlikely) or to express a regret: > *'If only I'd known, I wouldn't have done it!'* > *'If only Pete were here, it would all be different!'* > *'If only he didn't snore!'*
4 **If you could** (or **would**) Used in polite requests: > *'Pass me that glass, if you could.'*
5 **It's not as if** Used to introduce a possible explanation for something although the speaker knows that this is not true: > *'I don't know why she is so worried about Paul. It's not as if they're close friends.'*
6 **(Well) if** ... Used to introduce (an exclamation): > *'If it isn't spotty Brian from London! What are you doing here in Ibiza?'* > *'Well, if this doesn't beat everything!'*
7 **What if** ... *see* **What 15.**

IMAGINE

1 **Just) imagine (that)!** An expression of surprise: sometimes expressing disapproval of what is being mentioned: > *'Just imagine! After all these years of buying British, he's now bought a foreign car!'* > *'My dad's a driver on one of the new fast trains!' 'Imagine that! I thought he was a ticket-collector!'*
2 **You can't imagine** Used when the speaker is emphasising that something is extremely good or extremely bad: > *'You can't imagine my delight when I saw what Hugo gave me for my birthday – a brand new car!'*

INCH

1 **Every inch** Completely; exactly: > *He looked every inch the model English gentleman: bowler hat, dark coat, and umbrella.*
2 **Give someone an inch and they'll take a mile** If you do someone a small favour or give him or her a small amount of freedom, then he or she will take advantage of you and try to take a lot more. The expression derives from *give someone an inch and he'll take an ell*, deriving from Old English *eln*, forearm or the measure from the elbow to the fingertips.

INCLINE

I'm inclined to ... An expression used to make an opinion sound less strong: > *'I'm inclined to think you're right and Sheila's wrong.'*

INSTANCE

1 **For instance** Used to introduce a specific example that illustrates or explains an argument, opinion, etc.: > *They're planning to redevelop the old industrial areas, the former gas works and the steam laundry, for instance.*

2 **In the first instance** As the start of a series of actions: > *Enquiries should be made in the first instance to the General Secretary.*

IT

1 **If it hadn't been for** Used to describe something or someone that is the only reason that is preventing something from happening: > *'We'd have got here earlier if it hadn't been for the road-works on the motorway.'*

2 **It's me** I am at the door; it is me speaking: > *There was a knock on the door. 'Who's there?' Kitty asked.* *'It's me,' replied Annette, as she came in.*

3 **It's not that ...** Used when giving one reason among many for something: > *'It's not that I don't want to study; I just find reading pages of textbooks every day extremely boring.'*

4 **That's it** *see* **That 17.**

5 **This is it** *see* **This 2.**

6 **Who is it?** Who is at the door?; who is speaking?: > *There was a knock at the door. 'Who is it?' Bill called out. 'Cathy!' 'Come in, then.'* > *'753111,' John answered the phone, 'who is it?'*

J

JACK

1 **Before you can say Jack Robinson** *see* **Robinson.**

2 **I'm all right, Jack** I'm doing very well: used to show that you care only about yourself and not at all about other people: > *'We're going to make sure that our union gets the highest pay settlement this year. Workers in other industries don't count; it's "I'm all right, Jack" that's important.'* The phrase comes from the title of a film *I'm All Right, Jack* (1960).

JEEPER

Jeepers (creepers)! *Slang, chiefly American* An expression of surprise, sometimes also used for emphasis: > *'Jeepers creepers, Aaron's coming down the drive – we'd better move!'* *Jeepers* is a euphemism for *Jesus*.

JIFFY

Just a jiffy *see* **Just 3a.**

JIGGER

I'm jiggered! *Old-fashioned* Used to express surprise, anger, etc.: > *'It's Pete! Well, I'm jiggered! Who would have thought of meeting you here!'* > *'I'm jiggered if I'll let him get away without being punished!'*

JIMINY

By Jiminy! *Old-fashioned* An expression showing surprise, also used to add force to a statement: > *'By Jiminy – you're right, that is Margaret over there! I wonder what she's doing here!'* *Jiminy* is a shortened form of *Jesus Domine*, Jesus Lord.

JINGO

By jingo! *Old-fashioned* An expression of surprise, excitement, etc.: > *'By jingo, the bus is on time!'* >

'By Jingo, Mary's passed her driving test!' Originally, perhaps a euphemism for *Jesus*.

JOB

1 **(And a) good job too** *see* **Good 2.**
2 **Don't give up the day job** *see* **Day 2.**
3 **Jobs for the boys** Work given to one's friends, especially when they may not be the best people to do it.
4 **(That's) just the job** That is exactly what is needed: > *'A glass of cold milk! Just the job on a hot day like this!'* > *'So I could stay with you in Birmingham and then drive up to Edinburgh the next day? That's just the job!'* Also (*old-fashioned*) **That's (just) the ticket.**

JOIN

1 **If you can't beat 'em, join 'em!** *see* **Beat 3.**
2 **Join the club!** *see* **Club.**

JOKE

1 **Beyond a joke** Too unreasonable to become worrying: > *'They're always putting up the price of petrol. It's getting beyond a joke.'*
2 **It's** (or **it was**) **no joke** It is (or was) something serious: > *'It's no joke walking along a country lane in the dark.'* > *'It was no joke carrying all your suitcases from one side of the station to the other – what did you put in them?'*
3 **Joking apart** (or **aside**) Seriously: > *'Joking aside, has anyone got any real suggestions as to what we might use the patch of ground for?'*
4 **You must be joking!** I cannot seriously believe what you're saying; I am very surprised: > *'Goldie's just won first prize in the*

beauty competition!' 'You must be joking!' Also **You're joking!:** > *'Have I told you we're emigrating?' 'You're joking!'*

JOVE

By Jove! *Old-fashioned* An expression of surprise, excitement, or sometimes approval; also used to add force to a statement: > *'Isn't that plane Concorde?' 'Yes, by Jove, I think you're right!'* > *'By Jove, I'll get you back for what you've done to me, if it's the last thing I do!'* *Jove* comes from Old Latin *Jovis*, Jupiter. Also **By thunder!**

JOY

1 **Full of the joys of spring** Very happy and bright; sometimes said to someone who is obviously very cheerful when you yourself are not feeling at all like this: > *'You're full of the joys of spring this morning, aren't you?'*
2 **No joy** *British* No success or luck: > *'Did you manage to find the book you were looking for?' 'No joy!'* Also, more fully, *I got no joy; I didn't get any joy.*

JUDGEMENT

1 **Against your (his, her, etc.) better judgement** Though you think (he or she thinks, etc.) something is not sensible or wise: > *'Against our better judgement, I have to admit, we let them stay here and now see what a disaster it's turned out to be.'*
2 **Judgement on you** *School slang, becoming old-fashioned* It is as if you were being punished by God: said when something bad happens to a person after they

have done something bad themselves: > *'I got my homework back. The mark was only three out of ten.' 'Judgement on you!'* Carol replied, *'you should not have cheated and copied it!'* > *'I've just got absolutely soaked running for the bus!' 'It's a judgement on you for breaking Mrs Jones' window!'*

JUMP

1 **God (and) jump in the lake!** *see* **Lake.**

2 **Jump to it!** Get going on something; hurry; show that you are willing to obey: > *'You'd better start cleaning the office! Jump to it! The manager will be here in half an hour!'* > *'We'll have to jump to it to get our work finished by the time Pete comes round for us!'*

3 **Take a running jump!** Go away: used as a rude expression when you are very annoyed with someone: > *'You've really got on my nerves this morning!' 'Yes, and you've got on mine!' 'Why don't you take a running jump!'* > *'And then she told him to go and take a running jump – you can imagine what sort of an effect that had!'*

JUST

1 **Isn't (wasn't,** etc.) **it (he, she,** etc.) **just!** Yes, I agree; very much so: used to express complete agreement, but sometimes also indicating the opposite: > *'Wasn't that book interesting?' 'Wasn't it just! Once I started it, I couldn't put it down!'* > *'Isn't Perry helpful around the home?' 'Helpful? Isn't he just – he sits there all the time, watching the television, and never even asks if he can help at all!'*

2 **It's just that** Used when giving an explanation to someone, often used when someone may be thinking of another explanation and/or to stop someone becoming angry: > *'It's just that I've been hurt before and that's why I don't want to get too involved with you.'*

3 **Just a moment**

a Wait a moment, please: > *'Just a moment, please – I'm still dealing with another customer!'* Also **Half a mo** (*very informal*); **Half a moment; Half a tick** (*very informal, British*); **Just a jiffy** (*old-fashioned, very informal*); Just a second; Just a tick (*very informal British*); One moment: > *'I'll be with you in just one moment.'*

b I wish to make a comment or objection: > *'Just a moment! What about the plans for the other side of the building? Has everyone forgotten them?'* Alternatives to *moment* are *minute* and *second*.

c An expression of surprise or amazement: > *'Just a moment! Aren't you the chap we met in the bank? Yes, look, your beard's falling off!'* Alternatives to *moment* are *minute* and *second*.

4 **Just as well** *see* **Well 4.**

5 **Just so** *British, old-fashioned* It is exactly as you say; I agree; that's right: used to express complete agreement: > *'I'll come and pick you up at six o'clock and then we can drive on to Ralph's together.' 'Just so!'* Also **Quite (so):** > *'I always think that a cup of tea is the most refreshing drink there is.' 'Quite so!'* > *'I'm sure Harvey's the best tennis-player we've ever had, isn't he?' 'Quite!'*

6 **Just the thing!** *see* **Thing 9.**

KEEP

1 **How are you keeping?** *see* **How 6.**

2 **I (or we) mustn't keep you** Used as a way of ending a conversation before saying goodbye.

3 **Keep one's fingers crossed** *see* **Finger 2.**

4 **Keep smiling!** Take things easy; don't worry!: used to describe an optimistic approach to life even when things are going wrong: > *'Whatever troubles you may be going through, remember, "Keep smiling".'*

5 **Keep taking the tablets!** *see* **Tablet.**

6 **Keep you shirt (or hair) on!** *see* **Shirt 1.**

7 **You (he, she, etc.) can keep ...** I do not want (what is being offered) in the least: often said in a rude tone: > *'You can keep your burnt pie – I'm going out for a take-away!'* The stress falls on *keep*.

8 **You can't keep a good man down** *see* **Man 10.**

KEEPER

Finders keepers *see* **Finder.**

KETTLE

1 **A watched kettle (pot) never boils** Constantly waiting for something expectantly makes it seem to take even longer.

2 **That's a different kettle of fish** *see* **Story 2a.**

3 **That's (or it's) a fine kettle of fish** That's an awkward situation: > *'It's a fine kettle of fish you've got us in – stuck way out in the country with no petrol!'* Alternatives to *fine* are *nice* and *pretty*.

4 **The pot calling the kettle black** *see* **Pot 2.**

KICK

For kicks Just for the excitement: > *The boys stole the car and drove it round town just for kicks.* Also **For the hell of it.**

KID

1 **(And) no kidding!** I mean exactly what I say!; I am not joking: > *'I'll beat you in the long jump today – no kidding!'*

2 **No kidding?** I'm surprised at what you're saying; is it really true?: > *'Have you heard, Janet? My cousin's going to work in the States for the whole of next year.' 'No kidding?' 'Yes – she goes in January.'* > *'I've lived here all my life!' 'No kidding? Then how come you don't know where the railway station is?'*

3 **You're kidding!** I don't believe you!: > *'Pearl's just won first prize in a swimming competition!' 'You're kidding! She's about as athletic as an apple pudding!'* > *'You're kidding! You say you heard the Beatles at a concert – live? You're not old enough, surely?'* Also **You've got to be kidding; You must be kidding.**

KILL

1 **If it kills me** Even if it is very difficult: > *'I'm going to finish this essay tonight, even if it kills me.'*

2 Kill two birds with one stone *see* Bird 2.

KIND

1 **A kind (or sort) of ...** A vague or unusual type of (something): > *'I had a kind of feeling you'd be offered the job.'* > *'He always has a sort of mental blockage when it comes to buying other people presents.'*

2 **Kind of thing** *see* Thing 10.

3 **Kind (or sort) of ...** An expression used to make a statement or opinion sound less certain or definite; rather; to some degree: > *'That kind of explains it.'* > *'We felt kind of sorry for him.'* > *'It was sort of the size of that bag.'* Also written and pronounced (*slang*) *kinda, sorta.* These phrases are American in origin.

4 **Would you be so kind as to do something** *Formal* Used as a polite way of asking someone to do something: > *'Would you be so kind as to close the window, please.'* Also **Would you be kind enough to do something:** > *'I wonder if you would be kind enough to ask him for me.'*

KITE

Go fly a kite! *Slang, chiefly American* Go away!: > *'I'm tired of you telling us what to do, Goldie. Go fly a kite!'*

KNIFE

Before you can say knife *see* Robinson.

KNOB

And the same to you with brass knobs on *see* Same 2b.

KNOCK

1 **Knock it off!** *Slang* Stop it!: > *'Knock it off, you two. Can 't you see I'm trying to work?'*

2 **Knock, knock** Used as the first set of words of a joke (a knock-knock joke): > *'Knock, knock!' 'Who's there?' 'Lettuce!' 'Lettuce who?' 'Lettuce in and you'll know!'*

KNOT

Get knotted! *Slang* An expression of contempt used to show that you disapprove of something or that you do not want to do something: > *'Can I borrow your pen?' 'Get knotted! You never gave me back the last one you took!'* > *'I told her to get knotted!'*

KNOW

1 **And I don't know who (or what)** And many other people (or things) also: > *'There was the mayor, the school governors, the chaplain, and I don't know who at the dinner.'* > *'In the room, books, packs of cards, empty boxes, and I don't know what, had just been thrown about.'*

2 **As you know** You know this already, but I am telling you again: used to introduce further information: > *'As you know, Pete's got a place at university. Well, he starts next month.'*

3 **Don't I know it**
   a Unfortunately, I know it: used when the speaker has to do or has done something unpleasant: > *'I've got to wash all those dishes, don't I know it.'* > *'I got up at five o'clock this morning to finish my work, and don't I know it.'*

b Yes; I agree; I know it already: > *'She's angry with you!' 'Don't I know it! She just threw something at me!'*

4 Don't you know *Becoming old-fashioned* An expression used to show strong emotion: > *'It's such a nuisance, don't you know, travelling by train.'*

5 For all I (you, etc.) **know** *see* **All 16.**

6 For aught I know *see* **Aught.**

7 He (she, etc) **didn't want to know** *see* **Want 1.**

8 Heaven knows *Also* **God knows; Goodness knows; (The) Lord knows**

a I do not know; it is impossible to say: > *'Heaven knows where Leslie's got to – should have been here two hours ago!'* Often used with *only*: > *'God only knows how I'm going to explain why I'm late!'*

b Certainly: used to add force to a statement or opinion: > *'I hope you pass the exam. Heaven knows, you've tried hard enough!'* > *'Goodness knows, we were poor enough already before we were robbed!'*

9 How was I (he, she, etc.) **to know!** I (he, she, etc.) cannot be blamed for something; it is not reasonable to expect that I (he, she, etc.) should know something: > *'How was I to know that you'd asked her already?'* Also **I wasn't to know.**

10 I didn't know you cared! *Humorous* I had no idea that I meant something to you!; used between friends: > *'Here are some chocolates for you, Julie!' 'I didn't know you cared!'*

11 I don't know

a A cry of exasperation or surprise: > *'I don't know! You children are really getting on my nerves this morning!'* > *'Well, I don't know! Imagine her entering a beauty competition with a figure like that!'* The stress falls on *I*.

b I'm not sure: > *'I don't know that I care for the colours of that room.'* > *'I don't know if I can be home for six, but I'll do my best.'*

12 I don't know about that Used to show disagreement with what has just been said: > *'Robert's getting on very well at school these days, isn't he?' 'I don't know about that – though he's certainly not bottom of the class any more.'* The speaker can also use words used by the previous speaker: > *'That new dictionary looks very helpful.' 'I don't know about helpful, though it's certainly got lots of details about the words: it's just that it's all too difficult for me to understand.'*

13 I don't know, I'm sure I don't understand what is happening: said with an impatient tone: > *'What's this country coming to? – / don't know, I'm sure!'*

14 I don't know that I think that is not really true: > *'Tom's quite a good friend, isn't he?' 'I don't know that – he's never helped me much.'*

15 I knew it I was sure this would happen: > *'I knew it! As soon as I left the room, you stopped working!'*

16 I know

a Used to introduce an idea that is suddenly thought of: > *'I know, why don't we go to Brighton this afternoon?'*

b Used to agree with someone: > *'The match has been postponed till next Saturday.' 'I know.'*

c Used to show that you understand what someone is experiencing: > *'I know, Anne, what you're going through right now. Believe me, I do.'*

17 I know the feeling *see* **Feeling 2.**

18 I know (what) Used to introduce a new idea or suggestion: > *'I know what, let's go and see Pat tonight.'* Also **(I) tell you what; I'll tell you what:** > *'I tell you what, we'll have a cheap holiday and stay at home this year – that'll save us some money.'* > *'Tell you what,'* I said to encourage her, *'let's go and watch a film.'*

19 I (you, etc.) wouldn't know As is to be expected, I am (you are, etc.) not in a position to know: sometimes used to show scorn: > *'Is this the way to the station?' 'I'm sorry, I wouldn't know – I'm a stranger here myself.'* > *'Of course you wouldn't know what it was like spending all day at home doing the housework, would you?'*

20 I'd have you know Used to add emphasis to a statement, and also often to contradict what has just been said: > *'The car doesn't look too clean, does it?' 'I'd have you know I've just spent an hour washing it!'*

21 If you must know Used to express impatience or annoyance at having to tell someone some information: > *'Why won't you tell us where you met her?' 'If you must know, I met her at church.'*

22 Knowing you (him, her, etc.) Because I am familiar with your (his, her, etc.) real character, I am sure that: > *'Knowing Shirley, she'll be late.'* Also **If I know you (him, her, etc.); You know what he (she, it, etc.) is:** > *'If I know the weather, it'll rain on sports day – it does every year.'* > *'You know what Perry is, he always has some excuse for missing a French test.'*

23 Not if I know it *see* **Help 4.**

24 Not that I know Used to say no but also to say that one is not sure because one does not know all the facts: > *'Does she have a boyfriend?' 'Not that I know of.'*

25 That's all you know (about it) You are more ignorant about it than you think: > *'Pete's started to go out with my sister!' 'That's all you know about it! It's been going on for weeks!'*

26 There's no knowing (or telling) No one can say: > *'There's no knowing what we could do to help, if we had more money.'* > *'You'd better take your boots with you. There's no telling how deep the snow will be if it keeps falling like this.'*

27 Well, what do you know (about that)! An expression of surprise: > *'I've been to America for the weekend!' 'Well, what do you know!'* Sometimes written: *'Well, what d'you know!'* This phrase is American in origin.

28 What does he (she, etc.) know What right does he (she, etc.) have to make comments on something, since he (she, etc.) has no understanding of it.

29 You don't know when you're well off You are more fortunate than you realise: > *'You don't* *know when you're well-off. You've got a good job, a house, a colour television; just think of what the rest of the world has got compared with you!'* Also **You don't know you're alive** (or **born**): > *'Why are you moaning? You've passed your exams, got into college, and you're doing pretty well – you don't know you're alive!'*

30 You know

a An expression used while the speaker is thinking about what to say next or about what has already been said: > *'I sort of kept asking myself, you know, if only Karen hadn't married Derek, what might have happened ...'* > *'Then this car came along, you know, and well, just knocked her over.'* > *'Paul started off the game well enough, you know, he scored a goal in the opening minutes.'*

b An expression used to introduce a suggestion, to make it seem less strong: > *'You know, I think we should be going.'* > *'You know, we could always try the other supermarket down the road.'*

c An expression used to add emphasis to part of what is said: > *'You'll have to work harder, you know, if you want to pass your exams.'* Also **Do you know:** > *'Do you know, that's the sixth time this morning that the phone has rung.'* > *'Do you know, I think I will go to her party after all, in spite of the way she's treated me.'* The stress in both these phrases falls on *know*.

d An expression used to make what the speaker is saying less definite: > *'I think it's more or less*

a crime, you know, to kill those seals.'

e An expression used to remind the hearer of something he or she already knows or should know: > *'How can a chap like me get another job? I'm over fifty-five, you know.'* > *'Which book are you talking about?' 'You know, the one you borrowed from the library last week.'*

f An expression used to introduce an explanation or a subject which the speaker assumes is known by the hearer: > *'You know the road going up the hill? Well, the post office is up there on the right.'* > *'You know the difference between a gorilla and an ape? Well, which one's that, then?'*

31 You know something (or **what**)? Used to introduce something that the speaker thinks important: > *'You know what? I've never told you this before, but this is my second marriage.'*

32 You know what I mean Used to suggest that the listener understands what one is saying, and so needs not give any further explanation: > *'John's very absent-minded, you know what I mean?'*

33 You know what you can do with ... *Slang* A rude expression indicating contempt towards (someone or something): > *'I'm fed up with your Aunt Agatha! You know what you can do with her!'* > *'Your pen never works! You know what you can do with it!'*

34 You never know Things in the future are uncertain; perhaps: *'Do you think you'll be able to come* *and stay with us in Malaysia sometime?' 'You never know! My firm might give me a job there!'* Also **You never can tell:** > *'You'd*

better take an umbrella; you never can tell if it's going to rain.'
35 **You never know your luck** *see* **Luck** 12.

LADY

1 **Ladies and gentlemen** An expression used to address a meeting of adults of both sexes: > *'Ladies and gentlemen, we welcome to our gathering tonight Miss Jane Hunt, President of the local horticultural society.'* > *'Before your very eyes, ladies and gentlemen, these rabbits will disappear as I say these magic words.'*

2 **Ladies first** An expression used by a polite man who wants to allow a woman to go through a door before him: > *'Ladies first,' said Mr Harrington, holding the door open for Mrs Giles.*

3 **Your good lady** *Chiefly humorous* Your wife: > *'How's your good lady?'* Also **Your (good) lady wife.**

LAKE

Go (and) jump in the (or a) lake! Go away!: used when you are very annoyed with someone: > *'How dare you speak to me like that!' 'Go and jump in a lake!'*

LANDING

Happy landings! *Old-fashioned* An expression used when drinking with others; good health.

LARGE

By and large *see* **Whole.**

LAST

Last but not least Used to introduce an important item that comes last in a list: > *'The group included Harriet, June, and last but not least, Avril.'* Also **Last but by no means least.**

LATE

Better late than never The fact that someone has eventually arrived or something has happened late is better than that person not coming at all or than something not happening at all. In reality the expression is often used to express slight displeasure at someone's late arrival.

LAUGH

1 **Don't make me laugh!** I don't believe you for one moment; what you're saying is ridiculous: used with a rather critical or even scornful tone: > *'Did I tell you I'm going to buy a brand new sports car?' 'Don't make me laugh! You've not got enough money for your bus fare into town!'*

2 **Have (or get) the last laugh** To be successful at the end of a competition, etc., or be proved right in the end: > *'Everyone made fun of John's invention, but he's had*

the last laugh – think of the money he's made out of it!'

3 You have to laugh Used when one is in a. disappointing situation but also when one can see the situation's amusing aspects: > *'The car wouldn't start so I walked all the way to the hospital in the pouring rain. When I got there my appointment was cancelled as the doctor's car had broken down on the motorway! You have to laugh.'*

4 You're (or you'll be) laughing! You will be in a fortunate position, with no further worries: > *'If you get that amount of money for your new job in Saudi, you're laughing!'*

LAY

1 Lay it on (thick) To exaggerate, often when you are praising: > *'I know you think he's a good musician, but there's no need to lay it on.'* Also **Pile it on (thick).**

2 Lay off! Stop being annoying!; leave alone!; stop!: > *'Lay off me, will you!'* > *'Lay off or I'll hit you!'* > *'You'll have to lay off smoking or it will kill you.'*

LEAST

1 At least
a Being the lowest number or amount: > *There were at least 100 people present.*
b Being the lowest level of activity, although greater activity could be undertaken: > *'To improve security, at the (very) least we should install better locks.'*
c Used when referring to an advantage that exists alongside disadvantages that have been

mentioned: > *'He may have broken his arm in the crash but at least he is still alive.'*
d Used when correcting or changing something slightly that one has just said: > *'They're getting on fine together, or at least it appears they are.'*

2 That's the least that I (or we) can (or could) do Used to acknowledge someone's thanks: > *'Thanks for coming to Roshan's funeral.' 'That's the least I could do.'*

3 To say the least see **Put 3.**

LEAVE

1 Leave a lot to be desired Not to be as good as it should be: > *The standard of hygiene in many restaurants leaves a lot to be desired.*

2 Leave it at that To say or do nothing more; take a matter no further: > *'I think I've given you a strong enough warning; we'll leave it at that for the moment.'* > *'Let's leave it at that; we've worked hard enough today.'*

3 Leave off! Stop!: > *'Leave off doing that, will you?'* > *'Leave off interrupting me whenever I'm talking!'*

4 I must love you and leave you see **Love 3.**

5 Take it or leave it see **Take 8.**

LEG

1 Break a leg *Humorous* An expression used to wish someone good luck. The expression may possibly derive from the German *Hals und Beinbruch*, 'May you break your neck and your leg.'

2 Not have a leg to stand on To have no reasons, defence, or other support for an opinion or action: > *'Some friends of mine saw you take the watches so you haven't got a leg to stand on.'*

3 **Shake** (or **show**) **a leg!** *Slang* Hurry up!: > *'Shake a leg, there! We've got to get this work done soon, you know!'*

LESS

1 **Less of ...** Stop (something): > *'Less of your cheek, young man!'* Also **Less of that** (or **it**)**!; None of ...** : > *'We'll have none of that sort of thing in this class, thank you!'*

2 **Less than ...** Not having a particular quality that is mentioned; not at all: > *The receptionist was, to put it mildly, less than helpful.*

LET

Let alone *see* **Mention 3.**

LIBERTY

What a liberty! An expression used when someone does something improper or rude: > *'What a liberty! He's taken my car without even asking my permission!'* > *'Who does she think she is? She just walked past me without even saying a word! What a liberty!'*

LIE

I tell a lie An expression used to correct what the speaker has just said: > *'I saw him yesterday – no, I tell a lie – it was the day before.'*

LIFE

1 **For dear life** With great force, as if despairing: used when something is important or urgent: > *'He ran for dear life away from the scene of the crime.'* > *'When the horse began to gallop, she held on to the reins for dear life.'*

2 **For the life of me** (**him, her,** etc.) Though trying very hard: > *'I can't for the life of me remember her name.'*

3 **Get a life!** An expression of criticism, disrespect, or scorn for someone because he or she is boring or foolish.

4 **It's a dog's life** It's a life full of unhappiness and worries: > *'It's a dog's life running a small business – no holidays, so many forms to fill in, little money in the end – I sometimes wonder why I bother.'*

5 **Not** (or **never**) **on your life!** Most certainly not!: > *'Would you ever think of disobeying a commanding officer?' 'Not on your life!'* > *'Surely you'd like to be our new representative for the Arctic region, John?' 'Never on your life!'* Also (*slang, old-fashioned, British*) **Not on your nelly!**: > *'Do you really expect me to believe that excuse?' 'Not on your nelly!'* *Nelly* is short for *Nelly Duff*, which is rhyming slang for *puff*, itself a slang word for *life*.

6 **Run for your life!** *see* **Run.**

7 **That's life!** That's the way things happen!: > *'It's a pity Colin and Rowena got divorced, but then that's life!'* A translation of the French *c'est la vie!*

8 **This is the life!** An expression of contentment with one's present state: > *'A sandy beach, plenty of hot sun, lots of nice people! This is the life!'* The phrase dates from the early 1900s and became more current in World War I.

9 **To save his** (**her,** etc.) **life** Despite every attempt or consideration: >

'He couldn't play cricket to save his life.'

10 **Upon my life!** *Old-fashioned* Used to express surprise or to strengthen a statement or command: > *'Upon my life, I didn't realise how stubborn you could be!'* > *'Upon my life, we were lucky to come out of that crash with only a few cuts!'*

11 **What a life!** An expression of discontent: > *'What a life! I get up at half-past five every day, work solidly for eight hours, come home, have my meal and go to bed. It's all so monotonous!'*

12 **You (can) bet your life** *see* **Bet 6.**

LIGHT

Strike a light! *see* **Strike.**

LIKE

1 **... and the like** And similar things and people: > *Hot drinks such as tea, coffee, hot chocolate, and the like.*

2 **I (we, etc.) should (or would) like to** I (we, etc.) want to: > *'I should like to thank you very much for coming to speak to us this evening, Miss James.'* > *'Would you like to drink a cup of coffee yet?'*

3 **I'd like to see ...** I'd be surprised if (something actually happened): used to express impatience: > *'If he thinks he's so smart, I'd like to see him come round and mend this bike; I can't.'*

4 **If you like**
   a If you do not want anything else: used to express agreement with or approval of a suggestion: > *'I'd thought of asking Julie to give me some driving practice. What do you think she'd say?' 'I'll ask her, if you like.'*
   b An expression used to emphasise a statement: > *'I may be mean with money, if you like, but my wife certainly isn't.'* In this sense, the stress falls on *like.*
   c If I may express this in a rather strange way: > *'This is our house, if you like, but we've not yet made it into our home.'*

5 **Like it or not** Used to refer to an unpleasant situation that cannot be changed and has to be faced up to: > *'Like it or not, we've signed a contract to stay in this house for six months, so let's make the best of it.'* Also **Whether you like it or not.**

6 **That's more like it!** That is better; that is nearer what is needed: used to express satisfaction that things have improved or that what was wanted has actually happened: > *'I got sixty per cent in my history test this week.' 'That's more like it! That's a lot more than you've had recently.'*

7 **(Well) I like that!** An expression showing annoyance, dislike, or surprise: > *'I said this department store wouldn't have what we were looking for!' 'Well, I like that! It was you who suggested that we come here!'* The stress falls on *like.*

8 **What's he (she, you, etc.) like?** Expressing slight annoyance or impatience at someone's actions, habits, etc., often in a slightly humorous way: > *'Now then class, settle down, and we'll carry on with the sponge cake. If you've already creamed the sugar and margarine, it's time to add the eggs.' 'Do we crack them first, miss?' asked Darren. 'Ooh, what is he like?' said Kirsty.* The stress falls on *like.*

LIKELY

1 **A likely story!** *see* **Story 1.**

2 **Not likely** Certainly not; that is impossible: > *'Would you be willing for your name to be put forward as chairman of the committee?' Pete asked. 'What, me? Not likely!' Bob exclaimed and walked out of the room.*

LIMIT

The (absolute) limit *see* **End 4.**

LINE

1 **All** (or **right**) **down** (or **along**) **the line** Completely; in every part: > *The politician supported the government's actions all down the line.*

2 **Hard lines!** *see* **Luck 1.**

LIP

My lips are sealed I will not say anything about it: > *'OK – it's a secret, remember – don't tell anyone!' 'Right, my lips are sealed!'*

LITTLE

A little goes a long way A brief experience of someone or something is as much as one can reasonably tolerate; a small amount of something or a quality lasts a long time: > *'To be honest, at our age a little of Anita goes a long way.' > You'll find that a little of this new gloss paint goes a long way.*

LIVE

1 **As I live (and breathe)** *Old-fashioned*

a An expression of surprise: > *'As I live and breathe, if it isn't Josh Harrington! I've not seen you for years!'*

b An expression of firmness or boldness: > *'As I live and breathe, this will be the last time I come through these gates again!'*

2 **Live and let live** An expression that people should be allowed to behave how they want to and be tolerant of others' behaviour.

3 **Long live ...** May (someone or something) live or last a long time: an expression of loyalty, but sometimes used in a humorous way: > *'Long live the Queen!' > 'Long live the party!' > 'Long live anarchy!'*

4 **You've** (**he's, she's,** etc.) **not** (or **never**) **lived** You (he, she, etc.) have not really known life to the full: used in connection with a particular experience, place, or person: > *'You've never flown in an aeroplane before? You've never lived!' > 'You've not lived until you've seen the Niagara Falls – they're magnificent!' > 'She'd not lived before she met him.'*

LIVELY

Look lively! *see* **Look 6.**

LO

Lo and behold! *Often humorous* An expression of surprise at the appearance of an unexpected person or thing: > *'I'd just come in, when, lo and behold, your old friend Mandy came to the door!'*

LOAD

1 **Get a load of this!** *Slang* Listen to this!; look at this!: > *'Get a load of this – it's the new record I've just bought!'*

2 **What a load of (old) cobblers!** *Slang, British, old-fashioned* What

nonsense!: > *'Our car goes much faster than yours!' 'What a load of old cobblers! Ours will beat yours any day!'* Often shortened to *Cobblers!*

LOAF

Use your loaf! *Slang* Be sensible; show some common sense: > *'Use your loaf! Can't you be more tactful?'* *Loaf* is from *loaf of bread*, which is rhyming slang for *head*.

LONG

1 **As broad as it is long** see **Broad**.
2 **So long** Goodbye until we next meet: used between friends: > *'So long, Tom! See you next week!'* > *'I'm going now, but I'll be back again tomorrow. So long!'*

LOOK

1 **Be looking for a fight** (or **trouble**) To behave in such a way that may provoke an offensive or violent response: > *'Are you looking for a fight?' 'No!' 'Then shut up!'* > *Three youths were going round the streets late at night – you could tell from their faces that they were looking for trouble.* Also **Be spoiling for a fight**.
2 **I'm** (or **we're**) **just looking** In a shop, said by the speaker to indicate that he or she is simply browsing and does not plan to buy anything immediately: > *'Can I help you?' 'No, we're just looking, thanks.'*
3 **It's** (or **that's**) **your** (**his, her,** etc.) (**own**) **look-out** That is something that you (he, she, etc.) alone is responsible for: > *'If you don't do any revision for the exams, it's your own look-out.'* > *'That's her look-*

out, cycling without any lights at night.'

4 **Look after yourself!** Take care!; said when saying goodbye to someone: > *'Look after yourself, Julia!' 'Yes, I will, thanks. Cheerio.'*
5 **Look here!** An expression used to introduce a complaint, warning, or suggestion: > *'Look here, young man, I've had about enough of all this noise; now turn that radio down, or I'll report you.'* > *'Look here, why don't we go to Blackpool for the day? We've got some money and I've always wanted to see the lights.'* Also **See here!**: > *'Now see here! I won't have you speaking to my daughter like that! Apologise at once!'*
6 **Look lively** (or **smart**)! Be quick; hurry up!: > *'Look lively – teacher's coming!'* > *'You'll just catch the bus if you look smart.'*
7 **Look out!** Be careful; take care!: used as a warning: > *'Look out, Colin, that ladder's not secure.'* Also used on a grander scale: > *'Look out world, here I come!'* the great stunt man used to cry as he performed his daring acts. > *'Look out, prime minister, these new parties mean business!'*
8 **Look sharp!** see **Sharp 1**.
9 **Look what you've done!** An expression of mild rebuke: *'Look what you've done! You've woken baby up after we've spent an hour trying to get him to go to sleep.'*
10 **Look who's talking!** see **Talk 6b**.
11 **Look you!** Pay attention to what I am saying!: > *'Look you, take my advice, or you'll regret what you're about to do.'*

LORD

1 **Good Lord!** *see* **Good 7.**

2 **Oh Lord!** *see* **God 18.**

3 **(The) Lord knows** *see* **Know 8.**

LORRY

It (or they) fell off the back of a lorry *Euphemistic* It was (or they were) stolen: > *'Where did you get those coats from? 'Oh they just fell off the back of a lorry!'* Also in the form of a question *Did it fall off the back of a lorry?*

LOSE

1 **Get lost!** *see* **Lost.**

2 **What you lose on the swings you gain on the roundabouts** *see* **Swing.**

LOSS

... is a dead loss (Someone or something) is very bad or useless: > *'You're a dead loss, I must say, coming now that I've finished all the work.'*

LOST

Get lost! *Slang* Go away! stop annoying me (us, etc.)!: > *'Get lost, I'm trying to work!'*

LOT

1 **A fat lot ...** Very little; none at all: > *'A fat lot of good you are!'* > *'He gave us a pat on the back. That's a fat lot of encouragement. His time and money are more important to us than his words!'* > *'Have you read Roland's book?' 'Roland's written a book? A fat lot he knows about anything!'*

2 **A (fat) lot you care!** *see* **Care 1.**

3 **That's your (or the) lot** You have had all you are going to have; there is no more; this is the end: > *'Well, that's the lot for today – I'm off home now.'* > *'Well, that's your lot. I've checked all the lists for you and the total amount is correct.'*

LOVE

1 **For the love of God** (or **Mike**) *Old-fashioned* An expression used to add strength to a question, request, etc.: > *'Where for the love of God are my keys? I can never find them when I want them!'* > *'For the love of Mike, stop complaining, and get on and do some work!'* Mike comes from *St Michael*.

2 **I love you, too!** An expression used to show displeasure at something that someone has said or done that is unkind: > *'I'll have my meal now and you can wait for yours!' 'I love you, too!'* > *'You're absolutely hopeless, aren't you!' 'I love you, too!'*

3 **I must love you and leave you** I have to go now: > *'Time's getting on – I must love you and leave you!' 'OK; see you next week!'*

4 **My love** A way of addressing one's husband or wife, or very close friend: > *'You are beautiful, my love.'* > *'My love, shall we go out for a meal on Saturday?'*

LUCK

1 **Bad luck!** An expression of sympathy about someone's misfortune: > *'Bad luck! How awful that you didn't pass the exam!'* Also **Hard luck!; Tough luck!; Hard lines!** (*British, old-fashioned*): > *'I've just heard they're not picking me for the football team.' 'Hard luck!'*

2 **Better luck next time** I'm sorry that you didn't do well this time and wish you success when you try again: > *'Sorry you failed your driving test, Harry. Better luck next time!'*

3 **For luck** To be lucky: sometimes offered as the supposed reason for doing something extra: > *'I used to put a little coin in my handkerchief for luck before I took an exam.'* > *'I've already eaten two pieces of cake, but I think I'll have another one for luck!'*

4 **Good luck!**
a I wish you well: > *'Good luck, Andy!'* my friends all shouted as the train pulled out. > *'Good luck to you at college!'* Also **The best of luck.**
b An expression used before drinking: > *Mary raised her glass, 'Good luck!' she said.*

5 **It's the luck of the draw** You must take things as they come: > *'I wish I hadn't been chosen to be in John's team!' 'You'll just have to accept it – it's the luck of the draw!'*

6 **Just my (his, her, etc.) luck!** This is typical of my (his, her, etc.) misfortune: > *'Just my luck! The day I wanted to travel by train was the day of the national rail strike.'* > *'Just our luck to choose a hotel that was still only half built when we arrived!'*

7 **Knowing my luck** Used to express an expectation of misfortune because the speaker is usually unlucky.

8 **No such luck** Unfortunately not; used to express disappointment: > *'Can you take this Saturday off to help me move some furniture?' 'No such luck – I'm sorry but I've got to work.'*

9 **Some people have all the luck!** *see* **People.**

10 **With any luck** An expression showing hope: > *'With any luck we should be there by two o'clock.'* Alternatives to *any* are *a bit of* and *a little bit of:* > *'With a little bit of luck I'll have finished the painting this afternoon.'*

11 **Worse luck** Unfortunately: > *'Do you know Robert Hampshire?' 'Yes, I have met him before, worse luck.'*

12 **You never know your luck** You may be lucky: > *'Let's have another go on the space invader! I may beat you this time!' 'You never know your luck!'*

LUCKY

1 **Who's the lucky girl** (or **man**), **then?** Who have you just become engaged to?: an expression used on hearing that someone has got engaged: > *'Who's the lucky man, then, Cathy?'*

2 **You should be so lucky!** Why ever should something as good as that happen to you!: used as a humorous reply: > *'When I got there I thought you were going to give me some money.' 'You should be so lucky!'*

3 **You'll be lucky!** Good luck; I wish you well: used when the speaker doubts whether something will really happen: > *'I'm going to ask the manager for a pay rise.' 'You'll be lucky! At the moment the firm hasn't any extra money for its employees!'*

M

MACKEREL

Holy mackerel! *see* **Holy.**

MAD

Like mad Very fast; very much: > *'We ran like mad away from the scene of the explosion.'*

MAIN

In the main Generally: > *In the main, most parents are supportive of teachers but there are a few exceptions.*

MAKE

1 **As ... as they make 'em** Used to express an extreme degree of quality of someone or something, usually of bad characteristics: > *'Your new girlfriend's as cheeky as they make 'em, isn't she?'* In this phrase *'em* is almost always used instead of *them*. Also **As ... as they come:** > *'That chap's as stupid as they come.'*

2 **Don't make me laugh!** *see* **Laugh 1.**

3 **It makes you go blind** An expression used humorously to describe the results of over-indulgent actions: > *'I wouldn't drink too much, if I were you – it makes you go blind, you know!'*

4 **Make it snappy!** *Slang* Be quick!: > *'Pie and chips, please, and make it snappy: I'm in a hurry!'*

5 **Make no bones** (or **mistake**) **about it!** Do not doubt this at all; this is certainly true: used to emphasise a statement or promise expressed plainly and directly: > *'Make no bones about it, my boy, I'm going to see you're punished properly this time!'* > *'Make no mistake about it, you're bound to have an accident if you drive so fast down the motorway.'* > *'I shall be coming back, make no mistake about it!'*

6 **Make yourself at home!** *see* **Home 3.**

7 **That makes two of us!** The same applies to me; that is true of me, too: > *'I'm going up to Birmingham University in October!' 'That makes two of us – I am as well!*

MAN

1 **Be a man!** Act in a manly way: used especially to emphasise such qualities as a brave or independent spirit: > *'Be a man! You can beat him easily!' > 'Go on, be a man, accept the bet!'*

2 **Go man, go!** An expression of encouragement: > *'You can beat Perry – go man, go!'* Originally, from the language of American jazz.

3 **I'm** (or **he's**) **your man** I am (or he is) the person needed to do that particular job: > *'I'm your man! I'll accept that offer and start immediately!' > 'If you want any plumbing work done, then he's your man.'*

4 **Man alive!** An exclamation showing amazement, surprise, or pleasure: > *'Man alive! What are you doing here?'*

5 **May the best man win!** An expression wishing that the better or best person in a group might be the successful one: >

'I'd like to wish you every success!' *'Thank you, and may the best man win!'*

6 **My good man** *Old-fashioned* An offensive expression used to show that the speaker thinks he or she is more important than the man he or she is speaking to: > *'Look here, my good man! How dare you speak to me like that!'*

7 **Oh man!** *Slang* An exclamation expressing excitement, surprise, pleasure, etc.: > *'Oh man, was I pleased to see her!'* > *'Oh man, you really get on my nerves, you know!'*

8 **Old man** *see* **Boy 2.**

9 **Who's the lucky man then?** *see* **Lucky 1.**

10 **You can't keep a good man down** A saying that you can't stop a man with firm, determined intentions from doing what he wants: sometimes used ironically: > *'I hear Bill's company have launched yet another new product.' 'Yes – you can't keep a good man down!'*

MANNER

In a manner of speaking To express something in this particular way, to be used with a description that is not strictly or literally true: > *In a manner of speaking a company's subcontracted workers may be thought of as employees.*

MARINE

Tell it (or that) to the marines! *Old-fashioned* I don't believe what has just been said: > *'I've just been to tea at Buckingham Palace! 'Tell that to the marines!'* The phrase comes from the fact that at one time marines were thought to be stupid by regular sailors, and therefore likely to believe something obviously foolish.

MARK

1 **Mark you** *see* **Mind 12.**

2 **On your mark(s), (get) set, go!** *see* **Ready 1.**

MATTER

1 **As a matter of fact** *see* **Fact 1.**

2 **For that matter** *see* **Fact lb.**

3 **It doesn't matter**
a Used to tell someone that one is not angry or upset with them and that there is no need for them to be concerned: > *'I'm sorry, the meat's been overcooked.' 'It doesn't matter.'*
b Used as a reply when offered a choice between two things to show that one does not mind which one one will have: > *'Coffee or tea?' 'It doesn't matter.'*

4 **No matter!** It is not important: > *'I've just broken one of your mugs!' 'No matter! They were only cheap ones!'*

5 **No matter how (who, what,** etc.) It makes no difference how (who, what, etc.): > *'No matter who phones, say I'm not in.'* > *'No matter how hard I try, I still can't do crossword puzzles.'* > *'I'm going tomorrow, no matter what.'*

6 **What matter?** That need not worry or upset us: > *'What matter if there's a strike, we'll muddle through somehow.'*

7 **What's the matter?** What is wrong?; what is causing you trouble or pain? > *'What's the matter with you?' 'Nothing.'* > *'What's the matter with her this*

morning? She's so grumpy with everyone.' > 'What's the matter with having a good time once in a while?'

MAY

May I (we, etc.) ... ? Used in making a polite request or asking for permission: > *'May I come in for a minute, please?' 'Yes, of course you can.'* > *'May I make a suggestion? Why don't we vote now rather than continuing the discussion further?'*

MAYBE

That's as maybe! *see* **That 13.**

MEAN

1 **And I don't mean maybe** *Chiefly American* I mean exactly what I say: > *'I want this work done for ten this evening, and I don't mean maybe!'*

2 **Do you mean to say?** *see* **Say 4.**

3 **Do you see what I mean?** *see* **See 3.**

4 **I mean** An expression used to keep the attention of a listener, and making a slight pause; often the speaker wants to clarify what has just been said or give additional information, and rephrases the sentence: > *'It's no good just saying we're suffering from the recession. I mean, the people we do business with are only interested in seeing our products.'* > *'To rehearse for the concert ... , I mean ... we had to play for two hours.'*

5 **I mean (to say)** *see* **Say 12.**

6 **I see what you mean** *see* **See 5.**

7 **What do you mean ...?** Used to comment, in an annoyed tone, on something that has just been said: > *'I didn't know you could be so stupid.' 'What do you mean, stupid? I passed more exams than you, remember?'*

8 **What do you mean by ... ?** What is the purpose of (doing something)?: used to ask the reasons or justification for some behaviour; sometimes said in an annoyed tone: > *'What do you mean by getting me up in the middle of the night?'* > *'What do you mean by that? Please explain, as I'd like to know!'*

9 **You mean** Used as part of a question as a check that one has understood clearly what someone has said: > *'What did they do with the money?' 'The lottery money, you mean?'*

MEANS

1 **By all means** Certainly; yes; of course: > *'Can we come aboard?' 'By all means! You're most welcome!'* > *'By all means use my name when you apply for the job.'*

2 **By no means** Not at all: > *'That's by no means the last you've heard of this.'* Also **Not by any means.**

MEET

1 **Pleased** (or **nice, glad**) **to meet you!** An expression used as a reply in an introduction of one person to another: > (Robert talking to William) *'William, I'd like you to meet Mr Jones.'* (William to Mr Jones) *'Pleased to meet you, Mr Jones.'* (Mr Jones to William) *'Pleased to meet you!'* > (Colin talking to John) *'How do you do, John.'* (John to Colin) *'Glad to meet you, Colin.'* Also **Nice meeting you.**

2 **Until** (or **till**) **we meet again!** *Rather formal or literary* An expression used when saying

goodbye to someone: > *'Until we meet again, farewell!'* Also (*more informal*) **Until** (or **till**) **the next time!**

MEMORY

If my memory serves me right ... If I am remembering (something) correctly: > *'If my memory serves me right, Harold Wilson became Prime Minster in 1964.'*

MENTION

1 **Don't mention it!** *Polite* There is no need to thank me or apologise: > *'Thanks so much for lending me your book!' 'Don't mention it!'* > *'I'm so sorry I trod on your toe!' 'Oh, don't mention it!'*

2 **I hate to mention it, but ...** A polite expression used to draw attention to (something that the person being spoken to has, perhaps deliberately, forgotten or not noticed): > *'I hate to mention it, but what about the money you owe me?'* Also **If you don't mind my mentioning it:** > *'If you don't mind my mentioning it, your tie isn't quite straight.'*

3 **Not to mention ...** To say nothing of (something very obvious that it only needs to be named); in addition: > *'It was an awful hotel, with poor meals, hopeless service, not to mention the noise outside.'* Also **Let Alone; Not to speak of; To say nothing of ...**

MERCY

1 **Be thankful** (or **grateful**) **for small mercies** Not to complain about an unpleasant situation, but instead to be happy that the situation is not even more unpleasant: > *'As well as our luggage being thousands of miles away, the plane could have been hours late. I suppose we should be thankful for small mercies.'*

2 **For mercy's sake!** *see* **Goodness 1.**

MIGHT

Might I (**you,** etc.) **...?** Used in making a request or asking permission for something: > *'Might I be able to leave a little earlier tonight, please?'* > *'Might it not be helpful to look at last year's figures and compare them with this year's?'* This is rather more hesitant than *may.*

MIKE

For the love of Mike *see* **Love 1.**

MILD

To put it mildly *see* **Put 3.**

MILK

Get off and milk it! *see* **Get 10.**

MIND

1 **Do** (or **would**) **you mind ...?** Used in making a polite request: > *'Do you mind if I smoke?' 'No, that's quite all right.'* > *'Would you mind opening the window, please?' 'Yes, it is a bit hot in here, isn't it?'* Also **Would you ... ?** > *'Would you be quiet a moment, please?'*

2 **Do you mind!** Please stop that!: used to show annoyance when one has been offended: > *'Do you mind! That's my parking space you've taken!'*

3 **Don't mind me** (**him, her,** etc.) **a** Don't pay any attention to or worry about me (him, her, etc.): > *'Just carry on working! Don't*

mind her!' > *'Don't mind me – I can manage quite well while you're away!'*
b An expression used when one is annoyed at someone's rudeness, thoughtlessness, or when one thinks one is not being fairly treated: > *'Don't mind me, will you? I just type your letters, make you drinks, wait on you hand and foot, and you pay me next to nothing for all this!'*

4 **Great minds think alike** *Humorous* An expression used to praise oneself when two people both have the same idea, opinion, etc.: > *'Let's go to Brighton this afternoon!' 'Great minds think alike – I was just about to suggest that myself!'* A common reply to this phrase is *Fools seldom differ*.

5 **(I) don't mind if I do** Yes, I would like that, thank you: > *'Have another cake.' 'Thank you. I don't mind if I do.'*

6 **I wouldn't mind ...** Used in making a polite request: > *'I wouldn't mind a nice cup of tea.' 'All right, I'll go and make one for you.' 'Thank you.'*

7 **If you don't mind my mentioning it** *see* **Mention 2**.

8 **If you don't** (or **won't**) **mind** An expression used in making a polite request or command: > *'Please wait over there, if you don't mind.'* > *'If you won't mind, I'll see you in a few minutes.'*

9 **It's all in the mind** What is happening to you is all in the imagination: > *'I think Jane's in love with me!' 'It's all in the mind!'* > *'I feel awful with this stomach ache.' 'It's all in the mind; you're perfectly all right really.'*

10 **Mind how you go** Take care of yourself!; be careful: often used when saying goodbye: > *'Mind how you go! See you next week!'*

11 **Mind (out)!** Be careful: > *'Mind out! Don't go too near the edge!'* > *'Mind! The plate's hot!'*

12 **Mind (you)** Note what I'm saying: an expression used to qualify, disagree with, or emphasise something that has just been said: > *'Our baby's very sweet, but mind you, we do have a lot of nappies to wash.'* > *'I wouldn't help everyone, mind.'* Also **Mark you**.

13 **Mind your back(s)** *see* **Back 6**.

14 **Mind your head(s)** *see* **Head 3**.

15 **Mind your own business!** *see* **Business 2**.

16 **Mind your step!** *see* **Step 1**.

17 **Never mind** Don't worry or be troubled about; take no notice of: > *'Do what the doctor says; never mind the advice of your friends.'* > *'Never mind about yesterday; it's today I'm interested in!'* > *'I've hurt my finger.' 'Never mind, I'll kiss it better.'*

18 **Never you mind** It is no concern of yours and you are not going to be told: > *'Where did you two go last night?' 'Never you mind!'*

19 **The mind boggles** I am surprised, confused, or overwhelmed (by something): > *'The mind boggles at how she managed to bring up seven children by herself.'* > *'Three bathrooms and seven bedrooms in that house! The mind boggles!'*

MINUTE

1 **... in a minute!** An expression used to show annoyance or anger at something that has just been said: > 'Your hair needs cutting!' 'I'll cut you in a minute!' The particular part that is found annoying is repeated before the phrase *in a minute!*

2 **Just a minute** see **Just 3.**

3 **There's one born every minute** see **Born 4.**

4 **Wait a minute** see **Wait 4.**

MIRROR

It's all done by (or **with**) **mirrors** An expression used when something clever or ingenious has been done: > 'You see that new machine I've made for brewing tea?' 'Yes, how does it work?' 'Ah! It's all done by mirrors, you know!'

MISSIS

The missis My (or your) wife: > 'How's the missis?' Also **The wife.**

MIST

Scotch mist *Old-fashioned* The very thing you are talking about, that you are pretending is not there: used in stating firmly that something does in fact exist, despite the other person's ignorance or disbelief: > 'I've lost my keys again!' 'What do you think these are, then? Scotch mist?'

MISTAKE

1 **And no mistake** Without any doubt: used to emphasise what has just been said: > 'It's boiling hot today, and no mistake!' > 'This is the biggest orange I've ever seen, and no mistake!'

2 **Make no mistake about it!** *See* **Make 5.**

3 **There's no mistake about it!** There is no doubt about it; it is certain: > 'There's no mistake about it – this is quite simply the best car on the market, sir!' Also **There's no mistaking ...**

MISUNDERSTAND

Don't misunderstand me Used when one wants to correct a possible wrong meaning that someone may have understood from what one has said: > 'I'm not condoning violence, don't misunderstand me.'

MODESTY

In all modesty Used with a description of one's own achievements, abilities, etc. to try not to sound too proud: > 'In all modesty, I must say I played the title role rather well.'

MOMENT

1 **Just a moment** see **Just 3.**

2 **Never a dull moment!** Life is so busy: an expression used in times of much action, excitement, or danger: > 'As a teacher, it's all go from the moment I come into school to when I leave.' 'Yes, never a dull moment!'

3 **Not believe** (or **think**) **for a moment** Not to believe something at all; used for emphasis: > 'I don't believe for a moment that this company will ever make a profit.'

4 **One moment** see **Just 3a.**

5 **Wait a moment** see **Wait 4.**

MONEY

You pays your money and you takes your choice There are a number of different ways of doing something, courses of action, or opinions, that could be followed, any of which is as good as any other: often used humorously > *'You could go to London or Manchester to study for your degree – you pays your money and you takes your choice!'* Originally, the words of a nineteenth-century rhyme.

MOON

1 **Once in a blue moon** Extremely rarely: > *This machine is well-known for its efficiency. It only goes wrong once in a blue moon.*

2 **Over the moon** Very happy and excited: > *'Rosalind's over the moon about her new job!'*

MORE

1 **And what's more** Used to add something to what has just been said; moreover: > *'The price is too high, and what's more the style is too old-fashioned.'*

2 **More or less** Used to make an opinion sound less strong: > *'This is more or less the best book on the market on that subject.'* > *'It's more or less a day's journey to see the grandchildren.'*

3 **That's more like it!** *see* **Like 6.**

MORNING

1 **Good morning** *see* **Good 9.**
2 **Morning all!** *see* **All 14.**
3 **The top of the morning (to you)!** *see* **Top 2.**

MOSES

Holy Moses! *see* **Holy.**

MOTHER

1 **Be mother** To act as host or hostess by doing something, especially pour out the tea: > *'Who's going to be mother?' 'I'll be mother!'*

2 **Oh mother!** *Becoming old-fashioned* An exclamation of surprise, distress, etc.: > *'Oh mother! What are we going to do now?'* > *'Oh mother! Those children have broken another pane of glass!'*

3 **Some mothers do 'ave 'em!** An expression used when someone has made a silly or foolish mistake or blunder: > *'Trust Jim to be so clumsy! Some mothers do 'ave 'em!'* The phrase was made popular by a television comedy series, *Some Mothers Do 'Ave 'Em*, which began in 1974. Also **We've got a right one 'ere.**

4 **Who's she? The cat's mother** *see* **Cat 3.**

MOUTH

Shut your mouth! *see* **Shut.**

MOVE

Get a move on! Hurry up!: > *'Get a move on or you'll miss the bus!'*

MUCH

1 **It's a bit much** Your expectations are too high: > *'It's a bit much that you want this shirt now, when you know I've not done the ironing.'* > *'You come in late and want your dinner immediately – it really is a bit much, you know!'*

2 **Much as** Used to introduce a fact that stands in contrast to what has just been said or will just be said; although: > *'Much as I would*

have liked to have helped them, we had to go and take Freddy to the doctor.'

3 Much less Used to state that one thing is even less true than another thing: > *'He can scarcely reach the pedals, much less drive a car.'*

4 So much for ... This is now the end of (an idea): used when finishing talking about something, and often said in a resigned tone: > *'So much for my idea of going to town. It's snowing hard again, so we'd better stay in.'*

5 Too much *Slang, chiefly American* Used to express the speaker's enjoyment of or delight at something: > *'This music's too much, man!'*

MUD

1 Here's mud in your eye! *Old-fashioned* An expression used when taking a drink with other people: originally, referring to the muddy conditions of the soldiers fighting in Flanders in World War I.

2 (It's) as clear as mud *Humorous* What you have said is not at all clear: > *'Is my explanation clear?' 'Yes, as clear as mud, thanks!'*

MUGGINS

Muggins here *Slang, British* A way of referring to oneself: > *'Go on, you go out and enjoy yourselves, while muggins here stays at home and does all the work!'* > *'Who's going to do the washing-up?' 'Muggins here, I suppose, as usual!'* *Muggins* was probably originally a surname.

MUM

Mum's the word Don't say anything to anyone: > *'I don't want her to know about the present till Christmas Day!' 'OK! Mum's the word!'* *Mum* comes from the sound made when one's lips are closed.

MURDER

1 Get away with murder Not to be punished for one's actions; used as a complaint that someone is uncontrollable and can do whatever he or she wants: > *'Some teachers let their children get away with murder.'*

2 Scream (or **shout**) **blue murder** To be extremely noisy as a protest about something disliked: > *'If she gets promoted above him, he'll scream blue murder.'*

MURGATROYD

Heavens to Murgatroyd! *see* **Heaven 8.**

MUSIC

Face the music To have to meet the unpleasant effects that your own actions have brought about: > *'Joe was caught taking Petra's bike, and now he's got to face the music.'*

MUTTON

Mutton dressed (up) as lamb *Derogatory* Used to refer to a woman who is wearing a lot of make-up and showy clothes to make her look younger than she really is.

MY

1 My, my! An expression of surprise, pleasure, etc.: > *'My, my! How nice to see you again after all these years!'* > *'My, my! Who's* *grown so much, then: You're a big boy now, aren't you?'*

2 **Oh my!** An expression of surprise, disbelief, or annoyance: > *'Oh my, it must be all of five years since we last saw you!'* > *'Oh my, when are you going to turn that radio down?'*

NAME

1 **In heaven's name** see **Heaven 9**.

2 **... is my middle name** I am noted for my (characteristic): often used in humorous contexts: > *'I gave a good speech tonight!' 'Modest, aren't you?' 'Yes, modesty is my middle name!'*

3 **... or my name's not ...** I'm certain of (something): > *'I'll do that for you immediately, sir, or my name's not Peter Perkins!'*

4 **Take my (your,** etc.**) name in vain** *Humorous* To mention my (your, etc.) name to someone else, sometimes disrespectfully, without that person's knowledge: > *'Yes, when we came to discussing the photographs, I heard them taking your name in vain.'* > *'Hello, Ken!' Pete called out. Ken turned round to see who it was and said, 'I thought I heard my name being taken in vain!'* Originally, *take God's name in vain*, to use the name of God without proper reverence.

5 **The name of the game** *Slang* The main point: > *'The name of the game in this business is speed – if we can get our offer to the client before everyone else, then we're more likely to get the contract.'*

6 **What name shall I say?** What is your name?: used at reception desks, on the telephone, etc.: >

'I'll put you through to Mr Longfield. What name shall I say?'

7 **What's in a name?** It is not what a thing is called that matters, its character or quality is far more important. From *Romeo and Juliet*, by William Shakespeare, Act 1, Scene 4.

8 **You name it** Whatever you need, mention, etc.: > *'This is one of the best-stocked department stores in the country. You name it, we'll have it!'* > *'Pete's an expert on films: you name it, he's seen it!'*

NAMELESS

..., who shall be (or remain) nameless An expression used when you don't want to mention someone's name although you know it: used when someone has done something wrong or when you don't want to embarrass them: > *'And someone, who shall remain nameless, broke that window!'* Also **... , without mentioning any names.**

NATURE

Nature calls I must go to the lavatory: > *'Sorry, nature calls, I must leave you for a moment.'* Also **Answer (or obey) the call of nature:** > *'I must answer the call of nature – I'll be back in a minute.'*

NAUGHTY

Naughty, naughty! An expression used to show annoyance or impatience when criticising a child: > *'Naughty, naughty, Eric – why did you have to empty all your toys out of the box?'* Also used humorously to show disapproval of something: > *'Naughty, naughty! We know what you two are up to!'*

NEAR

1 **As near as damn it** Almost exactly, but not quite; very nearly: > *The hall was full, as near as damn it.* Also spelt *As near as dammit.*
2 **Nowhere near** *see* **Anything 3.**

NECESSARILY

Not necessarily Possibly, but not definitely: > *'Will prices go up again next year?' 'Not necessarily.'*

NEED

1 **Need I ask** Used when the speaker already knows the answer and therefore asking a question is not necessary: > *'Who will go for us this time?' 'Pat, need you ask? It'll be her as usual.'* Also **Need I say more; Need I go on** Used when it is not necessary for the speaker to continue saying something, since the next stages are already familiar to both speaker and listener.
2 **That's all I needed!** This is the last thing I wanted!; this is the worst thing in a series of bad events or circumstances: > *'What a day it's been – Rod had an accident on the way to school, the car's broken down, and now you say you're leaving me! That's all I needed!'* Also **That's all I need.**

3 **Who needs ...?** Used to say that something is unnecessary or boring: > *'I'm fed up with our leaders. Politicians, who needs them?'*

NELLY

Not on your nelly! *see* **Life 5.**

NERVE

What a nerve! What cheek or impudence!: > *'What a nerve! She's the richest person I know and now she asks me if she can borrow some money!'* Also **He's (she's, etc.) got a nerve!; Some nerve!; The nerve of it!:** > *'He's got a nerve, hasn't he, coming in here, taking my car keys off the desk without even asking!'*

NEVER

1 **Now or never** *see* **Now 3.**
2 **Well I never (did)!** *see* **Do 21.**

NEW

What's new?
   a *Chiefly American* Used as a friendly greeting: > *'What's new?' 'Not much.'*
   b *Ironic* Nothing is new; this situation is familiar: > *Owing lots of money? Feeling desperate? What's new?*

NEWS

1 **I've (or we've) news for you** I'm going to tell you something that will surprise you: > *'You know we'd invited one or two friends for a small celebration drink tonight – well, we've got news for you – we've invited the whole class and we're all going out for a slap-up meal!'*
2 **That's news to me!** I've not heard that!; often showing some

disbelief: > *'Did you know Rob's just got engaged to Susie!' 'That's news to me – I thought he was going out with Sheila!'*

NEXT

1 **Next please!** Ask the next question; the next person can come now, please: > *'Next please,' the man behind the counter in the post office called out.* > *'Thank you for raising such an interesting subject. And now, next please!'*

2 **Who's next?** Who's got the next question?; whose turn is it next?: > *'Who's next?' the chairman asked. 'Yes, I'd like to ask our speaker what he thinks about the state of the economy.'*

NICE

Nice one Used to show that you find something that has just been done or said clever or amusing: > *'I got a reduction on this CD-ROM, just because the box was damaged.' 'Nice one.'* A shortened form of the catchphrase *Nice one, Cyril.*

NIGHT

1 **Good night** *see* **Good 10.**

2 **Night night** An expression used to children to wish a good night's rest: > *'Night, night, darling; sleep well!'*

No

1 **I wouldn't say no** *see* **Say 17.**

2 **No, repeat, no** *see* **Repeat.**

3 **Not take no for an answer** Not to accept a refusal but to insist on someone agreeing to something: > *'Go on, you must stay and have dinner with us. We won't take no for an answer.'*

4 **Oh no!** An expression of sorrow at someone's misfortune, a disappointment, etc.: > *'Harry's had to go back into hospital, I'm afraid.' 'Oh no, how awful – I am sorry.'* > *'Oh no, that's the third time the line's engaged; how can I get in touch with him?'*

NONE

1 **None of ...** *see* **Less 1.**

2 **None too ...** Not at all: > *'I can tell you, he was none too happy about being woken up at 2 in the morning.'*

NOSE

It's no skin off your nose *see* **Skin.**

NOSEY

Nosey got shot! *British school slang, old-fashioned* Don't interfere in affairs that do not concern you or you will suffer harm yourself: > *'What were you saying about me to June?' 'Mind your own business! Nosey got shot!'* Often said touching the nose with one's forefinger. *Nosey* comes from *nosey parker,* a person who pries into other people's affairs; *Parker* as a surname seems to have been freely chosen. The expression is sometimes alluded to in the phrase *You know what happened to Nosey.*

NOT

1 **a** Used for emphasis to express *'no'*: > *'You don't think Melanie should go instead of Rob?'; 'No, not at all!'*

b **Not at all!** *Polite* There is no need to thank me or apologise: > *'Thank you for a lovely meal!' 'Not*

at all; we enjoyed having you!' >
*'I'm sorry I'm a bit late.' 'Not at all
– do come in!'*

2 **Not half** *see* **Half 5.**

3 **Not only ... but also** *see* **Only 2.**

NOTHING

1 **If nothing else** *see* **Else 1.**

2 **It was** (or **it's**) **nothing** There is
no need to thank me or praise
me: often said in either a self-
effacing or an embarrassed way:
> *'Thank you for all the help you've
given us over the last few days –
you've been tremendous!' 'It was
nothing – all I've done is cook a few
meals and tidy up a bit.'* > *'I thought
you acted the star role marvellously!'
'Oh, it was nothing, really!'*

3 **Nothing doing** *see* **Do 15.**

4 **Nothing like** *see* **Anything 3.**

5 **Nothing of the sort** Used when
the speaker is emphatically
refusing permission or saying
strongly that something is not
true: > *'I'm going to stay over at
Beth's tonight, Mum. Her parents
are away, so there'll be plenty of
room.' 'You'll do nothing of the sort.'*

6 **Nothing ventured, nothing gained**
A saying that if you are not
prepared to make an effort or
take risks, you cannot expect to
get results: > *'I'm not sure whether
Pete will let me borrow his motorbike.' 'Ask him – nothing ventured,
nothing gained.'*

7 **Thank you for nothing** There is
nothing to thank you for: used
after someone has unexpectedly
been snubbed or received a
refusal or rebuff: > *'I can't get that
coat cleaned for you by tonight, I'm
afraid.' 'Well, thank you for nothing!'*

8 **There's nothing for it** An
expression of resignation, used
when the speaker has reluctantly
to do something: > *'There's
nothing for it – we'll just have to
sell the car to pay off our debts,
that's all.'*

9 **There's nothing in it**
a The story, rumour, etc., is
untrue: > *'Have you heard about
Rob and Sheila?' 'Yes, but there's
nothing in it, I'm sure!'*
b The competitors in the race
are very close to each other: >
*'There's nothing in it as they're
coming up to the last hedge!'*

10 **There's nothing to it** It really is
very easy: > *'This is how you ride
a bike ... You see, there's nothing to
it. Now you try!'*

11 **Think nothing of it!** *Polite* There
is no need to thank me: >
*'Thank you very much for all
your help!' 'Think nothing of
it! You'd do the same for me!'*
Also used to apologise when
someone thinks they have been
rude: > *'I really am very sorry I
forgot your name just now!' "
Think nothing of it – it happens to
all of us!'*

12 **To say nothing of ...** *see* **Mention 3.**

NOW

1 **Now for ...** And now let us have,
see, or concern ourselves with
(something else): > *'I think we've
finished with that point. Now for
the next item on the agenda.'*

2 **Now, now!**
a An expression of comfort or
sympathy, as to a child: > *'Now,
now, Harriet! It's all right! There's
no need to cry!'*

b An expression used as a warning or mild rebuke: > *'Now, now, you two; don't start fighting again!'*

3 Now or never This is the moment to act; if we don't act now, we never will: > *'If we don't buy that car now, we never will – it's now or never!'* Also **Now for it:** > *I went into the interview room with my knees shaking – 'Now for it!' I thought.*

4 Now then Used to arouse someone's attention to what is about to be said or to the next point in the argument: > *'Now then, what's all this about?'* > *'Now then, why did you want to see me?'* > *'There we were, we'd climbed halfway up. Now then, it started to*

snow – so what do you think we did?' Also **Right then.**

NOWHERE

Nowhere near *see* **Anything 3.**

NUMBER

Number one A way of referring to oneself: > *'I can certainly assure you I'm looking after number one all right.'*

NUTSHELL

In a nutshell To summarise one's thoughts in a brief, clear manner: > *'In a nutshell, we're losing money and the shop will have to close in a month.'* Also **To put it in a nutshell.**

OBLIGE

1 I'd be obliged if ... A polite way of asking someone to do something: > *'I'd be obliged if you'd keep this matter to yourself for a few days.'*

2 (I'm) much obliged (to you) A polite way of thanking someone for doing something: > *'I'm much obliged to you for all your help!'*

ODD

Oddly enough *see* **Enough 5.**

ODDS

1 It makes no (or little) odds It makes no (or only a little) difference: > *'It makes little odds which party we vote for – nothing ever seems to change much!'* > *'It*

makes no odds which road we take, we'll come to the same place in the end.'

2 What's the odds? What does it matter?: > *'What's the odds? Whatever we do, we're bound to lose money!'*

OFF

1 It's (or that's) a bit off It's most unsatisfactory: said as a complaint: > *'It's a bit off not letting us know you'd be coming on a later coach – we've been waiting around for two hours!'*

2 Off with ... A request to remove something: > *'Off with your coats – they're soaking wet!'*

3 Off with his (or her) head! *see* **Head 4.**

4 **Off with you (him, her, etc.)!** Go away!: > *'Off with you! What are you doing here, anyway?'* Also **Be off with you!**

5 **They're off!** The horses, runners, etc., have set off!: > *'They're under starter's orders ... and they're off!'*

OFFENCE

No offence Used when the speaker does not wish to make someone angry or upset by what he or she has said or done although this could be considered rude: > *'I hope you don't mind if I go and sit with Ed for a moment, no offence to you of course.'* > *'I wouldn't worry about what she said – she meant no offence.'*

OH

1 **Oh for ...!** *see* **For.**
2 **Oh, yeah!** *see* **Yeah.**

OK

OK *see* **All 6.**

OLD

1 **Any old** Used to emphasise that what something is like is not important: > *'You can wear any old clothes.'* > *'We can go to any old café for a meal.'*

2 **Any old how** Any way, especially in a careless way: > *'We can paint the back of this cupboard any old how, as no one will ever see it.'*

ON

1 **It's (just) not on!** This is unacceptable or unsatisfactory: often used of someone's behaviour: > *'It's just not on, son, coming home so late without even ringing – your mother was worried stiff about you.'*

2 **On, on!** Go on; come on: > *'On, on! The fight is not yet over!'* Sometimes used with a name: > *'On, Henry, on!'*

3 **On with ...** Let's continue (something): > *'On with the show!'*

4 **You're on!** I'll accept your offer: used in making a bet or coming to an agreement: > *'I bet I can get to the windmill before you!' 'Right, you're on!'* > *'OK, so let's say £1,000 for the car then.' 'All right, you're on!'*

ONCE

1 **At once** Immediately: > *'Can you come and see me at once?'*

2 **Once again!** Please repeat this: > *'That was fine; now, once again, "The rain in Spain falls mainly on the plain."'*

3 **Once upon a time** *see* **Time 8.**

ONE

1 **A good one** *see* **Good 1.**

2 **... for one** As far as (someone) is concerned: > *'I, for one, don't think it's a good idea.'* > *'Who's for going to the park? Audrey, for one – anyone else?'*

3 **Got it in one** *see* **Get 15.**

4 **It's all one to me** I don't mind: used to express agreement with any of the choices offered, and often also a lack of interest in all of them: > *'It's all one to me where we go – round the shops, to the museum again; I'm getting rather bored with all this sightseeing anyway.'*

5 **One for ...** Take one spoonful for (a particular person): used to encourage children to eat their food: > *'One for Auntie Julie – there, that's right! Good!'*

6 One for the road One more drink before going home or going on a journey: > *'I think I'll be going home in a minute.' 'What about having one for the road?' 'No, hanks, I'm driving.'*

7 One to (for, etc.) ... The kind of person (to do something): > *'He's not usually one to talk about people behind their backs, but I did hear him being rather nasty about Peter, you know.'* > *'I'm not really one for eating lots of cakes, but since you insist, I think I will have another one.'*

8 The one and only Used in announcing or presenting an actor, singer, etc.: > *'And now, ladies and gentlemen, the star of tonight's show, the one and only Rob Robertson!'*

9 We've got a right one 'ere *see* **Mother 3**.

ONLY

1 If only ... *see* **If 3**.

2 Not only ... but also Besides ... is true in addition: > They not only broke the world record but also raised a lot of money for charity.

3 Only just Almost not: > We only just got through the winter.

4 The one and only *see* **One 8**.

OOPS

Oops a daisy! *Becoming old-fashioned*
a An expression used when helping someone into or out of a car, climb over something, etc.: > *'Oops a daisy ... Are you all right? Now you're in OK; are you comfortable enough?'*
b An expression used when someone falls down, drops something, or makes a mistake: > *'Oops a daisy! That was a silly thing to do, wasn't it!'*

OPEN

Open sesame! *Often humorous*
A supposedly magical or mysterious formula used to gain entrance to something inaccessible: > *He cried out, 'Open sesame!' and the rock moved aside to show a cave full of riches.* From the words used by Ali Baba in the *Arabian Nights* to open the door of the treasure cave.

ORDER

Order! Order! An expression called out at a formal meeting when someone has broken the rules of the running of that meeting: > *'Order! Order!' the chairman shouted, trying to make himself heard above the unruly noise.*

OUGHT

You ought to ... *see* **Want 3**.

OUT

1 ... out! A slogan used to show disapproval of (someone) and often seeking the removal of a leader from an official position: > *'Smithson, out! Smithson, out!' the crowd all chanted as the minister drove past.*

2 Out with it Say what you've got to say or what's on your mind: > *'Don't just stand there! Out with it! Who won?'* > *'Out with it, John! What's troubling you?'*

3 Out you go! Go out!: > *'Out you go, Rover!' Jim said to his dog, as he shut the door.*

OVER

1 **Over and out** The expression used at the end of a conversation on a radio transmission, etc.: > *'Alice two. Will go to scene of accident. Over and out.'*

2 **Over (to you)** You speak now; I await your reply: used in radio transmissions, etc.: > *'Come in, please, over.'* Also used in wider contexts: > *'We've done all we can, boys – it's now over to you to see if you can put into practice what we've been trying to teach you.'*

OWE

How much do I owe you? How much do all these things, this service, etc., that I am buying, cost?: > *'That's it – I'll take all these, please. Now how much do I owe you?'* > *'Thanks for doing the roof and guttering. How much do I owe you for it all?'*

PACK

Pack it in (or **up**)! Stop what you're doing; often used when something foolish is being done: > *'Pack it up, will you! You're so noisy I can't hear myself think!'* > *'It's so hot in here! Let's pack it in and go home!'*

PAIR

I've only one pair of hands You are asking me to do too much work: a complaint: > *'Rob, could you do the washing-up, and then make a start on the housework, please?'* *'Wait a minute, I've only one pair of hands, you know!'*

PARDON

(I) beg your pardon

a *Formal* I did not hear what you said exactly; I did not understand what you said: could you repeat it please > *'I beg your pardon: what did you say? I didn't catch it properly.'* Also (*informal*) **(Beg) pardon**; (*American*) **Pardon me?**

b I am sorry: > *I accidentally pushed Jo as I passed her, so I said to her, 'I beg your pardon.'* Also (*informal*) **(Beg) pardon**: > *Harry belched rather too loudly. 'Pardon!' he exclaimed.*

c I disagree with what you said; I think you're wrong: > *'I beg your pardon, but what you're saying is really the opposite of the truth.'* Also **Pardon me.**

PART

1 **For the most part** Usually, generally: > *For the most part the children here are very happy.*

2 **It's all part of the service!** see **Service 2.**

PAY

1 **I wouldn't have it if you paid me!** see **Have 5.**

2 **You pays your money and you takes your choice** see **Money.**

PEARL

Pearls of wisdom Clever and shrewd remarks, quotations, but often used humorously to mean the opposite of this; silly comments: > *'Ross, have you any other pearls of wisdom you'd like to share with us?'*

PECKER

Keep your pecker up! *see* **Chin.**

PEG

Bring (or **take**) **down a peg** (or **two**) To make someone think they are less important: > *'I'm glad Petra told him off – it's about time someone brought him down a peg or two.'*

PENNY

1 **A penny for your thoughts!** What are you thinking about: said to a person who has been quiet for a long time and looking deep in thought: > *'A penny for your thoughts, Martin! You've not said a word all evening!'*

2 **The penny dropped** *British* The meaning of what is being said is finally understood: > *We tried to suggest that she might give us a lift home, but she didn't seem to understand. Then suddenly the penny dropped and she said, 'Can I take you home now?'*

3 **Two a penny** Very cheap or common: > *'University degrees are two a penny these days.'*

PEOPLE

Some people have all the luck! A saying used when someone else is fortunate, and often when the speaker has been unlucky; said in a resigned tone: > *'I see Perry's got himself a new girlfriend – some people have all the luck!'*

PERISH

Perish the thought! *see* **Thought 4.**

PERMIT

Permit me *see* **Allow.**

PERSON

1 **I'd be the first (person) to ...** I am willing to (support some statement, decision, etc.) wholeheartedly: > *'Minister, what are your views on the economy?' 'Well, I'd be the first person to admit that things aren't exactly right.'* > *'I'd be the first to say we must decide on our priorities immediately.'*

2 **I'd be the last (person) to ...** I am unwilling to (do something): > *'I'd be the last person to criticise someone else for their failures.'*

PETE

For Pete's sake! *see* **Goodness 1.**

PEW

Take a pew Used as an invitation for someone to sit down.

PHRASE

To coin a phrase To make up an expression: but often really used with a very common or trite expression: > *'To coin a phrase, we could kill two birds with one stone, by visiting friends and doing the shopping when we go there.'*

PICK

1 **I've a bone to pick with you** *see* **Bone 2.**

2 **Pick and choose** To choose very carefully: > *'He likes to pick and choose before buying a new shirt.'*

PIECE

1 **A piece of the action** *see* **Action 1.**
2 **... is a piece of cake** (Something) is very easy: > *'I think swimming is a piece of cake.'*

PIG

Pigs might fly A saying showing that the speaker thinks that it is highly unlikely that something will happen: > *'I might get a job one day soon!' 'And pigs might fly!'* Also **If pigs could fly.**

PILE

Pile it on (thick) *see* **Lay 1.**

PIN

1 **Not care (or give) two pins** *see* **Damn 6.**
2 **You could hear (or have heard) a pin drop** It is (or was) extremely quiet: > *'When he started to tell us about how his son died, there was a sudden hush – you could have heard a pin drop.'*

PINK

Strike me pink! *see* **Strike.**

PIP

Pip, pip! *British, old-fashioned* A cheerful greeting or expression used when saying goodbye: > *'Pip, pip, old fellow!'* Perhaps originally from an imitation of the sound of a motor-car horn.

PIPE

1 **Pipe down!** Shut up; be quiet: > *'Pipe down, will you, I've got my work to do!'*
2 **Put that in your pipe and smoke it!** *Old-fashioned* Think about what I've said!; you'll have to accept it even though you don't like it: used after a statement that the speaker knows will be found unpleasant and said in a defiant tone: > *'You can't spend any more money, as we simply haven't got any more! So you can put that in your pipe and smoke it!'*

PITY

1 **For pity's sake!** *see* **Goodness 1.**
2 **More's the pity** Unfortunately; that is indeed something to be sorry about: > *'There's a rumour going round that they're getting divorced, and it's true, more's the pity.'*

PLACE

In the first place *Formal* The first reason is ...: > *'What do you think were the reasons for the war starting?' 'Well, in the first place, the people were oppressed for a long time.'*

PLAGUE

(A) plague on you (him, her, etc.)! *Old-fashioned* Used to express anger or disgust at someone or something: > *'A plague on you! Why do you always turn up so late?'*

PLAY

1 **Play it by ear** *see* **Ear 3.**
2 **Two can play at that game** *see* **Game 4.**

PLEASE

1 **If you please**
   a Used in making a polite request: > *'Step this way, ladies and gentlemen, if you please.'*
   b Used with something unreasonable or unbelievable:

said with an indignant or angry tone: > *'He crashed my car, and now, if you please, he expects me to pay the repair bill!'* > *'I want you to do it now, not tomorrow, if you please!'*

2 Please God see **God 19.**

3 Please yourself Do what you like; it doesn't matter to me: > *'Please yourself when you start – eight or nine o'clock, as long as you do your eight hours' work, I don't mind.'*

4 Pleased to meet you! see **Meet 1.**

5 We aim to please see **Aim.**

PLEASURE

1 (It's) a pleasure! *Polite* I was pleased to help, etc., you; there is no need to thank me: > *'Thank you, Marjorie, for all the help you've given us since we moved in!' 'It's a pleasure!'* Also **My** (or **our**) **pleasure!**

2 May I have the pleasure (of the next dance)? *Formal* May I ask you to dance with me?: > *Robin plucked up courage and eventually asked, 'May I have the pleasure?' 'Certainly!' Sally replied.*

3 With pleasure *Polite* Yes, certainly: > *'Could you post these letters on your way home, please?' 'With pleasure!' answered John, eager to please as ever.*

POINT

1 Beside the point Irrelevant: > *'How do we get to Nicole's is beside the point. What matters is, do we need to go anyway?'*

2 In point of fact see **Fact 1b, 1c.**

3 More to the point Used when the speaker thinks that what he or she is about to say is more important than what has just been mentioned: > *'Is it going to cost £400 or £600?' 'More to the point, who's going to pay for it?'*

4 Not to put too fine a point on it To speak frankly and honestly: > *'Not to put too fine a point on it, your work has been unsatisfactory recently.'* > *'We're most unhappy about the lack of clear religious teaching in our schools, not to put too fine a point on it.'*

5 Point taken I accept what you are telling me: often used when acknowledging a correction: > *'When was the last time we beat them – the late 1970s, wasn't it?' 'Surely not, what about 1982?' 'Point taken, yes, I'd forgotten about that!'* Also **I take your point.**

6 That's not the point What you are saying is not important or not really relevant to what is being talked about: > *'Since the early 1970s, since the price of oil went up so much ...' 'That's not the point; we've always had economic difficulties; we don't put enough money into building new factories.'*

7 That's the (whole) point That is the essence or the main thing in what I am trying to tell you: often used when the hearer is only slowly understanding an explanation: > *'That's the whole point, with the tax going down, the goods will cost less, don't you see?'*

8 The point is ... Used to direct the hearer's attention or to introduce a statement with emphasis: > *'The point is do you want to go or not, not whether we can make all the necessary arrangements.'*

9 You've (got) a point there What you've said is true, I think; I'd not thought of that before: > *'Do you know, you've got a point there – I think I might just try washing my hair with beer – Id never even thought of that.'*

10 You've made your point You have told us your argument and so we know it already: often also implying a request to be quiet: > *'Yes, Henry, you've made your point, so now let's hear what other people have got to say about it!'*

POISON

What's your poison? *Often humorous* What would you like to drink?: > *'Let me get you one – what's your poison?'* Also **Name your poison.**

POSSESS

What (ever) possessed you (him, her, etc.) ...? Why did you (do something): often used of strange, unusual, or foolish actions: > *'Whatever possessed her to do that? She must have been mad'* > *'What possessed you to behave in such a stupid way?'*

POT

1 A watched pot never boils *see* **Kettle 1.**

2 The pot calling the kettle black One should not criticise someone for a particular fault when one has that fault also.

POWER

More power to your elbow! *Becoming old-fashioned* An expression of encouragement: > *'More power to your elbow! Keep on revising and you'll soon know it all!'*

PRAISE

1 Praise be *Old-fashioned*
a An expression of true thankfulness to God: > *'Praise be! God has saved His people!'* Also **Praise be to God!** (*old-fashioned*); **Praise the Lord!**
b An expression of thanks, relief, etc.: > *'I've finished my work at last, praise be!'*

2 (That's) praise indeed! That is a true compliment: but also often used when the opposite is intended: > *'She's the best student I've ever had!' 'That's praise indeed!'* > *'Jo's not a very good actor, is he?' 'Praise indeed, eh! After all, you're no great Laurence Olivier yourself, are you?'*

PRESERVE

Saints preserve us! *Becoming old-fashioned* An expression of surprise, annoyance, impatience, fear, etc.: > *'You say you want some more money? Saints preserve us, woman, you'll be asking for every penny I ever earned next!'* Also **God preserve us!; Heaven preserve us!**

PRESTO

Hey presto! *see* **Hey.**

PRESUME

... I presume Am I right in thinking that you are (a particular person)?: > *'Mr Smith, I presume?' 'Yes.' 'Then come in!'* Probably patterned on the words *Doctor Livingstone, I presume* spoken by Henry Stanley when he met David Livingstone in central Africa in 1871.

PRICE

What price ... ? *Chiefly British* What are the chances of (something) happening now?: > *'What price freedom of speech if we can't say what we want about the government?'* > *'What price success if it gives you a nervous breakdown?'*

PROBLEM

No problem! That will present no difficulties!: > *'One double room with shower? No problem! Let me see – ah yes, room thirty-six is free.'*

PROMISE

1 **I promise you** I assure you: used to emphasise a statement, threat, or warning: > *'I didn't mean to do it, I promise you!'*
2 **Promises, promises!** All you do is make promises, you never keep them!; I don't believe the promise you're making this time, because you've always broken them before: > *'We'll go abroad for our holiday this year!' 'Promises, promises!'*

PROUD

I hope you feel proud of yourself! *see* Hope 1.

PULL

Pull the other one (it's got bells on)! I cannot believe what you're saying: used humorously to express ridicule or scorn: > *'I hear Mark's putting his car in for the London to Brighton race!' 'Pull the other one! I don't believe it would get as far as the end of his drive!'* The phrase is a development of *pull someone's leg*, to make fun of someone.

PURPOSE

Accidentally on purpose *see* Accidental.

PUSH

1 **At a push** Just about; with difficulty: > *'I'll be able to get the work done by five for you at a push.'*
2 **Push off!** Go away: > *'Push off, will you – can't you leave us alone?'*

PUT

1 **Put 'em up!** *see* Hand 5b.
2 **Put it there!** Let's shake hands on this!: said by a person as he or she puts out his or her hand for the other person to shake it: used when coming to an agreement or reconciliation, or as an expression of admiration: > *'OK, so £500 it is, put it there!'* > *'I think that's settled all our differences, hasn't it? Put it there, then John!'* Also **Stick it there!**
3 **To put it mildly** Without exaggerating: > *'These books are very, very expensive, to put it mildly!'* Also **To say the least.**

Q

QUESTION

1 **Ask a silly question (and you get a silly answer)!** An expression said in reply to a question whose answer is obvious: > *'What are you doing up that ladder?' 'Ask a silly question! What does it look like I'm doing? I'm painting the house, of course!'* Also used in the proverb *Ask no questions and (you'll) be told no lies.*

2 **(That's a) good question** Used as a reply to a question when the speaker does not know the answer: > *'So are we to expect, Minister, that the cost of inflation will remain stable over the next year?' 'That's a good question.'*

QUITE

1 **Quite a ...** A (person or thing) of a special or unusual type: sometimes used to hurt someone's feelings: > *'Your wife's quite a girl, isn't she?'* > *'It really was quite a shock to get the news.'* > *'Quite a little man about town, aren't we, going to all these clubs every day!'* Also (*chiefly American*) **Quite some**: > *'That's quite some library!'*

2 **Quite (so)** *see* **Just 5.**

3 **When you've quite finished!** An expression used to stop someone continuing doing something: > *'When you've quite finished, children ... thank you, we'll now start again!'* Also **When you're quite ready!**

R

RACE

It's anyone's race *see* **Anyone 2.**

RAIN

1 **Come rain or shine** Whatever the weather; whatever happens: > *'I'll see you again on Tuesday, come rain or shine.'*

2 **It never rains but it pours** Several bad things seem to happen or several things seem to go wrong at the same time.

RATE

At any rate Anyway: said before the main point is mentioned, to bring out a contrast with something just said: > *'What a terrible thing to have to go through! At any rate you're all right, now; that's the most important thing.'*

RATHER

... would rather ... *see* **Would 3.**

READY

1 **Ready, steady, go!** The words the starter says before a race, to get the competitors to start: > *'Now come on everybody, up to the line – ready, steady, go!'* Also **On your mark(s), (get) set, go!**

125

2 When you're quite ready! *see* **Quite 3.**

REALLY

1 Not really An expression of doubt or surprise: > *'Are you happy to be here?' 'Well, no, not really.'*

2 (Oh) really An expression of surprise, doubt, interest, etc.: > *'I've been promoted!' 'Oh really? That's good!'* > *'He's away at the moment.' 'Oh really!' 'Yes, he's been away about a month.'* > *'I collect old model cars.' 'Oh really, how interesting!'*

3 (Well) really! An expression showing slight disapproval or annoyance: > *'Well really! Who'd have thought he'd end up in prison?'* > *'Really! I'm surprised at you. I find your attitude wholly objectionable!'*

REASON

1 For no apparent reason Without a clear reason that can be understood easily: > *The train stopped, started, and then stopped again for no apparent reason.*

2 It stands to reason (that) It is reasonable and obvious from what is stated (that): > *'It stands to reason that if the government lowers taxes, then its income will be less.'* > *'I won't do the work unless you pay me promptly – it stands to reason – I've got a wife and two children to support, you know.'*

3 Ours (is) not to reason why We have no right to ask questions; our only responsibility is to continue doing what we have been asked to do: > *'Why on earth are they getting rid of this new metric size and going back to the old ones?' 'Ours is not to reason why!'* Also

Ours is not to reason why, Ours but to do or die, adapted from *The Charge of the Light Brigade,* by Alfred, Lord Tennyson.

RECKON

I reckon Used to make an opinion sound less strong: > *'It's time to go now, I reckon.'* > *'I reckon they'll be here soon.'*

RED

Was my face red! *see* **Face 5.**

REGARD

1 As regards Used to refer to a particular topic; regarding: > *As regards the weather in the southeast tomorrow, it will stay dull and cold.* Also **In regard to; With regard to.**

2 With kind (or best) regards Used at the end of a letter to show friendly but slightly formal feelings: > *I look forward to hearing from you. With kind regards, Graeme.*

REMAIN

It remains to be seen Something has not yet been decided; it is not known: > *It remains to be seen what the response to the company's new model will be.*

REMEMBER

Here's something to remember me by An expression said when giving someone something such as a present, but also a punch or blow: > *'Here's something to remember me by!' 'Oh – a book on the English countryside! How lovely!'* > *'Here's something to remember me by,' he shouted as he hit the man in the chest.*

REMOTE

Not have the remotest idea *see* **Foggiest.**

REPEAT

No, repeat, no Definitely no: > *'No, repeat, no, I can't come to your concert. We've got to go to a parents' evening at school.'*

RESPECT

With (all due) respect Used when politely disagreeing with what has been said: sometimes used in formal situations: > *'I'm sure I could drive better than you.' 'H'm, with respect, how many times did you have to take your driving test?* > *'With all due respect to the last speaker, I must point out that the lessons we can learn from history are rather different from those that he gave us.'*

REST

1 **A change is as good as a rest** *see* **Change 1.**
2 **... and the rest is history** Used to say that the speaker does not need to relate the remainder of the events in a story because it is already well-known: > *They met in their first year at university, and the rest, as they say, is history.*
3 **Give it a rest!** Stop it; stop talking!: > *'Give it a rest, Ron, we all know you can play the piano, but we'd like some peace and quiet, too!'*
4 **(May God) rest his (her,** etc.**) soul** *see* **Soul 2.**
5 **(You can) rest assured** You can be certain: > *'Rest assured, we are doing all we can to find your son.'* > *'You can rest assured that no efforts are being spared to provide you with the finest accommodation in town.'*

RETURN

Many happy returns (of the day)! An expression of greeting on someone's birthday, to wish happiness: > *'Many happy returns, darling! May you have a lovely birthday!'* > *'Let me wish you many happy returns of the day!'*

RHUBARB

Rhubarb, rhubarb The noise made by performers in a play, etc., to make, rather humorously, the sounds of a normal conversation.

RICH

That's rich! That's ridiculous: said about something that is contrary to what is expected: > *'An Englishman teaching a Scotsman how to make kilts – that's rich!'*

RIDDANCE

Good riddance! An expression used to show pleasure at being rid of someone or something: > *'David's leaving next week!' 'Good riddance!'* > *'Thank heavens we've finally sold that car – good riddance to it!'* Sometimes in the phrase *Good riddance to bad rubbish!*

RIDICULOUS

From the sublime to the ridiculous *see* **Sublime.**

RIGHT

1 **All right** *see* **All 6.**
2 **I'm all right, Jack** *see* **Jack 2.**
3 **It's all right** *see* **Well 3.**
4 **Right enough** *see* **Sure 8.**
5 **Right on!** *Slang* An expression of agreement or approval: > *At the rally the speaker asked the crowd, 'We all want cheap fares, don't we?'*

The whole crowd shouted back, 'Right on!' > *'You played real bad,' said Dad. 'You're right on there, father,' she replied.* This phrase is American in origin.

6 **Right then** *see* **Now 4.**

7 **Right you are!** All right, OK: used to show agreement with an order or suggestion and a willingness to do what is asked: > *'Two coffees, please.' 'Right you are!'* > *'You can come on Tuesday, if you want.' 'Right you are, then – see you next week!'* Also **Right oh!**

8 **That's** (or **it's**) **all right** *see* **All 23.**

9 **(That's) right!** Yes; what you say is correct: an expression of agreement or approval: > *'So your first book was published last year?' 'That's right!'* > *'You're filming a new series of the programme, I gather.' 'Right; we've just started the third episode.'*

10 **Too right!** Used to express strong agreement: > *'I'm a bit of a fool, aren't I, coming out here and forgetting my map!' 'Too right you are!'* Also **Too true!**

RING

1 **Don't ring us, we'll ring you** *see* **Call 1.**

2 **That rings a bell** *see* **Bell 3.**

3 **You rang, sir?** *Formal* What may I do for you?: said by a butler, etc., in answer to the ringing of the bell: > *'You rang, sir?' 'Yes, Smithy, may we have some port?'*

RIP

Let her rip Let the car, boat, etc., go at full speed: > *'Let her rip, Joe, we're out in the country now!'*

RISE

Rise and shine *Often humorous* Get out of bed quickly and look fresh!: > *I was lying in bed asleep and suddenly I heard Dad shout, 'Rise and shine!'*

ROAD

One for the road *see* **One 6.**

ROBINSON

Before you can (or **could**) **say Jack Robinson** *Becoming old-fashioned* Very quickly: > *'I'll be downstairs before you can say Jack Robinson.'* > *'Before you could say Jack Robinson, he'd taken my wallet and dashed out of the room.'* It is not known who Jack Robinson actually was. Also (*rare*) **Before you can say knife.**

ROLL

Roll on ... Used to express a wish for the quick approach of (a time or occasion): > *'Roll on spring! The winter's so long!'* > *'Roll on the year that I retire!'* > *'Roll on the weekend!'*

ROOM

There's no room to swing a cat Used to describe a place that is very small or very crowded: > *'Their new kitchen is so tiny – there's no room to swing a cat in there!'* The *cat* in this expression probably originally referred to the *cat-o'-nine tails*, a whip that was used to punish disobedient soldiers or sailors.

ROUNDABOUT

Swings and roundabouts *see* **Swing.**

RUB

There's the rub *Becoming old-fashioned* That is the central point of the matter, the one on which the difficulty or problem comes: > *'Yes, I think we've agreed on how long it will take to build. Now what about the cost?' 'Ah, there's the rub – our figures don't seem to tally on this.'* From *Hamlet*, by William Shakespeare, Act 3, Scene 1: *To sleep! perchance to dream; ay, there's the rub.*

RUN

Run for it! Move as fast as you can to escape from the danger: > *'The house is on fire! Don't go and collect your things! Just run for it!'* > *'Run for it! They're after us!'* Also **Run for your life!**

SAFE

Better safe than sorry It is better to be cautious and take steps now to avoid possible difficulties later on.

SAINT

1 **Saints alive!** *see* **Aunt.**
2 **Saints preserve us!** *see* **Preserve.**

SALT

The salt of the earth An expression used to describe people who are very kind or reliable, or have other very good features: > *The newspaper described the youth group who helped in the local old people's home as the salt of the earth.* From the Bible, Matthew, chapter 5, verse 13.

SAME

1 **All the same**
a Not making any difference at all: > *'If it's all the same to you, I think I'll go now!'* > *'It's all the same whether we go by train or coach.'*
b Even so; nevertheless; in any case: > *'I know he's rich, but all the same, it doesn't mean he's got an endless supply of money, you know!'* > *'Despite his unfaithfulness, I shall go on loving him all the same.'*

2 **(And) the same to you**
a I wish you the same thing: said in reply to a greeting or wish: > *'Happy Christmas!' 'The same to you!'*
b I wish you the same thing: said in reply to an unkind wish or insult: > *'I wish you'd go and jump in a lake!' 'The same to you!'* To strengthen this expression *(And) the same to you with (brass) knobs on* is used: > *'You're the biggest idiot I've ever met! Why don't you go and put your head in a bucket!' 'The same to you with brass knobs on!'*

3 **Same here** The same applies to me; and the same for me: > *'I'm fed up with revising!' 'Same here! Let's go and watch television.'* > *'Can I have pie and chips, please?' 'Same here!' 'OK, two pie and chips coming up!'*

4 (The) same again An order for another drink, dish, etc., of the same kind as the previous one: > *'The same again, please, Jan!'*

SAVE

To save his (her, etc.) life *see* Life 9.

SAY

1 And so say all of us *Sometimes humorous, becoming old-fashioned* An expression of agreement or approval by everyone present: > *'I'm sure we'll want to express our deepest gratitude to our guest speaker tonight!' 'Yes! And so say all of us!'* > *'For he's a jolly good fellow, and so say all of us!'*

2 As you say You are right; I'll do what you ask: often used when the speaker is really not willing to do something: > *'That's absolute nonsense!' 'As you say, sir!'* > *'We must leave at once. Come on; pack your bags!' 'As you say!'*

3 Confucius, he say ... *see* Confucius.

4 (Do) you mean to say? Used to express surprise, disbelief, etc.: > *'You mean to say you're leaving us?'* > *'Do you mean to say I've come all this way for nothing?'*

5 Don't say ... An expression of impatient surprise or annoyance: > *'Don't say I've gone and locked my keys in the car!'* > *'Don't say you can't help me now after you promised you would!'*

6 Easier said than done It is simpler to talk about something, make a suggestion, etc., than to actually do it: > *'Why don't you update your computer software? There's a new version now with really good graphics features.' 'Easier said than done.'* > *Not being deeply emotionally hurt a few times in your life is easier said than done.*

7 How say you? *British* The formula spoken by the clerk of the court to the defendant, when the charge is read out at the start of the trial: > *'How say you? Are you guilty or not guilty?'*

8 I can't say A way of making a negative expression seem less strong: sometimes said in a rather reluctant tone: > *'To tell you the truth, I can't say I like your choice of wallpaper!'*

9 I couldn't say I don't know: > *'How many people came to the party?' 'I couldn't say – perhaps twenty, perhaps forty – it's difficult to tell.'*

10 I dare say *Chiefly British* It is quite likely, I think; probably: > *'We've run out of sugar, but I dare say there's some in the cupboard.'* > *'I dare say you're hungry after your long walk!'* Sometimes written *I daresay*.

11 I (he, she, etc.) said Used in reporting a conversation: > *'I said to the lady downstairs, "What about your bunions?" and so she told me about all the illnesses she'd ever had.'* Also used by the speaker to make a quotation of one's own words, to show that the quotation applies to oneself: > *'All of us have bad days!' remarked the presenter at the end of the programme, when so many things had gone wrong.* Also **Said I (he, she, etc.); Says I (he, she, etc.)** (*nonstandard*); **I (he, she, etc.) says** (*nonstandard*): > *'I spoke to the fellow who knows the*

*boss and I says to him, "When am
I getting my pay rise, then?"'*

12 I mean to say
a An expression of surprise,
disbelief, disgust etc.: > *'Well I
mean to say! Who does she think
she is? Coming in here and telling
us how to run the kitchen!'*
b An expression used to clarify
or expand on a previous
statement: > *'I was standing by
the pond, that's all. I mean to say,
I was just looking at the ducks,
when suddenly this man came up
and pushed me in!'* Often
shortened to *I mean*.

13 I must say An expression used to
add force to an often critical
opinion or statement: > *'It's not
the most exciting novel I've ever
read, I must say, but it wasn't too
bad.'* > *'You've been a great help, I
must say! You might as well not
have come for all the support
you've given!'*

14 I say *British, rather old-fashioned*
a An expression of surprise: > *'I
say, look at the time – it's nearly
midnight; we must be going
home!'*
b An expression used to attract
someone's attention: > *'I say,
Colonel, just look at that Rolls-
Royce, it's like the one we had
before the war!'*

15 I say, I say, I say! Used to
introduce a joke: especially in
theatrical contexts: > *'I say, I say,
I say! Can you sing* Faust*?' 'Yes –
and I can sing slow, as well!'*
Made more current by the
variety duo Harry Murray and
Harry Mooney in the 1930s.

16 I wouldn't say Used to introduce

a statement or opinion that is
then further qualified: > *'I
wouldn't say we're not happily
married – it's just that we do seem
to have more than our fair share of
quarrels.'*

17 I wouldn't say no A polite way of
saying yes: > *'Would you like
another piece of cake?' 'I wouldn't
say no!'*

18 I wouldn't say that A polite way
of disagreeing with someone: >
*'So you think £100 will be
enough?' 'I wouldn't say that – I
was thinking of nearer £500!'* >
*'Pete's helped you quite a bit since
you moved in, hasn't he?' 'I
wouldn't say that – I think he's
come in only once, that's all!'* Also
I'm not saying that.

19 If I may (or **might**) **say so** A
polite expression used to make
an opinion or statement sound
less strong: > *'If I may say so,
that jacket doesn't quite fit you.'* >
*'I'm not sure he's the right person
to ask, if I might say so.'*

20 I'll say! Yes indeed: a strong
form of agreement: > *'Do you
want to go to the seaside?' 'I'll say!'*
> *'Were they happy at the thought
of going away on holiday?' 'I'll say
they were!'*

21 I'll say this much I will say only
this, and no more: used to state
the positive side of a person or
thing: > *'I'll say this much for him
– he's always honest, even if he is
poorly dressed.'*

22 I'm not just saying this I really
mean what I'm saying: > *'We've
appreciated your help enormously,
and I'm not just saying this.'*

23 It's easy for you to say *see* **Easy 4.**

24 (Let's) say Let us suppose: > *'We'll meet, say, at six o'clock.'* > *'What if I were to offer you, let's say, £1,000 for the whole lot?'*

25 Needless to say Used when one is saying something that is obvious, expected, or already known: > *'Needless to say Frances won as usual.'*

26 Never say die! *Becoming old-fashioned* Do not despair!; do not give up hope!: > *She spoke to me gently, 'Never say die! It won't last forever!'*

27 Sad to say Used to describe an unfortunate or tragic situation: > *'She collapsed suddenly and, sad to say, she died ten days later in hospital.'*

28 Say again? *see* **Come 2.**

29 Say no more Your intended meaning is clear just from what you've said: > *'I saw her going into his room at ten o'clock last night.' 'Say no more!'* Also (*rather more formal*) **Enough said.** This phrase is sometimes written *'nuff said.*

30 Say something Say a few words; make a short speech: > *'Go on, say something – we can't just sit here with everyone looking at us expectantly!'*

31 Say what you like Even though you may not agree with what is being said: > *'Say what you like, it won't make me change my mind!'*

32 Say when Please tell me when to stop or start something: used especially when a host is pouring a drink for someone: > *'Say when!'* ... *'Right, that's enough thanks!'* > *'Say when!'* ... *'When!'* > *'As soon as you're ready, say when, and I'll switch on!'*

33 Says (or sez) you (he, she, etc.)! I don't believe that; I strongly disagree with what you (he, **she**, etc.) have just said: said in a rude, sneering, or scornful tone: > *'Our team'll win today!' 'Says you! We'll eat yours easily!'* Also **Says (or sez) who?:** > *'I'm taking Jo to the party.' 'Sez who? She's my girlfriend, not yours!'* The spelling **sez** is nonstandard.

34 That is (to say) An expression used to clarify or expand on something that has just been said: > *'He didn't sign the register, that is to say, I've no record that he ever did.'* > *'We're leaving on 2 March, that is, Friday.'* Abbreviated to *i.e.*, Latin *id est.*

35 That's what you say! I think there might be other opinions as well as yours: used to express doubt about the truth of a statement: > *'That's what you say, but I'm sure your sister wouldn't agree with you!'*

36 They say People in general say; it is an opinion that is widely held: > *'They say, "Nothing succeeds like success" and I'm certainly proving it in my business!'* > *'They say that if it rains on St Swithin's Day, the rain will continue for the next forty days.'*

37 Though I say it (or so) myself An expression used with a statement of boasting, to make this seem less strong, but also to give self-assurance: > *'I think I've made a good job of decorating this room, though I say so myself.'* Also **Though I says it as shouldn't.**

38 **To say the least** *see* **Put 3.**

39 **What can I say?** I am lost for words; I can't think how to express my thoughts: > *'Well, what can I say? I'm overwhelmed by all the kindness you've shown me! However can I say thank you?'*

40 **What did I say!** What I say has now come true!: > *'There you are! What did I say! I said they'd been meeting secretly, and now it's come out that they have! It's just as I thought!'* Also What did I tell you!

41 **What do you say?**
a Do you like it?; do you agree with my suggestion?: > *'How about each putting in £100? What do you say?' 'OK, it's a deal!'* Also **What would you say?:** > *'What would you say to going to Brighton for the afternoon?' 'Yes, that's fine by me!'* > *'What would you say to another cup of tea?'*
b Said to encourage a child to say please or thank you: > *'Can I take another banana?' 'What do you say?' 'Please!' 'Right, OK, then – help yourself!'*

42 **You can say that again!** I agree very much with what you've said: > *'I don't think he looks after his wife.' 'You can say that again: he goes out drinking with his friends every night.'* Also **You said it!:** > *'That exam was very hard, wasn't it?' 'You said it!'*

43 **You could say that** I agree with you partly: > *'He's plump isn't he?' 'You could say that, but he's not too fat, really.'* The stress falls on *could*.

44 **You don't say?** Used to show surprise at what has just been said: > *'We're thinking of emigrating to Australia next year.' 'You don't say? I thought you were very happy here.'* The stress falls on *don't*.

SAYING

As the saying goes An expression used with a fixed phrase such as a proverb or idiom: > *'There were ten of us working there, but everything seemed to go wrong, and the project was abandoned – too many cooks spoiling the broth, as the saying goes.'*

SCORE

On that score On the subject of that: > *'How are you off for money?' 'Oh, you needn't have any worries about us on that score.'*

SCOTT

Great Scott! *Old-fashioned* An expression showing great surprise or astonishment: > *'Great Scott! That car's going very fast!'* The origin of this phrase is uncertain but it seems likely that Scott was General Winfield Scott (1786-1866), soldier and nominee in a US presidential election.

SCOUT

Scout's honour! *see* **Honour 3.**

SEAL

My lips are sealed *see* **Lip.**

SEARCH

Search me! I do not know the answer; I do not know what to do: > *'Where's Barry got to?' 'Search me! I've no idea!'* > *'What shall we do next?' 'Search me! Haven't you got any bright ideas?'*

SECOND

1 **Just a second** *see* **Just 3.**
2 **Wait a second** *see* **Wait 4b, c.**

SEE

1 **As far as I can see** To the best of my understanding or judgement: > *'As far as I can see, the only honourable course of action open to you is to resign immediately.'*

2 **As I see it** In my opinion: > *'As I see it, you can either invest the money or spend it!'* > *'As I see it, the best thing to do is to take half an hour's exercise every day, and then you'll feel a lot better.'*

3 **Do you see (what I mean)?** Also **Don't you see?**
   a Do you understand what I'm trying to explain?: > *'If we extend the shelves this way, then that'll give us a lot more room – do you see what I mean?'*
   b It is as I said; didn't I tell you that this was so?: > *'Do you see what I mean, whenever these two get together, they always start to fight. Just look at them now!'*

4 **I see** I understand your explanation: > *'If the government lowers taxes ...' 'Oh, I see – you mean then the price will come down.' 'Exactly!'*

5 **I see what you mean**
   a I understand what you're trying to explain: > *'This cogwheel turns this bigger one.' ... 'And the whole thing moves round – I see what you mean.'*
   b It is as you said; you are quite right: > *'I see what you mean – Peter's ears do stick out a little, don't they? I'd not noticed that before.'*

6 **I wouldn't be seen dead** *see* **Dead 2.**
7 **I'd like to see ...** *see* **Like 3.**
8 **I'll (or we'll) be seeing you!** Goodbye: used between friends: > *'I'll be seeing you then, Jackie!' 'Right oh, Mark!'* Also shortened to **Be seeing you!**: > *'Be seeing you, Alf!' 'OK, be seeing you!'*
9 **I'll (or we'll) see** Used to show that the speaker does not wish to make a decision immediately: > *'Can Rachel stay the night?' 'We'll see.'*
10 **I'll (or we'll) see (about that)** I (or we) may do something, but are unable to make a decision or commitment at the moment; it depends on various things: > *'We may come round tonight. We'll see.'* Also **I'll (or we'll) have to see (about that).** This phrase is used to show near-refusal: > *'Do you think I could borrow some money?' 'I'll have to see about that.'*
11 **Let me (or let's) see** An expression used to give the speaker time to think what to say next: > *'Let me see, when would he have been born? It must have been about 1900.'* > *'Do you know that smell?' 'Ah! Let me see ... Yes, it's rotten eggs!'* > *'Let's see, there must be a way out of here somewhere!'* Also **Let me think**: > *'Let me think; I may be able to see you on Friday.'*
12 **Long time no see** *see* **Time 6.**
13 **See here!** *see* **Look 5.**
14 **See you later!** Goodbye: used between friends: > *'See you later, Peter!' 'Yes, goodbye!'* Also (*slang, becoming old-fashioned*) **See you later alligator!** *Alligator* is rhyming slang for *later*. Also **See you!; See you around!**

15 **So I see** What you say is obvious: used in reply to an apology or an excuse that may be rejected: > *'I'm sorry. I'm late.' 'So I see!'* > *'I'm afraid I've brought in all this mud onto your carpet!' 'So I see!'*

16 **We'll (soon) see about that?** I will put an end to that!: > *'You say the kids are playing behind the sheds again – we'll soon see about that!'*

17 **(You) see** An expression used in an explanation, reminding the hearer of something that has just been said or that the hearer already knows, sometimes making what is said sound less strong: > *'I was coming down the road, see, and then this car suddenly came towards me.'* > *'I had to go and talk to Mr Smith – that's why I'm five minutes late, you see.'* > *'You see, I know this town very well.'*

18 **You see if ...** An expression stating that the speaker will be proved right by (events to come): > *'He'll quietly forget about all that money he owes you, you see if he won't.'*

SENSE

In a sense In a particular way; partly: > *'It was, in a sense, my fault as I forgot to remind him.'*

SERIOUS

You can't be serious! You don't really mean that, do you?: used to try to dissuade someone from a course of action: > *'Climb that ladder? You can't be serious! You know I don't like heights!'*

SERVE

1 **If my memory serves me right ...** *see* **Memory**.

2 **It** (or **that**) **serves you** (**him, her**, etc.) **right!** That is a just punishment for what you have (he or she has, etc.) done: > *'I've just heard Rod failed his exams – I think it serves him right as he didn't do any work for them!'* Also **Serves you** (**him, her**, etc.) **right!**: > *'I've got such a pain in my stomach!' 'Serves you right for eating so many cakes!'*

SERVICE

1 **At your service** *Formal* I am (or we are) waiting for your instructions and will do exactly as you ask: used in polite or pompous contexts: > *'Should you require any assistance, all my staff are at your service.'* > *'At your service, sir!'*

2 **It's all part of the service!** A response made to someone saying thank you: used by shopkeepers, etc., or humorously in a wider context: > *'I want to thank you very much for seeing that I have all my shopping!' 'It's all part of the service, madam!'* > *'Thanks for looking after me so well during my stay here, son.' 'Ah, Mother! It's all part of the service!'* Also (in public contexts) **It's what we're here for!**

SEZ

Sez you! *see* **Say 33**.

SHAKE

1 **He's** (**she's, it's**, etc.) **no great shakes** He (she, it, etc.) has no skill, value, merit, or importance: > *'Ethel is no great shakes at speaking French but she can write it quite well.'*

2 Shake a leg! *see* **Leg 3.**

3 Shake hands *see* **Hand 8.**

SHALL

Shall we (I, etc.) ...? *Formal* Used in asking questions in a polite way: > *'Shall we have dinner now?'* > *'Shall I take you to the station?'*

SHAME

1 Shame on you! You should be ashamed: > *'Shame on you, Peter, for behaving like that – I'd have thought you'd know better!'*

2 Shame, shame! You should be ashamed of such behaviour: called out to a speaker at a public meeting or, usually humorously, by a theatre audience: > *The spokesman continued, 'I have to admit that we have made some administration mistakes ...' and this brought cries of 'Shame, shame!' from the audience.*

SHARP

1 Look sharp!
a Be quick; hurry up: > *'Don't walk so slowly! Look sharp!'* Also **Be sharp about it!**
b Be careful: > *'Look sharp! There's a lot of traffic about!'*

2 Sharp's the word! *see* **Word 13.**

SHINE

1 Come rain or shine *see* **Rain 1.**

2 Rise and shine! *see* **Rise.**

SHIRT

1 Keep your shirt on! There is no need to get so annoyed!; calm down! > *'Keep your shirt on, Rod! I only asked if I could borrow the car for this evening, not for you to give it to me for ever!'* Also (*British*) **Keep your hair on:** > *'What are you doing with my radio?' 'Keep your hair on! I'm just putting a new battery in it for you!'*

2 You (can) bet your shirt *see* **Bet 6.**

SHIVER

Shiver my timbers! *see* **Timber.**

SHOCK

Shock, horror *see* **Horror.**

SHOOT

1 Nosey got shot! *see* **Nosey.**

2 The whole bang shoot *Slang* Everything: > *'I want all your furniture and books – the whole bang shoot – out of there by ten o'clock tomorrow.'*

SHORT

1 In short Used to summarise something briefly and concisely: > *'In short, they quickly got engaged and were married later that year.'*

2 Nothing (or little) short of ... Used to emphasise how extreme something is: > *'It's nothing short of a miracle that she survived the accident.'*

SHOT

1 A shot in the dark A very rough guess or random action, made without any real thought: > *Because of pressure of time, the company's advertisements for their new ballpoint pen were just a shot in the dark.*

2 Not by a long shot *see* **Chalk.**

SHOULD

1 **I should ...** An expression used in giving advice: > *'I should get rid of that old car, if I were you, and buy yourself a newer one.'*

2 **Who** (*how, why,* etc.) **should ...?** An expression of surprise: > *'Who should come to see me but Pedro?'* > *'Why should she want to do that?'* > *'What should he suggest, but that we get married!'*

3 **You should ...** *see* **Want 3.**

SHOUT

It's my (or **your**) **shout!** It's my (or your) turn to buy a drink for the people in your group: > *'It's my shout! I'll get them this time. Same again for everyone?'*

SHOW

1 **Bad** (or **poor**) **show!** *Old-fashioned* Used to express sympathy with someone for something unfortunate that has happened: > *'Bad show, Milton! A pity Joe was a bit faster than you in the end!'*

2 **Good show!** *Old-fashioned* Used to express approval: > *'I hear Jack's coming back from India!' 'Oh, good show! I've not seen him for ages!'* > *'Jolly good show you turned up – I was just giving up all hope of ever seeing you again!'*

3 **It just goes to show** *see* **Go 17.**

4 **Show a leg!** *see* **Leg 3.**

SHUT

Shut up! Stop talking!; be quiet!: > *'Shut up, Ian, do you have to go on and on all the time?'* Also (*slang*) **Shut your face!; Shut your mouth!; Shut your trap!**

SHY

Once bitten, twice shy *see* **Bite 3.**

SIDE

On the other side of the coin Used to make a strong contrast with something just said: > *'It's cheap but on the other side of the coin, it's very fragile.'*

SIGHT

Out of my sight! Go immediately: > *'Out of my sight! I never want to see you again!'*

SIN

... for my sins! *Humorous* Used when the speaker considers what is being talked about as slightly disagreeable or as a gentle form of punishment: > *'He's left all the holiday arrangements to me, for my sins!'* > *'Is that pile of books all yours?' 'Yes, for my sins! I've got to mark them all for tomorrow!'*

SINK

Now we're sunk! All our efforts, hopes, etc., have failed us; we're in a desperate situation!: > *'Now we're sunk! We've run out of food and it's getting dark!'*

SIX

Six of one and half a dozen of the other *see* **Dozen.**

SIZE

That's about the size of it! That's a fair account of the matter, situation, etc.: > *'That's about the size of it – the roof will have to be repaired within a month or two, I'm afraid.'*

SKIN

It's (or that's) no skin off your (his, her, etc.) nose It doesn't bother or affect you (him, her, etc.) > *'Why shouldn't I come in late if I want to? After all, it's no skin off your nose, is it?'*

SKIP

Skip it! There is no need to bother about something, such as an apology or thanks; also used for dropping a subject of conversation: > *'Let me pay you back what I owe you – how much was it?' 'Oh, skip it – it doesn't matter!'* > *'Skip it! Can't you two talk about anything but politics?'*

SLICE

A slice of the action *see* **Action 1**.

SMART

Look smart! *see* **Look 6**.

SMILE

1 **Keep smiling!** *see* **Keep 4**.
2 **Take (or wipe) that smile off your face** *see* **Grin 2**.

SMOKE

Holy smoke! *see* **Holy**.

SNAPPY

Make it snappy! *see* **Make 4**.

SO

1 **Ever so** *see* **Ever 2**.
2 **How so?** *see* **How 13**.
3 **Is that so?** Is it really as you say: an expression of surprise: > *'Brian's coming to see us tonight, you know.' 'Is that so? I thought it was tomorrow!'*
4 **It is so!** Used to contradict a negative statement: > *'It's not raining, is it?' 'It is so!'*
5 **Just so** *see* **Just 5**.
6 **So be it!** *Formal* Let it be as you say: used in accepting something, sometimes in a resigned manner: > *'If that's what you want, so be it, though it's not what we'd have chosen for you!'* > *'So be it – the dead are now departed from among us and we must face the future with boldness.'*
7 **So there!** *see* **There 1**.
8 **So what?** *see* **What 6**.
9 **That being so** *see* **Case 3**.

SOCK

1 **Bless his (her, etc.) (little) cotton socks** *see* **Bless 4**.
2 **Pull your (his, her, etc.) socks up** To make a definite effort to improve one's work: > *The teacher told John to pull his socks up or he would have to leave.*
3 **Put a sock in it!** *Becoming old-fashioned* Be quiet! stop what you're doing!: > *'Put a sock in it! Why don't you two shut up? It's two o'clock in the morning, and I've got to be up at six!'*

SOME

Some ...
  a You are (or it is) no kind of a ... at all: said in an indignant or angry tone: > *'Some help you've been, I must say – you've just sat there and done nothing all afternoon!'* > *'Some people! You know you make me sick, Peter, the way you've treated me recently.'*
  b A (person or thing) of a special or unusual type: > *'That was some storm!'* > *'That was some game you played!'*

SOMETHING

1 Or something

a Used when the speaker disagrees with or does not fully believe the meaning of a particular word: > *'I thought jobs here were supposed to be well-paid or something!'*

b Or something very like it: used when the speaker is unsure of what is said: > *'I think he's studying sociology or something at university.'* > *'Are you trying to kill me or something, with all this work you keep on giving me?'*

2 Say something see **Say 30.**

3 Something tells me I think that: used when the speaker suspects something: > *'Something tells me those two are getting married soon.'* Also used in the past tense: > *'Something told me it wasn't safe to go into the room, so I stayed outside.'*

4 You know something? see **Know 31.**

SON

Son of a gun *Old-fashioned* A way of addressing a man in a friendly way: used by other men: > *'Come on, you old son of a gun, what have you been up to these last few years?'* The phrase was originally a term of abuse and meant 'the bastard son of a soldier or sailor'.

SORRY

1 (I'm) sorry!

a An expression used as an apology after the speaker has done or said something that may have annoyed someone else: > *'I'm sorry, I hope you've not been waiting long.'* > *'Sorry! Did I step on your toe?'* Also **So sorry!**

b Used to express polite disagreement, excusing of oneself, etc.: > *'I'm sorry, but it's getting late, and I think we'd better be going now.'*

2 You'll be sorry Used as a warning or threat that you will regret the unpleasant results of your actions: > *'If you're ever discovered stealing these computers, you'll be sorry.'*

SORT

1 A sort of ... see **Kind 1.**

2 It takes all sorts (to make a world) There are many different kinds of people; used to show that the speaker thinks that someone's tastes, habits, abilities, etc. are odd: > *Some people take active holidays, some people like a complete rest. It takes all sorts to make a world.*

3 Sort of ... see **Kind 3.**

4 Sort of thing see **Thing 10.**

SOUL

1 God bless my soul! see **Bless 2.**

2 (May God) rest his (or her) soul A wish that God would give a dead person's soul peace: > *'He's been dead twenty years, now, God rest his soul.'*

3 Upon my soul! see **Bless 2.**

SPEAK

1 Not to speak of ... see **Mention 3.**

2 So to speak If it may be described in this way: sometimes used to make an opinion sound less strong: > *'This machine's, so to speak, the Rolls-Royce of computers.'*

3 Speak for yourself! Do not imagine that other people agree with you!: > *'I think Catherine*

Cookson's books are the best I've ever read!' 'Speak for yourself – I'm sticking to Rudyard Kipling!'

4 **Speak of the devil!** *see* **Devil 6.**

5 **Speaking of** Used to link what the speaker is about to say with what has just been said: > *'And Jane went to see her friends, Vicky and Sarah.' 'Speaking of Sarah, whatever happened to her daughter?'* Also **Talking of.**

SPEECH

Speech, speech! We want you to give a speech!: > *They gave me my leaving present and there were cries of 'Speech, speech!' so I had to say a few words.*

SPEED

Full speed (or steam) ahead! Let's work or go as fast as we can!: > *'I've got to finish writing this in a few days, so it's full steam ahead!'* > *'Now we're out on the open seas – full speed ahead!'* Originally, *Full steam ahead!* was used of a steam engine on the railway, and *Full speed ahead!* of a ship.

SPENDER

The last of the big spenders! I see you are spending a lot of money: but only used ironically when a person is really spending very little: > *'This coat cost me all of £5!'* *'Ah – the last of the big spenders!'*

SPIT

Spit it out! Say what you've got to say or what's on your mind: > *'Come on, spit it out, old chap – we're all friends here; feel free to say what's troubling you.'*

SPOIL

Be spoiling for a fight *see* **Look 1.**

SQUARE

Back to square one We must go back to the beginning: > *I've spent years writing this book, and now I've been told to write it all differently, so it's back to square one, I'm afraid.'*

STAND

1 **It stands to reason (that)** *see* **Reason 2.**

2 **Stand and deliver!** Stop and hand over your valuable belongings to us: said in former times by highwaymen to travellers in carriages.

STAR

(You can) thank your lucky stars! Be very thankful; consider yourself very fortunate: > *'Thank your lucky stars that that car didn't run you down just then – it only just missed you!'* > *'You can thank your lucky stars your job's a lot easier than mine!'*

START

For a start Used to introduce the first of a series of reasons, points: > *'For a start, how much money do we have?'* Also **To start with.**

STATION

Action stations! *see* **Action 2.**

STEADY

Steady on *British* Stop what you're doing; slow down; be more moderate: > *'Steady on! I can't keep up with you fast walkers!'* > *'Steady on with the milk – it's the* *last carton we've got!'* > *'Steady on, old chap, there's no need to tell her everything about my past all at once!'*

STEAM

Full steam ahead! *see* **Speed.**

STEP

1 **Mind** (or **watch**) **your step!** Be very careful: used as a warning: > *'Mind your step, young Michael! There are plenty of people looking at your job enviously!'*

2 **Step on it!** Go faster: > *I got into the taxi quickly. 'Euston station, please, and step on it! My train goes in ten minutes!'* The phrase refers to pushing the accelerator on a car further down to make the car go faster.

3 **Step outside** Come outside and we can settle our differences: said as a challenge to a fight: > *Big Max was getting angry. 'Would you care to step outside and repeat that?' he called out to Dave, who looked absolutely terrified.*

4 **Step this way** *see* **Way 4.**

STICK

1 **Jolly hockey sticks!** *Old-fashioned* An expression showing pleasure or delight at something traditional or conventional: used to mock mildly the hearty atmosphere of British girls' public schools: > *'Term finishes in two weeks' time!' 'Ooh, jolly hockey sticks!'* Originally, coined by Beryl Reid in the radio programme *Educating Archie.*

2 **Stick 'em up!** *see* **Hand 5b.**

3 **Stick it there!** *see* **Put 2.**

STIR

Stir, stir! An expression used when someone is trying to cause an argument or trouble between other people: often said with a movement of one's arms, as if stirring a large pot: > *'Michael, what about you and Jane, then?' 'Stir, stir! There he goes again!'*

STONE

Stone the crows! *British slang, old-fashioned* An expression of surprise, shock, disbelief, etc.: > *'Stone the crows! Do you really expect me to believe that story?'* Also **Stone me!**: > *'Stone me! I've not seen one of those cars for years!'*

STOOL

Fall between two stools To be neither totally one thing nor another but partly both and therefore unsatisfactory: > *The book fell between two stools – the author tried to make it suitable for both students and lay people.*

STOP

1 **... full stop** That is the end of the matter: said at the end of a statement, to add force to it: > *'I'm not going to the party, full stop.'*

2 **Stop, thief!** *see* **Thief.**

STORY

1 **A likely story!** I don't believe what has just been said: > *'He says he was at church on Sunday!' 'A likely story – I bet he was playing football as usual!'*

2 **But that's (quite) another story**
   a That is very different from what has just been said: > *'He can write French well, but speak it –*

that's quite another story – he's hopeless at that!' Also **That's a different kettle of fish.**

b An expression used when the speaker reaches a very interesting point in a story but he or she does not describe further details at that time: > *'Do you see that barn over there? It's been there many years now. Of course, there once was another one, which was burnt down in a mysterious fire, but that's another story.'*

3 It's the same old story The usual bad or unpleasant situation that is happening now has happened before or in other places: > *It's the same old story – cutbacks in staffing and demands by the management for greater efficiency on the part of the remaining workforce.*

4 The story of my life! This continually happens to me; used to comment on unfortunate events: > *'That's the third time this year a girl has chucked me – it's the story of my life!'*

5 To cut a long story short I'll miss out the less important details to come to the main point in my description of the events: > *'Stephen met Claire one night at a party. They saw each other the next Saturday at the club dance, and, to cut a long story short, they got married last week!'*

STRAIN

Don't strain yourself! An expression used when someone is very slow at doing something: > *'It's taken you three hours to write ten lines. Don't strain yourself, will you?'*

STRANGE

Strangely enough see **Enough 5.**

STRANGER

Hello stranger! An expression said to someone whom the speaker knows quite well but has not seen for some time: > *'Hello, stranger! Where have you been these past few weeks?'*

STRENGTH

Give me strength! I need help and courage to bear what is going on: used when the speaker is annoyed or impatient: > *'You stupid boy! Can't you even tell me what twelve twelves are? Give me strength!'* Short for *God, give me strength.*

STRIKE

Strike me pink! *Old-fashioned* An expression of surprise, disbelief, etc.: > *'Strike me pink! So Andrew's finally passed his exam after all those attempts!'* Also **Strike a light!; Strike me dead!**

STUFF

1 Get stuffed! *Slang* A rude expression of strong contempt, used to show that the speaker disapproves of something or does not want to do something: > *'Can I borrow your pen again?' 'Get stuffed! You borrow my pens, pencils, rubbers, and dictionaries, and you never give any of them back to me!'* Also **Stuff it!; Stuff you!:** > *'I got up at six o'clock, travelled for three hours to get here, and now you tell me I needn't have come! Stuff you! Don't think I'm coming next week!'*

2 Stuff and nonsense! *Old-fashioned* That's stupid, foolish, untrue, etc.!: > *'They say he's the best wrestler in the area!' 'Stuff and nonsense! Our Harold could beat him any day!'* The stress falls on *nonsense.*

3 That's the stuff *Old-fashioned* That's the way to do it!; you're doing the right thing!: > *'That's the stuff! Some more good hits like that and we'll beat them hollow!'* The stress falls on *that's.* Also **Great stuff!**

SUBJECT

Change the subject To talk about a new topic, in order to avoid discussing something embarrassing: > *'Talking of school, Jenny, you never did tell us how you did in your history test.' 'Er, well let's change the subject! It's a nice day, isn't it?'*

SUBLIME

From the sublime to the ridiculous From something very good, or noble, to something of much poorer quality or silly: used when contrasting two very different things: > *'You had a Rolls-Royce, and now you've bought that old crock – that's going from the sublime to the ridiculous!'* > *'A talk on the merits of various educational methods, followed by two hours of rock music – that's going from the sublime to the ridiculous!'*

SUCH

1 Such as Used to introduce an example: > *Students are advised to buy good standard reference books such as a concise dictionary, thesaurus, and a compact encyclopedia.*

2 Such as it is (or **they are**) Used when the speaker does not think that the quality of something is very good: > *'You're welcome to use our caravan, such as it is.'*

SUCK

Yah boo sucks to you! *Becoming old-fashioned* An expression of defiance, disgust, or ridicule: > *'I told Auntie you didn't like the colour of my dress, but she said it was the nicest she'd ever seen, so yah boo sucks to you!'* Also shortened to *Sucks (to you)!*

SUFFICE

Suffice it to say I will just say: > *'Suffice it to say, she discovered she was pregnant, but had the baby and all is now well.'*

SUIT

Suit yourself! Do what you like; it doesn't matter to me: sometimes said in a rude tone: > *'Suit yourself – if you want to hang the picture upside-down, I don't mind!'* > *'Shall I have another cake, then?' 'Suit yourself!'*

SUM

To sum up To state the main points of an argument at the end of a talk, essay, etc.; to summarise: > *To sum up, there would be considerable savings to the company if Smith's computer system were installed.*

SUPPOSE

1 I don't suppose A polite way of making a request: used when the speaker hopes for a positive answer: > *'I don't suppose you could drive us into town, could you? We've got some shopping to do.' 'Yes, I think I could.'* > *'I don't suppose you could lend me £5?'*

2 I suppose

a A polite way of enquiring about something: > *'I suppose you'll not be staying to dinner, then, if you've got to be back soon?'*

b Used to make an opinion, statement, etc., sound less strong: > *'Being ill is just one of those things you have to put up with, I suppose.'*

3 I suppose so Used to express reluctant agreement: > *'We ought to be going now.' 'Yes, I suppose so.'*

4 Suppose we Used to make a suggestion: > *'Suppose we had enough money to buy a car, could we afford to run it?'*

SURE

1 (And) that's for sure That is certain: > *'He won't live much longer, and that's for sure.'*

2 As sure as ... Used to add strength to a statement: > *'As sure as I'm standing here talking to you, I tell you I did see a flying-saucer last night!'*

3 I don't know, I'm sure *see* **Know 13.**

4 I'm not (so) sure A way of expressing doubt or disagreement in a hesitant way: > *'I'm not so sure you've got your facts right there.'* > *'I thought that film was great!' 'I'm not so sure – parts of it were OK, I suppose.'* > *'Do you*

understand what I've said?' 'I'm not sure I do.'*

5 ... I'm sure

a I am certain (of something): > *'I shut the door, I'm sure.'* > *'It'll rain soon, I'm sure.'*

b *Humorous* I am sure it was not (as described): > *'We then had a lecture on his approach to socio-linguistics!' 'Fascinating, I'm sure!'*

6 I'm sure ... I am certain (of something): > *'I'm sure I shut the door.'* > *'I'm sure she'll be here any minute now.'*

7 Sure do! *see* **Do 16.**

8 Sure enough As was expected: > *'She said she'd come at ten o'clock, and sure enough, she arrived on time.'* Also **Right enough.**

9 Sure thing! *see* **Thing 13.**

10 To be sure

a Certainly it must be acknow-ledged that; > *'It's not the most beautiful car in the world, to be sure, but it's very economical, you know'*

b *Irish or old-fashioned* An expression of surprise or delight: > *'And there he was, to be sure!'* > *'It's Aunt Freda after all, to be sure!'*

SURPRISE

Surprise, surprise!

a This is a surprise: > *'Surprise, surprise! It's me! I'm back!'* > *'Close your eyes for a moment ... Now open them! Surprise, surprise! It's a present for you!'*

b An expression used when fears of something poor or disappointing are confirmed: > *'When we set up a stall in our local market to sell my wife's pottery, we didn't think we'd* *do very well and – surprise, surprise! – we didn't sell a thing!'*

SWEAT

No sweat It will be done easily; it will be no problem: > *'Will you fix my television by tonight?' 'Yes, no sweat – you can pick it up any time after three!'* > *'Build that house for you in two months ?' 'No sweat, man!'*

SWEET

Sweet enough already Used in a reply when not having sugar in coffee or tea, as a play on words to refer to one's pleasant and kind nature: > *'Do you take sugar in coffee?' 'No thanks, I'm sweet enough already.'*

SWING

Swings and roundabouts A saying that there are disadvantages, if one thing is done, that are equal to the advantages gained, if another is done. Also **What you lose on the swings you gain on the roundabouts.**

SYSTEM

All systems go! Everything is ready to start; you can start now: > *'The royal couple have just arrived – so it's all systems go for the celebrations!'* Used originally in the launching of space vehicles, when everything was ready for take-off.

TABLET

Keep taking the tablets! An expression used in response to someone's supposedly mad or crazy action: > *'I've just walked on the headmaster's ceiling!' 'Don't worry, Martha, just keep taking the tablets!'*

TAKE

1 **... I take it** *Formal* Am I right in thinking ... : used especially when the speaker assumes that someone is a particular person: > *'Mr Jones, I take it?' 'Yes.' 'Then come this way, please, sir.'* > *'May I take it that you'll be staying to dinner?'*

2 **It takes one to know one** You are as bad as the person you are complaining about: > *'Perry really is a fool.' 'It takes one to know one.'* Probably from the proverb *It takes a thief to catch a thief.*

3 **Point taken** *see* **Point 5.**

4 **Take a running jump!** *see* **Jump 3.**

5 **Take care!** *see* **Care 8.**

6 **Take it away!** An instruction to start playing or singing music: > *'From the thirteenth bar, take it away!'* > *'Take it away, Sam!'*

7 **Take it easy!**
   a There is no need to worry!: > *'Take it easy, Mary – Ruth is only a little late. I'm sure nothing's happened to her.'*

b Don't rush!; don't get excited!:
> *'Take it easy, Mark – the taxi won't be here for half an hour yet – there's no need to panic!'*

8 Take it or leave it It does not matter whether you accept something; it is only available on these terms: > *'I'll give you £100 for that desk!' 'No! £200 is the price. Take it or leave it – I'm not bargaining with you!'*

9 Take that! An expression said at the same time as hitting someone: > *'Take that, you stupid boy! Will you never learn to respect your elders?'*

10 Take that grin (or smile) off your face see **Grin 2.**

11 Take your (my, etc.) name in vain see **Name 4.**

12 We can't take you anywhere! see **Anywhere 2.**

13 (You can) take it from me You can believe me when I say this: > *'You can take it from me; they're up to no good, I tell you – I've met their sort before!'* Also **(You can) take my word (for it)**: > *'Take my word for it, if he says he'll do something, then he won't break his promise.'*

TALE

Thereby hangs a tale There is an interesting or unusual story connected with what has just been talked about: often only to suggest something further without actually saying anything more: > *'When they built the new library in less than three months, not everyone was happy about the building methods they used, and thereby hangs a tale.'*

TALK

1 It's easy for you to talk see **Easy 4.**

2 Now you're talking At last what you're suggesting appeals to me: > *'How much will you sell that car to me for?' '£600?' 'No!' '£500?' 'No!' '£250?' 'Now you're talking – it's a deal!'*

3 Talk about This is a very good (or bad) example of something: > *'Talk about a wonderful holiday! All our money was stolen!'* > *'Talk about pride – he's the most big-headed man I've ever met!'*

4 Talk of the devil! see **Devil 6.**

5 Talking of see **Speak 5.**

6 You can talk
a You are much more comfortably off than I am, not having to do the particular thing yourself: > *'I'm going to stay in bed late tomorrow.' 'You can talk – I've got to be up at six to go to work.'* The stress falls on *you*.
b You yourself are as guilty in the very matter you are complaining about in someone else: > *'Johnny's eaten all the cakes, Mummy.' 'You can talk, Peter – you've eaten all the bread and butter!'* The stress falls on *you*. Also **Look who's talking!; You can't talk!**

TASTE

There's no accounting for tastes A saying that people all have different likes and dislikes; often said by a speaker who disapproves of what has just been mentioned: > *'I've just bought their latest record.' 'Well, there's no accounting for tastes!'*

TEACH

That (or I) will teach you to (do something) That (or I) will make you regret doing something, so that you will not do it again: > *'So you were sick after eating all that chocolate – that'll teach you to spend all your pocket money on sweets!'* > *'I'll teach you to interfere in my business – you can pay me back for those useless machines you made me buy.'*

TEAR

That's torn it! That has spoiled our plans, etc.!; that has dashed our hopes!: > *'It's raining! That's torn it! We were hoping for good weather for the fête!'* > *'That's really torn it now! We'll never beat the other side now they know our secret!'*

TELL

1 **As far as I can tell** According to the information that I have, though I may not have all the facts: > *'As far as I can tell, they seem happily married.'*

2 **Do tell** Tell me about it: used to show interest and some surprise at what has just been said: > *'Have you heard about Ralph and Pauline?' 'No do tell!'* The stress falls on *do*.

3 **Don't tell me!** An expression of disbelief, surprise, etc.: > *'Don't tell me you've heard the news already! Yes, Marcia's expecting a baby!'* > *'Don't tell me you can't make the party after all the preparations we've made?' 'No, I'm sorry, but I'm busy tonight – I've got to work late!'* The stress falls on *don't*.

4 **I can tell you** Used to emphasise a statement: > *'It's boiling hot outside, I can tell you!'* The stress falls on *tell*.

5 **I can't tell you …** I'm overwhelmed by (something, usually something pleasant): > *'I can't tell you what it means to have company; I get so lonely here all by myself, you see.'* The stress falls on tell.

6 **I tell you** Used to add force to a statement: > *'I tell you I really did see a flying-saucer last night!'* The stress falls on *tell*.

7 **(I) tell you what** *see* **Know 18.**

8 **I told you so** I warned you that this would happen, you didn't listen, and now you see that I was right: > *'Jack's gone and broken a window!' 'There you are – I told you so – I said we shouldn't let him play near the greenhouse.'* > *'Daddy, my teddy bear won't squeak any more!' 'I told you so – you shouldn't keep on hitting him!'* The stress falls on *told*.

9 **I'll tell you what** *see* **Know 18.**

10 **I'm not telling!** I won't answer your question: > *'Where were you last night?' 'I'm not telling!'* Also **I'm not saying!**

11 **I'm telling you** Used to strengthen a previous statement that the speaker has made and that the other person is unsure of: > *'They needn't pay us any money if we're made redundant, you know' 'But surely we'd get something?' 'No, I'm telling you – we could be unemployed and get no money at all – there's no way round it.'*

12 **Something tells me** *see* **Something 3.**

13 Tell it like it is Just give us the straight facts in an honest way: > *'Tell it like it is, Dick, we want to hear it all, however bad it is.'*

14 Tell it to the marines! *see* **Marine.**

15 Tell me another! *Rather old-fashioned* I simply can't believe you: > *'Did you know that Jim's just got engaged to Sarah?' 'What? Tell me another! I thought he was going out with Judy last week!'*

16 That would be telling I am not telling you; used when the speaker wants to keep something secret: > *'Who were you with last night?' 'Ah! That would be telling!'* The stress falls on *telling.*

17 There's no telling *see* **Know 26.**

18 To tell (you) the truth *see* **Truth 2.**

19 What did I tell you! *see* **Say 40.**

20 You can't tell him (her, etc.) anything
a He (she, etc.) can't keep a secret: > *'You can't tell him anything. The moment he hears some bit of gossip, it's all round the town!'*
b He (she, etc.) knows everything: > *'You can't tell her anything! She's been to college and thinks she knows it all!'*

21 You never can tell *see* **Know 34.**

22 You tell 'em An expression used to encourage someone in what they are saying: > *'You tell 'em, Barnie!' the man shouted out to the speaker at the election meeting.* The stress falls on *tell.*

23 You tell me I don't know; I've no idea: > *'How can we possibly get through this week with just this amount of money?' 'You tell me.'*

The stress falls on *you* and *me.*

24 You're telling me! I know what you're saying very well already: > *'It's raining outside.' 'You're telling me – I've been out to get the paper and I'm absolutely soaked!'* > *'I don't think I've done this very well, have I?' 'You're telling me you've not – It's awful!'* The stress falls on *me.*

TEMPER

Temper, temper! There's no need to get so angry!: used mainly to children; but usually having the effect of making matters worse: *Sarah was slowly getting more and more annoyed. 'Temper, temper, Sarah!' Patrick called out, but she flew more into a rage.*

TEST

1 Just testing A reply to an answer given that corrects an error in the speaker's original statement or behaviour: often used humorously in an attempt to hide the speaker's ignorance or stupidity: > *'The Battle of Hastings was 1166, wasn't it?' 'No, 1066.' 'Oh, yes, just testing!'*

2 Testing, testing An expression used in testing a microphone or other broadcasting equipment: > *'Testing, testing, one, two, three; can you hear me at the back there?'*

THANK

1 I thank you ... *Formal* Please (do something): > *'I thank you not to walk on the grass.'*

2 I'll thank you to ... Used to strengthen a command, request, etc., implying criticism: > *'I'll* *thank you to mind your own business!'* > *'I'll thank you to shut the door behind you!'*

3 Thank God! Also **Thank heavens!**
a An expression of gratitude to God: > *'Thank God for life, and breath, and everything!'*
b An expression of gratitude: used especially to show delight or relief after some trouble has passed: > *'Thank God you're back – we were getting worried about you!'* > *'Thank heavens the weather stayed fine!'* > *'Thank God it's Friday!'* Also **Thank goodness!**

4 Thank you Also (*stronger*) **Thank you very much.**
a A polite expression of gratitude when accepting a present or service, or acknowledging praise: > *'Thank you for the flowers – they were lovely!'* > *'Thank you for coming!'* *'Don't mention it; thanks for having us!'* Also **Many thanks; Thanking you.**
b A polite way of accepting or refusing an offer: > *'Would you like some more tea?' 'No, thank you!'* > *'Can I get your coat?' 'Thank you – it's lucky I brought one as it's so cold!'*
c Used as a polite expression at the end of an announcement: > *'Please make sure you have all your belongings with you when you leave the train. Thank you.'*
d Used to stop something or to ask someone to leave: > *Patrick was playing the piano in the music competition. 'Thank you!' the judge called out, 'I've heard enough now!'* > *'Thank you, Bertram, that will be all! You may go now!'*
e Used after a statement to show delight, pleasure, or criticism: > *'Last year our sales of maps did very nicely, thank you very much.'* > *'Our football team is doing very well this season, thank you very much!'* > *'Leave my private life alone, thank you!'*
f Used to show displeasure at something: > *'I'll have my meal now and you can wait for yours!' 'Thank you, pal!'*

5 Thank you for nothing *see* **Nothing 7.**

6 Thank your lucky stars! *see* **Star.**

7 Thanks (or **thank you**) **for having me** (**us**, etc.) Thank you for your hospitality: said as you say goodbye to someone: > *'Thanks for having us, Jo – we've had a lovely time!' 'That's OK – see you again sometime!'*

8 Thanks to Because of: > *Thanks to all the hard work put in by the staff and pupils, the school play was a great success.* Note that *No thanks to* is used when someone did not help even when he or she could have done; in spite of: > *'It was no thanks to social workers that poor old Geraldine managed a fair living, after being left with three young children when Ross died. It was sheer hard work.'*
> *'We managed to get to London eventually.' 'Yes, but with no thanks to you. You weren't in the least concerned when you heard the car had had a puncture.'*

THAT

1 **Be that as it may** *see* **Be 3.**
2 **How's that?** *see* **How 15.**
3 **How's that for ...** *see* **How 16.**
4 **Is that so?** *see* **So 3.**

5 It is (or was) that Used to confirm and strengthen something that someone else has just said: > *'It's cold out, isn't it?' 'It is that!'* Also **That it is (or was)**: > *'It was a bright, crisp winter last year, wasn't it?' 'Yes, that it was!'*

6 That ...! *Formal* or *literary* Used in exclamations to express a wish: > *'That things should have come to this!'* > *'Oh, that I could be near my beloved!'*

7 That does it! *see* **Do 17.**

8 That is (to say) *see* **Say 34.**

9 That will do *see* **Do 18.**

10 That's a ... *see* **There 9.**

11 That's about it That is more or less everything: > *'Well that's about it for tonight, folks. We'll see you same channel, same time, next week!'*

12 That's all
a No more need be said or done; there is no alternative: > *'If we've not got any money, we won't be able to afford a holiday, that's all.'* Also **That's all there is to it**: > *'I saw you taking the money from the drawer. You can't say you didn't, because I caught you in the act, and that's all there is to it!'*
b Only: used at the end of a sentence for emphasis: > *'Can't we have a new car?' 'Sorry, but there just isn't the money!' 'I was just thinking, that's all.'*

13 That's as maybe! It is not yet definite that it is true: > *'When I'm at college next year ...!' 'That's as maybe, my girl! You've not passed your exams yet!'*

14 That's done it *see* **Do 19.**

15 That's ... for you *see* **There 10.**

16 That's how it is This is the position; these are the facts: said after an explanation: > *'My job's in Birmingham, and I have to travel up there every day – – that's how it is at the moment.'*

17 That's it
a That is the real problem: > *'That is – I just don't seem to have enough time these days to do all I want to do!'* The stress falls on *it*.
b That is the end; it is finished: > *'That's it – it's all over, and a remarkable victory for England in this competition at last!'* > *'That's tomorrow's weather forecast. And that's it from me until later.'*
c That is the right way to do it: used to show approval or encouragement: > *'That's it! Now keep on like that and you won't lose your balance!'* Sometimes also used to mean the opposite: > *'That's it! Go on – show us up in front of all our friends – that's typical of you!'* The stress falls on *that's*.
d Used to express annoyance at something: > *'That's it! I'm fed up with you children breaking things! You can go straight to bed!'*
e Used to express disappointment: > *'Well, that's it, then! If we're beaten as badly as that in every match this season, we'll never get promoted in the league!'* The stress falls on *it*.
f That is what is wanted: > *'Yes, that's it – a little screwdriver – Just what I need for my jobs around the house!'*
g What you say is right: > *'You mean he stole all that money?' 'Yes, that's it!'*

18 That's more like it! *see* **Like 6.**

19 That's that

a That is the end of the matter: said at the end of a statement; and often implying regret at a state of affairs: > *'Harry, you're not going to play football, and that's that!'* > *'The post has just gone!' 'Oh well, that's that, then – this letter will never get there in time!'*

b That is the end of the discussion: > *'Well, that's that for this week. We'll be back next Monday with another edition of World Vision.'*

c That is the end: said at the end of doing some work: > *'Phew! That's that! I'm glad I've finished that essay at last!'*

20 That's what it is (or **was**) That is (or was) the reason or explanation: > *'That cab driver didn't look very happy!' 'You drove straight out in front of him at the last set of traffic lights, that's what it was.'*

21 You do that *see* **Do 29.**

THERE

1 So there! Note what I'm saying or what has happened: said in a defiant tone: > *'You can stop boasting – I've beaten you now, so there!'*

2 There again Used to introduce a further explanation or reason: > *'How could I get to Basingstoke?' 'Well, you could drive down, or, there again, you could come by train and I'll meet you at the station.'*

3 There are ... and ... There are good and bad kinds of (things): > *'There are cars and cars.'*

4 There it is This is the problem; this is the state of affairs: > *'There it is, I'm afraid, the firm's run out of money, so we've got no choice but to make some of the workers redundant.'*

5 There, there! An expression of comfort or sympathy, as to a child: > *'There, there, dear! Don't worry!'* Also **There now!**

6 There you are

a An expression used when giving something to someone; this is what you wanted: > *'There you are, sir, your shoes, mended as you asked.'*

b An expression of triumph: used when one's opinion has been shown to be correct: > *'There you are – I said we'd win first prize this year!' she called out, smiling excitedly.* > *'Well, there you are, then! I knew all along he'd refuse.'*

c An expression used when finishing a presentation: > *'I hope you like my choice of records on this week's programme. There you are – and now, till next Tuesday, goodbye.'*

d An expression used at the end of an explanation: > *'Turn right at the traffic lights, then second left, and there you are, the library will be opposite you.'*

e An expression used to make clear that something cannot be changed: > *'That roof will have to be repaired within a month or two, I'm afraid – but there you are, you asked me what was wrong.'* Also **There we are.**

7 There you go again *see* **Go 22.**

8 There's ... Used in making a

suggestion: > *'Who could we ask to be chairman next year?' 'Well, there's Mr Smith for a start – he's shown signs of interest.'* The phrase *There's always ...* is used to introduce a suggestion that is a last resort but is known to be reliable: > *'Where else could we go?' 'There's always London – I'd quite like to go round some of the museums again.'*

9 **There's a ...** An expression of praise or encouragement to (a person or animal): > *'You eat all your cabbage now, there's a good boy!'* > *'Fetch it, there's a good dog!'* Also **That's a ...**: > *'Could you pass me that book, that's a good chap!'* > *'Now that's a good girl! Don't pull your sister's hair!'*

10 **There's** (or **that's**) **... for you** An expression used to emphasise (a particular quality): used to show enthusiasm, but also sometimes annoyance or resignation: > *'I arrived at the hotel, and a porter took my cases upstairs, someone ran my bath, and dinner was brought to my room – now, there's service for you!'* > *'That's gratitude for you – I've been working hard all day, and she's not said a word of thanks the whole time!'*

THICK

Through thick and thin In the good times and the bad times; always, whatever happens: > *'I'll stick by you, Sandra, through thick and thin.'*

THIEF

Stop, thief! The cry of a person who has been robbed when chasing the thief: > *'Stop, thief! Stop, thief!' the manager shouted, running out of his shop and going after the men who had stolen the jewels.*

THING

1 **All things considered** Taking everything into account: > *All things considered, this book is a very fair historical survey of the country's legal system over the last forty years.*

2 **(And a) good thing too** *see* **Good 2.**

3 **First things first** Things must be done in order of the most important first: sometimes used as a reminder of something obvious: > *'You must go and finish off your work, before you can go out to play. First things first!'* > *'I'd like to build a new boat!' 'First things first – have you got the time and the money?'*

4 **For one thing** Here's a reason: used to introduce a reason or explanation: > *'Why can't I get a motorbike?' 'For one thing, you're too young, and for another, you're not sensible enough yet.'*

5 **How are things?** *see* **How 6.**

6 **How are things going?** *see* **Go 14.**

7 **It's a good thing** It is fortunate: > *'It's a good thing these walls are thick, or our neighbours might hear what we're saying!'*

8 **(Just) one of those things** Something that is liable to happen and cannot be avoided: used of unpleasant things: > *'Being made redundant is just one of those things these days, I suppose.'*

9 **Just the thing!** That is exactly what we wanted: > *'Here's a screwdriver!' 'Ah, just the thing!'*

10 **Kind** (or **sort**) **of thing** Used to make something sound less certain or definite: > *'How long did it go on, kind of thing?'* > *'It was a big car, sort of thing, a Cadillac, perhaps.'*

11 **Old thing** *Old-fashioned* A way of addressing someone in a friendly way: > *'I say, old thing, what a funny hat you're wearing today!'*

12 **Other** (or **all**) **things being equal** Used to describe a possible situation; if there are no special reasons to consider: > *'All things being equal, I prefer to travel by car.'*

13 **Sure (thing)!** Yes; of course: > *'Can you come round tonight?' 'Sure thing! I'll be with you at six!'* This phrase is American in origin.

14 **That's the thing** *see* **This 2c.**

15 **The thing is ...** The real, most important, point, or idea is ...: > *'The thing is, I love him.'* > *'He said they'd come, but his brother said they wouldn't – the thing is, who am I to believe?'*

16 **These things are sent to try us** Used as a response when several bad or unpleasant events happen to someone: > *'The lock on the front door got stuck, I heard Jim's been made redundant, and Sue's got to go into hospital – that was enough bad news for one day.' 'These things are sent to try us, I suppose.'*

THINK

1 **Good thinking!** What a good idea!: > *'Why don't we go to Milton Keynes to do our Christmas shopping?' 'Good thinking! They've one of the best shopping-centres in the country!'* > *'As she's not here, she could have gone home earlier.' 'That's good thinking – let's go and see!'* The phrase was made more popular by *Good thinking, Batman* in the *Batman* strip cartoons.

2 **I don't think** *Humorous* An expression of disbelief in what has just been said: used to contradict the previous statement, often to criticise a person or thing: > *'She's good-looking, I don't think!'* > *'I thought the film was great!' 'Great, I don't think!'* The stress falls on *don't*.

3 **I should have thought ...** Used to express surprise (at something): > *'Isn't he here yet? I should have thought he'd be on time for his own wedding!'*

4 **I should think ...** Of course: used to support a previous statement strongly: > *'He's very proud of his first book!' 'I should think so, the years it's taken for him to write it!'* > *'Hot – I should jolly well think it was – it was baking in there!'*

5 **I think** Used to make an opinion sound less strong: > *'It's usual, I think, to decide how big a dictionary should be before you start to write it.'* > *'She's wrong, I think.'* > *'I think I'll go and have a wash.'*

6 **I thought as much** It is just as I expected: often used about something bad: > *'I thought as much – you've been out with that boy down the road again, haven't*

you? I can see it on your face!' >
'Did you have difficulty finding our
house? I thought as much, since you
were so late.'

7 **I thought I told you ...** Used as a
criticism when someone has
failed (to do something): > '*I
thought I told you to shut the door
behind you!*' Also used with other
verbs: > '*I thought I asked you to
come early this week!*'

8 **If you think (he or she thinks,** etc.)
that, you've (he's, she's, etc.) **got
another think coming** If you (he
or she) think(s) like that, then
you're (he's, she's) very much
mistaken: used to express strong
disagreement or disapproval of a
suggestion, statement, etc., in an
angry way: > '*If he thinks I'm
going to work for that miserable
wage, he's got another think
coming.*' Sometimes shortened to
You've (he's, she's, etc.) **got
another think coming.**

9 **Let me think** *see* See 11.

10 **Not think for a moment** *see*
Moment 3.

11 **(Now I) come to think of it** *see*
Come 15.

12. **That's what you think** That is
your opinion, but you are
probably wrong: often said with
a tone of contempt: > '*When I
get my extra money back from the
tax people, I'm going to spend it on
a new dress!*' '*That's what you
think – I'm keeping it to pay for
the repairs to the car!*' The stress
falls on *you*.

13 **Think nothing of it!** *see* **Nothing 11.**

14 **To think ...** Just imagine; just
consider (this): > *To think that
the Queen stayed in my hotel!*

What an honour!' > '*To think I
once was a millionaire, and now
look at my rags!*' Also **Just to
think of it!**

15 **What do you think?** Used to
introduce something surprising;
> '*What do you think? I've been
promoted!*'

16 **Who do you (does he, she,** etc.)
think you are (he or she is, etc.)?
A response to someone who has
a high opinion of themselves: >
'*Just look at her, dressed like that!
Who does she think she is?*'
Originally from the catch
phrase *Who do you think you are
– Clark Gable?*

THIS

1 **This is how it is** This is the
position; these are the facts: said
before an explanation is given: >
'*This is how it is: we can lend you
the money, provided you pay it back
in two years.*'

2 **This is it**

a This is what you've been
waiting for: used when introducing or showing something: >
'*And now, ladies and gentlemen,
this is it, the most successful one-
man action show in the world – -the
Owen Opie show!*' > '*This is it, the
finest vase of its kind in the
country!*'

b This is the crucial point: >
'*Well, this is it, then Robby!*' '*Yes,
my love, it's time to say goodbye!*' >
'*Well, this is it! It's now or never!*' I
thought as I went into the interview
room.

c That is indeed the reason: used
as a reply when the speaker
agrees with the statement made

by the previous speaker: > *'We've not got enough money to buy a house.' 'This is it – they cost such a lot of money, don't they?'* Also **That's the thing.**

3 **What's all this?** *see* **What 20.**

THOUGHT

1 **A penny for your thoughts!** *see* **Penny 1.**

2 **Don't give something another thought** Used to tell someone not to worry when he or she has apologised to you: > *'I'm really sorry we're so late.' 'Don't give it another thought, I quite understand.'*

3 **It's the thought that counts** Someone's attitude and motives are kind and generous even if his or her actual actions do not seem very important; or when only something inexpensive and small has been given as a present: > *'I couldn't really afford much for Gail's present this year.' 'I wouldn't worry, it's the thought that counts.'*

4 **Perish the thought!** *Becoming old-fashioned* I very much hope this is not so: used about something unpleasant or undesirable: > *'Sally's not back yet. If something should have happened to her, and perish the thought, you'll be to blame for not looking after her properly, you know.'*

THOUSAND

I believe you, thousands wouldn't! *see* **Believe 5.**

THRILL

Big thrill! How exciting!: but usually used when the opposite is true: > *'What's the next lecture, then?' 'Dr Stephens speaking to us on butterflies!' 'Oh, big thrill!'*

THUMB

1 **Thumbs down!** An expression showing disapproval of something: > *'It's thumbs down for the cuts in fares on public transport, as it's against the law.'* The thumb is held out and pushed down slightly.

2 **Thumbs up!** An expression showing satisfaction, agreement, or victory: > *'Thumbs up! We've got the go-ahead to make another film!'* The thumb is held out and stuck up slightly. The phrases in **1** and **2** come from the practice in ancient Rome, when the crowd would decide whether a defeated gladiator would be killed, in which case they would point their thumbs down, or be allowed to live, in which case they would point their thumbs up.

3 **Twiddle your (my, etc.) thumbs** To do nothing; wait for something to happen: > *'What do you expect me to do all day – just sit around, twiddling my thumbs?'*

THUNDER

By thunder! *see* **Jove.**

TICK

Half (or just) a tick *see* **Just 3a.**

TICKET

That's (just) the ticket *see* **Job 4.**

TIMBER

Shiver me (or my) timbers! *Old-fashioned* Used to express great surprise: used in rather humorous contexts: > *'Shiver me timbers! It's Captain Cook!'* Originally, this phrase was used by sailors to mean 'shatter the sides of my ship!'

TIME

1 **All in good time!** It will happen at the right time: said implying that the speaker does not want to be rushed and the person being spoken to should be patient: > *'Can you give me back the money and the books I lent you?' Jo asked hurriedly. 'All in good time!' Geraldine replied calmly.*

2 **(And) about time, too!** An expression used when someone or something that has been delayed actually comes, happens, etc.: > *'Good – I can see the bus coming – and about time, too!'* > *'Here's Peter! About time, too! We've been waiting ages for you!'* > Also used after *it's*: > *'It's about time you started taking your studies more seriously, isn't it?'*

3 **Any time!** There is no need to say thank you; do what you have done any time: > *'Thanks for a lovely evening!' 'Any time! It was very nice to see you again and have a good chat!'*

4 **At the same time** Used with two things that are both true but which seem to contradict each other: > *'I enjoyed the play but at the same time I found it rather uncomfortable.'*

5 **How many more times do I have to tell you?** Used to express impatience or annoyance at someone not obeying the speaker's instructions: > *'How many more times do I have to tell you? Always put things back in the place where you found them.'*

6 **Long time no see** It's nice to see you again after such a long time: > *'Hello there! Long time no see!' 'Yes, it is a while, isn't it?'* A translation of the Chinese *háo jiù b_jiàn*.

7 **Not before time** Used to emphasise that something should have come or have been done earlier: > *The government are responding to the report on airport security, and not before time.*

8 **Once upon a time**
a Used as a traditional way of beginning a children's story: > *'Once upon a time, there were three bears ...'*
b Used to refer to something that existed or was true a long time ago: > *'Once upon a time you could have bought a house for £1,000.'*

9 **There's no time like the present** Do not delay doing something; do it now: > *Don't wait till later to sort out your personal finances. There's no time like the present.*

10 **Time's up!** There is no more time allowed: > *'Time's up! Put your pens down please and leave the examination hall quietly.'*

11 **Until the next time!** *see* **Meet 2.**

12 **What time do you call this?** An expression used to show annoyance when someone arrives very late: > *'What time do you call this, Liam? You said you'd be back by 10 o'clock.'*

TIP

It's on the tip of my tongue I can't exactly remember it at the moment, although I'm thinking hard: > *'His name's on the tip of my tongue – ah, yes, Pressworth, that was it.'* Also used when the speaker is about to say something: > *'The words are on the tip of my tongue, but I don't quite know how to put what I want to say.'*

TOFFEE

... can't ... for toffee (A person) just can't (do something) at all: > *'He can't dance for toffee!'*

TOGETHER

All together now! *see* **All 9.**

TOKEN

By the same token In the same way; used to bring further evidence to support a point of view: > *If the regime has acted unlawfully in plotting to assassinate the president, then by the same token the government has acted illegally in trying to overthrow the regime's general.*

TONGUE

1 **Has the cat got your tongue?** *see* **Cat 1.**
2 **It's on the tip of my tongue** *see* **Tip.**

TOOTH

1 **Fight tooth and nail** To make the strongest possible effort in a confrontation: > *'We'll fight tooth and nail to make sure the motorway is not built through the countryside.'*
2 **Hell's teeth!** *see* **Hell 2.**

TOP

1 **On top of that** Additionally; often used to introduce a further reason after having given one already: > *'The firm went bankrupt as it ran out of money, and on top of that, there were just no more orders for its goods.'* > *'He broke his leg, and on top of that, caught smallpox.'*
2 **The top of the morning (to you)!** *Irish* An expression used when greeting people in the morning.

TORN

That's torn it! *see* **Tear.**

TOUCH

Touch wood *see* **Wood 2.**

TRAP

Shut your trap! *see* **Shut.**

TRICK

1 **For my next trick ...** *Humorous* An expression used, followed by a pause, after the speaker has failed to do something, dropped something, or missed a catch, etc.: > *The box fell heavily to the ground. 'Oops! For my next trick ... I'll balance it on my head!'* (Originally from the language of the entertainer, to announce the next trick.
2 **How's tricks?** A greeting; how are you?: used between friends who have not seen each other for some time: > *'Hello, Bill! How's tricks? It's ages since we had a chat, isn't it?'*

TROUBLE

1 **A trouble shared is a trouble halved** A saying that talking about your worries with someone will make them seem smaller.

2 **Be looking for trouble** see **Look 1.**

TRUE

1 **It just isn't true** An expression used to emphasise and add strength to a statement: > *'I'm so happy, it just isn't true!'* > *'It just isn't true how much work I've got to do this weekend!'*

2 **Too true!** see **Right 10.**

TRULY

Yours truly see **Yours 3.**

TRUST

Trust you (him, her, etc.) **to ...** You have (he or she has, etc.) as expected managed to (do something): used with things that have turned out badly: > *'Trust you to open your big mouth and let out the secret!'* > *'Trust Sarah to go and lose the keys!'*

TRUTH

1 **If the truth be known** If the real facts about something were to be made clear: > *'If the truth be known, that was the real reason for his resignation.'*

2 **To tell (you) the truth**
   a An expression used to make an apology for not fulfilling the other person's expectations in some way: > *'What did you think of the book I lent you?' 'To tell the truth, I've not had a chance to look at it yet.'*

b Used to introduce a personal comment on something that has just been said: > *'Sue pretended that she knew Paris well, but to tell the truth, it was the first time she had been there.'*

c A way of expressing something negative, making the whole statement seem less strong: > *'To tell you the truth, I don't really go for your choice of wallpaper somehow.'*

TURN

1 **That's a turn-up for the book!** That's very surprising: > *'Well, Jim's here early for a change – that's a turn-up for the book!'*

2 **Whatever turns you on!** *Slang* I don't find this interesting in the least, even if you do: > *'I think that that new record by the* Louts *is fantastic!' 'Whatever turns you on!'*

TUT

Tut, Tut! An expression of disapproval or criticism: > *'Tut, tut, Perry! I'm surprised at your behaving like that! I'd have thought you'd have known better!'*

Twenty-one
Twenty-one today! *Humorous* A birthday greeting said to a woman who is obviously over twenty-one.

TWO

Two can play at that game see **Game 4.**

UNACCUSTOMED

Unaccustomed as I am to public speaking ... I am not experienced at speaking in public, but ... : often used at the start of a speech as a mild apology: > *'Unaccustomed as I am to public speaking,' the best man began, and the guests at the wedding all cheered, 'it gives me great pleasure as a close friend of the groom to be part of this happy event.'*

UNCLE

(And) Bob's your uncle *see* **Bob.**

UP

1 **Up with ...!** A slogan used to show the speaker's approval of something or someone: > *'Up with the revolution!'* > *'Up with the workers!'*

2 **Up with you!** Get up!: > *'Up with you!' Mum shouted, as she pulled back the sheets, 'school begins in half an hour and you're not yet out of bed!'*

3 **Up yours!** *Slang* A rude expression used as a reply to express contempt, disagreement, or refusal and showing a disregard of the other person: > *'The car-park attendant told Andrew, 'You can't park here!' but he called back, 'Up yours!' and drove in.*

4 **What's up!** *see* **What 21.**

USE

Use your loaf! *see* **Loaf.**

USUAL

The (or my) usual A request for the drink, food, etc., that the speaker usually has: > *'The usual please, love.' 'Right, beans and chips coming up!'*

VIEW

In view of Taking into consideration: > *In view of the slight risk of infection, we advise against having contact with other people for a week.*

WAIT

1 I can hardly wait Used to show that the speaker is not really looking forward to something: used as a reply: > *'Mother's coming down from Glasgow next week to stay with us.' 'I can hardly wait!'*

2 I can't wait Used to show impatience and excitement in looking forward to something: > *'I can't wait to see her face when she opens her present!'* > *'I can't wait for the holidays to come!'*

3 (Just) you wait Used as a threat of punishment: > *'Just you wait – I'll get you back for this!'* > *'Just you wait till your father comes home!'*

4 Wait a minute (or **moment**)
a I shall not keep you waiting for a long time: > *'Wait a minute, while I just find your record card.'* > *'Wait a moment and I'll ask someone for you.'*
b I wish to make a comment or objection: > *'Wait a minute! Didn't we try that plan a few months ago and found it didn't work?'* > *'Wait a moment! I've got an idea!'* Also **Wait a second.**
c An expression of surprise or amazement: > *'Wait a moment! Haven't we met before? Ah yes, didn't we meet at that training camp in Hampshire?'* Also **Wait a second.**

5 Wait for it!
a Don't move, speak, etc., before the proper moment: > *'Right, class, go when I blow the whistle, wait for it ... now, go!'*
b Used to introduce something exciting: > *'He may be about to get the highest score in the whole history of the game – wait for it – yes, McDonald's done it!'*

6 Wait for me! Don't go so fast or go away so that I'm left behind!: > *'Wait for me everyone! I'm just coming!'*

7 What are you waiting for? Used to tell someone to hurry up or to do something immediately: > *'Well, what are you waiting for? Are you going to ask me out or not? Get on with it.'*

WAKEY

Wakey, wakey! *Often humorous* Wake up!: > *I was sound asleep in bed when suddenly my dreams were shattered by mother crying out, 'Wakey, wakey, Peter!'* The phrase was made more current by the radio and television programme, *Billy Cotton's Band Show*, first broadcast in 1949.

WANT

1 He (she, etc.) didn't want to know He (she, etc.) took no interest or notice in what was being said or happening: > *'There I was talking to her, but she just looked at me blankly – she didn't want to know.'* > *'The crowds just walked past the injured man – they just didn't want to know.'*

2 If you want Used as a response to a suggestion, sometimes showing slight unwillingness: > *'Let's go to the cinema, shall we?' 'If you want.'*

3 You want to ... Also **You ought to ... ; You should ...**
a A wish that the person the speaker is talking to would (do something): used to describe something that is special or unusual in some way: > *'You want to see the way she plays tennis!'* > *'He might think he's got a very good mark, but you ought to wait till you hear mine!'*
b A wish that the person the speaker is talking to would (do something): used as a warning or criticism: > *'You want to look where you're going, young man!'* > *'You should be more careful!'*

WART
Warts and all *see* **All 11a.**

WATCH
1 Watch it! Be careful!: > *'Watch it! The bottom of that box looks as if it might fall out!'* > *'You'd better watch it! Unless your marks improve, you'll be moved down a class!'*
2 Watch out! Be careful!: used as a warning: > *'Watch out! There's a car coming!'* > *'Watch out! There's a thief about!'*
3 Watch your step! *see* **Step 1.**

WAY
1 (Be) on your way! Go!: > *'On your way!'* the teacher shouted angrily to the boys playing around after school had finished.
2 By the way Used to introduce a new subject or something that the speaker had just thought of into a conversation: > *'By the way, how did you get on at the doctor's?'* > *'By the way, when you saw Ruth, did she say anything about coming round?'* The stress falls on *way.*
3 No way No; under no circumstances; what you're suggesting is impossible: > *'Will you lend me £50?' 'No way – you didn't pay me back the last time I lent you some, so I'm not giving you any more now!'* This phrase is American in origin.
4 Step this way *Formal* Please come this way; follow me: > *'Step this way, ladies and gentlemen, to see the world's biggest man-eating spider!'*
5 That's the way it goes *see* **Cookie.**
6 That's the way the cookie crumbles *see* **Cookie.**
7 There's (or there are) no two ways about it There is no alternative; it is definite; there is no other opinion: > *'There's no two ways about it – I'm afraid we shall have to follow the rules.'* > *'There are no two ways about it – as manager of our export section, you've been a dismal failure, and we must ask you to leave.'*
8 Way out *Slang* Very unusual, because it is very modern or even ahead of its time: > *'Wow! That dress is a bit way out, isn't it?'*
9 You can't have it both ways You cannot have the good points from both of two possible choices: > *'You've got to choose between staying in and getting your homework finished in time, or going out and enjoying yourself. You can't have it both ways.'*

WEATHER
1 Lovely (or nice) weather for ducks! *Humorous* Aren't we having rainy

weather at the moment!: > *Geoff passed Jill in the street. 'Lovely weather for ducks!' he called out from under his umbrella.*

2 **Under the weather** Not very well or not very happy: > *Robert was feeling a bit under the weather as he'd not had much sleep for several nights.*

WEAVE

Get weaving! *see* **Crack.**

WEEK

Any day of the week *see* **Day 1.**

WEIGHT

Worth its (his, her, etc.**) weight in gold** Very valuable: > *'He's worth his weight in gold – I don't know anyone who's more reliable.'*

WELCOME

You're welcome! *American* There is no need to thank me: > *'Thanks for your help!' 'You're welcome!'*

WELL

1 **(All) well and good** Used to express detached acceptance of a suggestion or decision: > *'If he offers me some more work, all well and good, if not I don't mind too much.'* > *'If you refuse to take my advice, well and good, but don't come crying to me in six months, saying it didn't work out.'* Also used to show dissatisfaction at the subject being discussed: > *'It's all well and good for you to just sit there and expect me to keep the house clean, when I've got my own job to do and I look after the children as well.'*

2 **I (he, she,** etc.**) may (might) as well** Used to show a slight unwillingness to do something: > *'We might as well buy the book. It's very cheap and I shouldn't think it's in the library.'* > *'I might as well not have cooked dinner for all the thanks you lot have shown.'*

3 **It's all very well** An expression showing discontent, dissatisfaction, or sometimes envy, at a reply or at someone's advice: > *'Why don't you work it out the way I've just shown you?' 'It's all very well for you to make suggestions, you don't have to sit down and do it!'* Also **It's all right:** > *'When do you go back to work?' 'Next week.' 'It's all right for some, isn't it – I'm going back tomorrow!'* Also used with a noun as subject: > *'These clothes are all very well for wearing in the summer, but they're not heavy or warm enough for the winter.'*

4 **Just as well** An expression used as a reply to show that something, such as an event or circumstance, was indeed fortunate: > *'We were too late for the concert!' 'Just as well – it wasn't very good anyway.'* > *'It's just as well you came – we needed someone with your experience.'*

5 **Oh well** Used to show a resigned acceptance of something bad: > *'Oh well, I shouldn't grumble, I suppose, this is the first time something like this has happened.'* > *'Oh well, it can't be helped.'*

6 **Very well** An expression showing acceptance of or agreement to something that has just been said, but often showing unwillingness also: > *'Please be*

*home early tonight – I want to wash
your hair.' 'Very well, mother!'* >
'I'm not sure I really want to take
your advice.' *Very well, then, if
you don't want to, I don't mind, but
don't say I didn't warn you!'*

7 **Well done!** *see* **Do 20.**

8 **Well I never did!** *see* **Do 21.**

9 **Well then** An expression showing
expectation of something: >
'Well then, what's your answer?' >
'Well then, what do we do now?'

10 **Well, well** An expression of
surprise: > *'Well, well, who'd
have thought those two would end
up getting married?'* Also **Well,
well, well.**

WELL-OFF

You don't know when you're well-
off *see* **Know 29.**

WHAT

1 **And I don't know what** *see* **Know 1.**

2 **And what's more** *see* **More 1.**

3 **For what it's worth** *see* **Worth.**

4 **I know what** *see* **Know 18.**

5 **Or what** Used when the speaker
is unsure of what is said: often
used when there are a number of
alternatives and there may be
more: > *'I've not seen her recently –
I don't know whether she's moved
away, whether I've upset her, or
what.'* Also **Or whatever.**

6 **So what?** What importance or
relevance does that have?: used
to show a lack of interest and
often said in an impolite,
unfriendly way: > *'I'm going to
New York on business next week.'
'So what – we've still got to stay
here and work all the same!'* > *'He*

*can have his suspicions if he wants –
so what? We don't care!'* Also (*more
formal*) What of (or about) it?

7 **That's what it is** *see* **That 20.**

8 **Well, what do you know (about
that)!** *see* **Know 27.**

9 **What ...!** Used to introduce an
exclamation: > *'What a fool I've
been!'* > *'What awful weather we're
having at the moment!'* > *'What
lovely flowers!'*

10 **What about...?** *see* **About 1.**

11 **What about that?** *see* **About 2.**

12 **What can I do for you?** *see* **Help 1.**

13 **What do you do (for a living)?** *see*
Do 23.

14 **What ho!** *Old-fashioned* An
expression of greeting or used
to attract attention: > *'What ho,
old chap!'*

15 **What if...?** What would or will
happen if (something were to
happen): > *'What if we bought a
new carpet – would it make any
difference to the room?'* > *'What if
the President were shot?'*

16 **What is it?** What do you want?:
> *'Herby, are you in there?' 'What
is it? I'm busy!'* Note also **What is
it now?** Why are you bothering
me again?: > *'Herby, are you still
there?' 'What is it now? You've
seen me once already today!'* The
stress falls on *now.*

17 **What is it to you?** Why are you
interested in this?: > *'How old
are you?' 'Why do you want to
know? What is it to you?'*

18 **What next?** What further
surprising or cheeky thing will
come now?. > *'What next? You'll
be asking us to pay you to take
these books away, instead of you
paying us!'*

19 **What with** Used to introduce a number of reasons for something, usually something bad: > *'What with one thing and another, over the last few weeks, I've not got round to ringing her up, I'm afraid.'* > *'We've had awful weather this year, what with all the snow and heavy frosts.'*

20 **What's all this?** What's going on?; what's the matter?: > *'What's all this, boys? Why aren't you paying attention and listening?'*

21 **What's up?** What is happening?; what's the matter?: > *'What's up? What's everyone looking at?'* > *'What's up with Rachel today?'* > *'What's up, Rolf? You look as if you've seen a ghost!'*

22 **What's yours?** What would you like to drink?: > *'What's yours, Nick?' 'Gin and tonic, please.'*

23 **You know what?** *see* **Know 31.**

24 **You know what you can do with ...** *see* **Know 33.**

25 **You what?** *Slang*
a Please repeat what you said as I didn't hear it properly: > *'The postman's at the door.' 'You what?' 'I said the postman's come.'*
b An expression of dismay, surprise, etc.: > *'You remember you still owe me £500?' 'You what! I paid that back to you, didn't I?'*

WHATEVER

Or whatever *see* **What 5.**

WHEN

Say when *see* **Say 32.**

WHERE

1 **Where do we go from here?** *see* **Go 23.**

2 **Where was I?** Used as a question to oneself when the speaker has forgotten what point in an argument he or she was thinking of: > *'Let me see now, where was I?'*

3 **Where were we?** What were we talking about before our thoughts were interrupted?: > *'Where were we? Oh yes, we were discussing the arrangements for the party next month.'*

WHO

1 **And I don't know who** *see* **Know 1.**

2 **Who goes there?** *see* **Go 24.**

3 **Who is it?** *see* **It 6.**

4 **Who's ... when he's (she's,** etc. **) at home?** *see* **Home 4.**

WHOLE

On the whole Generally speaking: taking everything into consideration: > *'On the whole, I'm inclined to agree with you, but we do see things differently in one or two places.'* > *'Britain is still an industrialised country on the whole.'* Also **By and large.**

WHY

Why not ...? Used to introduce a suggestion: > *'Why not take a chance on it?'* > *'Why not ask him for yourself?'*

WIFE

The wife *see* **Missis.**

WILL

1 **God willing** *see* **God 13.**

2 **Have ..., will ...** *see* **Have 2.**

3 **If you will** *Formal* If you want to

describe someone or something in this way: > *'Permit me to make a few comments about my spiritual life, my inner life, if you will.'*

4 **Will do!** *see* **Do 27.**

WIN

1 **May be best man win!** *see* **Man 5.**

2 **You can't win (them all)** An expression of resignation after a failure or series of failures: > *'We spent years campaigning for a bypass. Now it's been built, you hear the heavy lorries driving by so fast that it's as noisy as ever. You can't win, can you?'* Them is often shortened to *'em.*

WIPE

Wipe that grin off your face *see* **Grin 2.**

WOE

1 **Woe betide** *Rather old-fashioned* Punishment, misfortune, etc., will come: often used as a threat: > *'Woe betide if you arrive late!'* > *'Woe betide the man who fails to keep the rules!'*

2 **Woe (is me)!** *Archaic* An exclamation of sorrow or grief.

WOMAN

My good woman *Old-fashioned* An offensive expression used to show the speaker thinks that he or she is more important than the woman he or she is speaking to: > *'Look here, my good woman! No one has ever been so rude to me before in all my life!'*

WONDER

1 **I shouldn't wonder** I wouldn't be surprised; I'm fairly confident (that): > *'He'll have left that job by now, I shouldn't wonder.'* > *'I shouldn't wonder if he's at university – he was very clever, you know.'*

2 **I wonder if ...** A polite way of asking (something): > *'I wonder if you'd mind opening the window.'* > *'I wonder if I could see the doctor this evening.'* Also **I was wondering if ...**: > *'I was wondering if I might have another glass of wine.'*

3 **It's a wonder (that)** It's surprising that: > *'It's a wonder you're still living here after all these years!'*

4 **(It's) no wonder** (I am) not very surprised that ...; of course: > *'No wonder Jack couldn't come dancing with us; he has broken his leg, after all.'* Alternatives to *no* are *little* and *small*: > *'It's little wonder you're so thin – you never seem to eat much.'* > *'We've not had a new car for years. Small wonder, as we've hardly any money.'*

5 **The wonder is** What is surprising: > *'The wonder is that she remembered my name!'*

6 **Wonders will never cease** I am most surprised by what you have done, what has happened, etc.: > *'I've done the washing-up, Mum!' 'Wonders will never cease!'*

WOOD

1 **Not see the wood for the trees** To be so occupied with details that you do not look at what you are doing more generally: > *Many leaders get absorbed in small matters and so don't see the wood for the trees.*

2 **Touch wood** An expression used when the speaker hopes that things will be or continue as has just been said: used to bring

good luck; often said touching something near made of wood: > *'We've had no expensive repair bills on the car so far, touch wood!'* American equivalent *Knock on wood*.

WORD

1 **(Could I have) a word in your ear?** May I speak to you in private? :> *'A word in your ear, John? It's about those new contracts we mentioned.'* > *'Could I have a word in your ear, if you can bear to leave everyone here for a moment? It's rather urgent.'*

2 **Famous last words!** An expression used as a reply to a boasting, self-assured, or optimistic statement: often said as a warning or in a mocking, disbelieving tone: > *'Playing with matches is a good game!' 'Famous last words! You'll set fire to yourself if you're not careful.'* > *'I'll be back in half an hour!' 'Famous last words – you've said that before and you've been gone all morning!'*

3 **In a word** Used to summarise what has just been said or to give a very brief answer to a question: > *'Did you enjoy your meal with Freda?' 'In a word, no.'*

4 **In other words** An expression used to clarify or expand on something that has just been said: > *'Patrick works hard; in other words, he's an excellent student.'* > *'The first verse in the Bible begins "In the beginning God created ... "; in other words, it states firmly that God exists and that He acts.'* Also used as a reply: > *'I'm not very happy about what you're doing.' 'In other words, you don't*

trust me?' 'I wouldn't quite say that.'

5 **... isn't the word for it** An expression used to show that something is not put in an extreme enough way: > *'It's rather cold today, isn't it?' 'Cold isn't the word for it – it's absolutely freezing!'*

6 **Mark my words!** Take note of what I'm saying: often used as a warning or threat: > *'Mark my words, he'll let you down. He's worked for me in the past, so I know he's not very reliable.'* > *'He'll be back soon, mark my words – he never stays away for long.'* > *'Mark my words, never come near this house again!'*

7 **Mum's the word** see **Mum**.

8 **My word!** An expression showing surprise, annoyance, etc.: > *'My word! How nice to see you again!'* > *'My word, you've got a lot of explaining to do, you know!'* Also (*old-fashioned*) **Upon my word!**

9 **Not a word** Don't say anything (about something): > *'Here comes Mum, so remember, not a word about her birthday present!'* > *'Not a word to the others, OK?'*

10 **Not another word** Don't say anything more (about something): > *'So that's settled then, is it? Now, not another word about it!'* > *'Now goodnight, children, and I don't want another word out of you tonight.'*

11 **Not in so many words** Not quite the right or exact way of expressing something: > *'Would you say the talk was a success?' 'Well, not in so many words ... but it was quite useful, nevertheless.'* >

'We weren't invited in so many words; but she certainly told us she was having a party.'

12 **One more word out of ...** Be quiet; a threat or warning to (someone) that punishment will follow if there is not silence: > *'One more word out of you, and I won't let you go on the trip.'*

13 **Sharp's the word!** Be quick!:> *'Sharp's the word! We've got to go in a minute – come on and get ready!'*

14 **Words fail me** I am too surprised, shocked, angry, happy, etc., to express my thoughts adequately: > *'You say you spent £1,000 on that car! Words fail me! What a fool you are!'* > *'Words fail me! You come in here and expect me to give you all my attention for a whole hour. You know I'm busy, so just go!'*

15 **(You can) take my word (for it)** see **Take 13**.

WORK

(It's) all in a day's work see **Day 7**.

WORLD

1 **It's a small world!** An expression used when one meets in an unexpected place a person whom one knows: > *'Janet – how nice to see you! What are you doing here in Germany?' 'I'm on holiday too! It's a small world, isn't it!'*

2 **On top of the world** Very happy; very well: > *'I'm feeling on top of the world today – I've just heard I've passed all my exams!'*

3 **The world and his wife** Everyone: > *'It seemed that the world and his wife were at the reception!'*

WORRY

1 **Don't worry** There is no need for you to worry: > *'I can't quite reach the tin on the top shelf.' 'Don't worry, I'll get it for you.'* > *'I'll be fine, don't worry!'*

2 **Not to worry** There is no need to worry: > *'I've lost my ticket.' 'Well, not to worry, we can pay when we get to London.'* Also **No worry.**

3 **You should worry!** *Humorous* You certainly need not worry: > *'You should worry with a salary like that coming in every month! You don't know how lucky you are!'*

WORSE

(Things) could be worse A reply to a greeting such as 'How are you?', saying that one's health and well-being are really not too bad: > *'How are you, Jim?' 'Things could be worse – we're not managing too badly at the moment, thanks.'* Also **It could be worse.**

WORST

If the worst comes to the worst If all the better alternatives are impossible or if the worst possible things happens: > *'If the worst comes to the worst, and all the hotels are full, you could always stay with us, I suppose.'* > *'We'll have to close the whole business down, if the worst comes to the worst, and if there are no more orders.'*

WORTH

For what it's worth An expression used when the speaker is not sure of the importance of a statement, opinion, etc.: > *'For what it's worth, I don't really think she's the right girl for the job.'*

WOULD

1 If you would *see* If 4.

2 Would ... *Becoming old-fashioned* I wish: > *'Would that he were alive to see our new baby daughter!'* > *'Would that things were different!'*

3 ... would rather ... (Someone) would prefer to (do something): used to show a choice: > *'Would you rather go by train or coach?'* > *'I'd rather you came a bit earlier, really, if you can.'* > *'May I smoke?' 'I'd rather you didn't.'*

4 Would you ...? *see* Mind 1.

5 You (he, she, etc.) would ... An expression used to show annoyance at what someone has done because they often do it or is just the kind of thing they do: > *'You would go and spoil our plans again by telling us now that you can't come!'* > *'That's just like Jackie – she would forget to bring the tickets!'*

WRAP

Wrap up! *Becoming old-fashioned* Be quiet!: > *'Wrap up, Pete! Can't you stop moaning?'*

WRITING

Could I have that in writing An expression used when someone has made a compliment or said something flattering about the speaker: used humorously: > *'We've always found you to be a man of most remarkable abilities!' 'Could I have that in writing!'*

WRONG

1 Don't get me wrong *see* Get 1.

2 Two wrongs don't make a right It is not right to do something wrong in retaliation for something wrong done to oneself.

Y

YAH

Yah boo sucks to you! *see* Suck.

YEAH

Oh, yeah! An expression of rude disbelief: > *'If you don't shut up, I'll come and hit you!' 'Oh, yeah – really?'*

YEAR

Happy new year! An expression of greeting around the time of the beginning of a new year: > *'Happy New Year!' 'Happy New Year, everyone!'* they all cried, raising their glasses, as the clock struck midnight. > *'We wish all our friends a happy new year!'*

YES

Yes and no An ambiguous answer to a question, showing that the speaker wants to reply 'yes' to some aspects and 'no' to other aspects of the matter: > *'Would you like a job in London?' 'Yes and no – the salaries are high, and there's lots to do, but it's so noisy and busy.'* > *'Have you made up your mind whether to go?' 'Yes and no.'*

YESTERDAY

I wasn't born yesterday *see* **Born 2.**

YOU

1 **There's … for you** *see* **There 10.**
2 **You and your …** Used to express disapproval of what someone has said or done: > *'You and your idea of coming early to the exhibition – just look at the queue!'* > *'You and your statistics! Why don't you shut up about the gross national product and come down to earth?'*
3 **You there!** An expression used to call someone's attention: > *'Hey, you there! What are you doing with that picture?'*
4 **You're another!** An expression used as a reply to show that the accusation just made of someone else applies to them also: > *'I think Jim's rather a fool!' 'Yes, and you're another!'*

YOUNG

You're not as young as you used to be A polite way of saying that someone is getting older: > *'You shouldn't spend the whole day rushing round town like that – remember, you're not as young as you used to be!'* Also **You're not getting any younger.**

YOUR

1 **You and your …** *see* **You 2.**
2 **Your actual …** *see* **Actual.**

YOURS

1 **Up yours!** *see* **Up 3.**
2 **What's yours?** *see* **What 22.**
3 **Yours truly** *Humorous* A way of referring to oneself: > *'Who was it that was left behind to clear up the mess? Yours truly!'*

YOURSELF

How's yourself? *see* **How 6.**

Index

How to use the index

In the index the idioms in the dictionary are listed under subjects. If you are looking for a suitable idiom to express a particular topic or function of the language, you can consult this li s t. You will then be referred to the keyword in the dictionary where the idiom is listed. Note that the index does not include any style markers on levels of formality, etc.: guidance on this is given at the entries in the dictionary itself.

Index

Apologies

175

Index

Disapproval, slogans expressing

Disbelief

Index

No problem **Problem**
No sweat **Sweat**
There's nothing to it **Nothing 10**

Eating and drinking

After you with … **After 2**
Be mother **Mother 1**
Come and get it! **Come 3**
… coming up **Come 10**
Do the honours **Honour 2**
Here you are **Here 3a**
It's my shout! **Shout**
My compliments to the chef
  Compliment 1
One for the road **One 6**
Say when **Say 32**
Sweet enough already **Sweet**
The same again **Same 4**
The usual **Usual**
Time's up! **Time 11**
What's your poison? **Poison**
What's yours? **What 22**

Embarrassment

I almost died **Die 2**
It was nothing **Nothing 2**
Was my face red! **Face 5**
We can't take you anywhere!
  Anywhere 2

Emphasis

All of **All 4**
And all **All 11d**
And I don't mean maybe **Mean 1**
And no kidding! **Kid 1**
And no mistake **Mistake 1**
And that's flat **Flat**
Any old **Old 1**
Apart from **Apart b**
As a matter of fact **Fact 1b**
As sure as … **Sure 2**
By Jiminy! **Jiminy**
By Jove! **Jove**
Cross my heart **Heart 2**

Cross my heart and hope to die **Cross 2**
Do you know **Know 30c**
For dear life **Life 1**
For that matter **Fact 1b**
For the life of me **Life 2**
For the love of God **Love 1**
For the love of Mike **Love 1**
… full stop **Stop l**
God knows **Know 8b**
Goodness knows **Know 8b**
Heaven knows **Know 8b**
Honest to God **God 15**
I can tell you **Tell 4**
I must say **Say 13**
I promise you **Promise 1**
I tell you **Tell 6**
I'd … first **First 3**
I'd have you know **Know 20**
If you like **Like 4b**
I'll say this much **Say 21**
I'll thank you to … **Thank 2**
I'm telling you **Tell 11**
In actual fact **Fact 1b**
In all my born days **Day 6**
In fact **Fact 1b**
In heaven's name **Heaven 9**
In point of fact **Fact 1b**
Into the bargain **Bargain 1**
It just isn't true **True 1**
Little short of … **Short 2**
Lord knows **Know 8b**
Mark you **Mind 12**
Mind you **Mind 12**
No, repeat, no **Repeat**
Not believe for a moment **Moment 3**
Not to put too fine a point on it **Point 4**
Nothing short of … **Short 2**
Of course not **Course 2**
Rest assured **Rest 5**
So help me **Help 5**
So help me God **Help 6b**

Encouragements

Endearment

Endurance, limit of personal

Enquiries and asking for information

Index

Index

Greetings

Greetings, seasonal

Happiness *see* Pleasure and happiness.

Healthy, enquiries about

Health, replies to enquiries about

Help, asking for

Help, offering

Honesty

Hopes or wishes

Index

Impatience

Important things *see* Summarising and expressing important things

Indifference

Information, asking for *see* Enquiries and asking for information

Information, refusal to give

Interfere, requests not to

Index

Index

You should be so lucky! **Lucky 2**

You're laughing! **Laugh 4**

You've not lived! **Live 4**

Politeness

Age before beauty! **Age 2**

At your service **Service 1**

Be honoured (to do something) **Honour 1**

Could I … ? **Could 1**

Do you mind … ? **Mind 1**

Forgive me, but … **Forgive 1**

I don't suppose **Suppose 1**

I suppose **Suppose 2a**

I thank you … **Thank 1**

I wonder if … **Wonder 2**

I wouldn't mind **Mind 6**

I wouldn't say no **Say 17**

I wouldn't say that **Say 18**

If I may say so **Say 19**

If you could **If 4**

If you please **Please 1a**

If you would **If 4**

I'm afraid **Afraid**

I'm much obliged to you **Oblige 2**

I'm not saying that **Say 18**

I'm sorry! **Sorry 1b**

Ladies first **Lady 2**

May I … ? **May**

Might I … ? **Might**

Much obliged **Oblige 2**

No disrespect **Disrespect**

Present company excepted **Company 1**

Shall we … ? **Shall**

With all due respect **Respect**

Would you be good enough to … ? **Good 16**

Would you be so good as to … ? **Good 16**

Would you mind … ? **Mind 1**

You could … **Could 6**

You're not as young as you used to be **Young**

Praise *see* **Approval and praise.**

Promises

Cross my heart **Heart 2**

Cross my heart and hope to die **Cross 2**

God's honour! **Honour 3**

I promise you **Promise 1**

On my honour **Honour 4**

Promises, promises! **Promise 2**

So help me **Help 5**

Public, phrases in

Action stations! **Action 2**

Attention, please **Attention**

Going, going, gone **Go 11a**

Ladies and gentlemen **Lady 1**

Order! Order! **Order**

Shame, shame! **Shame 2**

Speech, speech! **Speech**

Testing, testing **Test 2**

The customer is always right **Customer**

Unaccustomed as I am to public speaking … **Unaccustomed**

Your attention, please **Attention**

Public transport, phrases on

All aboard! **Aboard**

All change! **Change 2**

Attention, please **Attention**

Thank you **Thank 4c**

Your attention, please **Attention**

Punishment

Are you looking for a fight? **Look 1**

Are you looking for trouble? **Look 1**

… for my sins! **Sin**

Here's something to remember me by **Remember**

His just deserts **Desert**

It serves you right! **Serve 2**

Judgement on you **Judgement 2**

Just you wait **Wait 3**

Step outside **Step 3**

Index

Index

Statements, alleged

Statements, contrast with previous

Statements, disagreement with

Index

It's all happening **Happen 2**

Well done! **Do 20**

What did I say! **Say 40**

What did I tell you! **Say 40**

You scratch my back and I'll scratch yours **Back 7**

Suggestions, agreement with

All right **All 6b**

And so say all of us **Say 1**

As you say **Say 2**

Be my guest! **Guest**

Fair enough! **Enough 4**

Good thinking! **Think 1**

Hands up! **Hand 5a**

I don't mind if I do **Mind 5**

I guess **Guess 2**

I suppose so **Suppose 3**

If you like **Like 4a**

If you want **Want 2**

I'll say! **Say 20**

It's a bargain! **Bargain 1**

Just so **Just 5**

Not half **Half 5c**

Now you're talking **Talk 2**

Put it there! **Put 2**

Quite so **Just 5**

Right on! **Right 5**

Right you are! **Right 7**

Same here **Same 3**

Stick it there! **Put 2**

Suppose we **Suppose 4**

Sure do **Do 16**

That's a bargain! **Bargain 2**

That's an idea **Idea 3**

That's fine by me **Fine**

Very well **Well 6**

You do that **Do 29**

You've got a point there **Point 9**

Suggestions, disagreement with

Absolutely not **Absolutely**

Anything you say **Anything 4**

Hang about **Hang 3b**

Hang on **Hang 3b**

I don't know about that **Know 12**

If you think that, you've got another think coming **Think 8**

If you want **Want 2**

I'm not so sure **Sure 4**

I'm sorry! **Sorry 1b**

Just a moment **Just 3b**

Like hell **Hell 3b**

Not if I can help it **Help 4**

Not if I know it **Help 4**

Not on your life! **Life 5**

Over my dead body **Body**

Say what you like **Say 31**

Says who? **Say 33**

Says you! **Say 33**

Sez you! **Say 33**

The hell you will **Hell 3b**

The very idea! **Idea 5**

Wait a minute **Wait 4b**

Wait a moment **Wait 4b**

What an idea! **Idea 5**

With all due respect **Respect**

You can't have your cake and eat it **Cake 2**

Suggestions, introducing

As regards **Regard 1**

Far be it from me **Far 2**

For a start **Start**

For one thing **Thing 4**

Guess what **Guess 1**

How about … ? **About la**

I mean to say **Say 12b**

I should… **Should 1**

I wonder if … **Wonder 2**

If I may be so bold **Bold**

If I were you **If 2**

In the first place **Place**

I've news for you **News 1**

Let's say **Say 24**

On the whole **Whole**

Speaking of **Speak 5**

Index

Index

Index